TO245068

Praise

"Playful and history-rich . . . Broadway-loving readers will appreciate the play-by-play (pun intended) of this fizzy book." —*New York Times*

"This deserves a standing ovation." —*Publishers Weekly*

"Fans of musical theater and dance are in for a real treat." —*Kirkus Reviews*

"An enjoyable and inspiring inside look at a life in the theater." —*Library Journal*

"Full of sharp, insightful humor." —*Vulture*

"Wow! A wide-ranging, entertaining memoir about her life on stage and screen. And yes, *Chita* is as wonderful as she is!" —*Town & Country*

"A captivating, stirring memoir [filled with] loads of dramatic incidents . . . Every fast-reading page is animated with her upbeat, outspoken spin on a spunky, fearless life where she blazed her own trail. Chita, take your well-deserved bow!" —Brian Bromberger, *Bay Area Reporter*

"Delicious! . . . One of the main and most delightful concepts of the book: 'Chita is sweet and kind,' she insists before admitting, 'Dolores [alter ego] is a bat out of hell.' Rivera's advice to us all comes from an Ebb lyric in the team's *70, Girls, 70*: 'Say yes!' Indeed, say yes to this marvelous memoir so that you can not only savor all there is to Chita but also understand where Dolores is coming from, too." —Peter Filichia, *Masterworks Broadway*

"This colorful and entertaining memoir—as vital and captivating as Chita herself—is the unforgettable and engrossing personal story of a performer who blazed her own trail and inspired countless performers to forge their own unique path to success."   —Richard Ridge, *Broadway World*

"Chita Rivera knows how to tell a story.... The book is a fast, fun read full of fabulous tales, smart and insightful. It may well make you laugh and cry. And I bet you'll be sad when it ends. I was."

—Wendy Caster, *Talkin' Broadway*

"Gripping, moving, insightful . . . wonderfully inspirational! Reading *Chita: A Memoir* is like going to the still center of Broadway creativity and the remarkable people who gave their all to make it happen. The details of her life are simply astounding!"   —Cahir O'Doherty, *The Irish Voice*

"Chita Rivera blazed a trail where none existed so the rest of us could see a path forward. She was part of some of the greatest musicals in the history of the form, from Anita in the trailblazing *West Side Story* through Claire Zachanassian in the underrated masterpiece *The Visit*, over sixty years later. She was a Puerto Rican Broadway icon and the original 'triple threat.' We're so lucky to be alive in the same timeline as Chita Rivera."

—Lin-Manuel Miranda

"A frank and fascinating memoir from one of the truly great artists of the American Theater. Lots of stories . . . Lots of insight . . . and quite a few caustic statements from Chita's alter ego, Dolores. An illuminating history and a guaranteed pleasure!"   —John Kander

CHITA

A Memoir

CHITA RIVERA

WITH PATRICK PACHECO

HarperOne

An Imprint of HarperCollinsPublishers

FIRST HARPERCOLLINS PAPERBACK EDITION PUBLISHED IN 2024

Designed by Nancy Singer

Page 305 is a continuation of this copyright page.

Library of Congress Cataloging-in-Publication Data is available upon request.

ISBN 978-0-06-322680-7

24 25 26 27 28 LBC 5 4 3 2 1

This book is dedicated with love and gratitude to
my parents, Pedro Julio and Katherine Anderson
my siblings, Carmen, Julio, Armando, and Lola
and
my daughter, Lisa

CONTENTS

Preface

WHY NOW?

had just gotten off the elevator on the floor of the School of American Ballet with Doris Jones, my dance teacher, when a door flung open and a female dancer came running out of a room crying and screaming, "I can't! I can't! I can't!"

I was all of sixteen at the time, and this outburst didn't do anything to calm my nerves about auditioning for placement in the school. I figured if she—tall, blond, and gorgeous—"can't," then I—short, brown, and wide-eyed—certainly couldn't. I turned to Miss Jones and asked why the young lady was bawling.

"Never you mind, Dolores," said Miss Jones. "Just stay in your own lane and look straight ahead."

Looking straight ahead was an early lesson I learned not only from Miss Jones but also, by example, from my mother, Katherine Rosalia Anderson. When my father, Pedro Julio del Rivero, died suddenly in 1940, she forged ahead with one goal in mind: to care for her five children. I was only seven at the time. Mother was helped in this by my maternal grandmother, Sarah "Sallie" Anderson, who was also widowed young. So I grew up in a household on Flagler Place in Washington, DC, led by two very strong, generous, and resilient women who never looked back in self-pity or regret. Their only agenda was to look to the future, teaching us to be citizens worthy of America's promise and good Catholic kids, worthy of heaven, even though I was one hellion of a kid myself. "Get on with it" might as well have been a motto stitched into the del Rivero coat of arms. I've followed it all my life.

So I don't mind admitting that this book you hold in your hands is a surprise to me. Just as that scared sixteen-year-old couldn't possibly have imagined how the next seventy-plus years of her life would turn out, it seemed impossible that my personal history would ever be put within a memoir. Oh, sure, from time to time, friends encouraged me to write about my life.

"Would anybody care?" I responded.

This isn't false modesty. It's a typical answer from someone who has always thought of herself as more of a dancer than a Broadway musical star. The natural inclination of dancers is to keep to themselves. It's the work that matters. We are always looking ahead to the next challenge, the next assignment, the next discovery. That explains, in part, why the one song I could never relate to was "I'm Still Here." It's brilliant, like all of Steve Sondheim's work. But I had always been "here." Never looking back. So how could I *still* be "here"?

Then Covid hit and, like the rest of the world, *there* I was. Maybe it *was* time to look back? Still, what would make my memoir matter? I have been incredibly lucky to have had the benefit of some of the best teachers and mentors in the business. The list is endless. Surely there'd be some value in passing on what I learned from them to succeeding generations? The idea of taking them into "the rooms where it happened," as Lin-Manuel Miranda so cleverly put it, was appealing.

I knew at the same time I'd have to lift the veil on my personal life. That, I wasn't too wild about. But I knew that was what readers would want. And maybe my crazy-quilt of a life, stitched together on fate, faith, impulse, and hope, could be of value as well. Like how I managed to balance a busy career, a husband, a child, lovers, family, and friends. How I tried to navigate, for better or worse, the creative conflicts, triumphs, flops, and vulnerabilities that are part of a life in the theater. I'd have to be as honest as I could when it came to the people I'd worked and played with, and that made me nervous. What helped me to come around was a question posed at the very beginning of the project:

"After seventy years in the public eye, what is it that people don't know about you, Chita?"

"I'm not nearly as nice as people think I am," I answered. So a solution to my hesitation to spill the beans was born. Prepare to meet Dolores. My given name, what my mother called me when I caused trouble, and, now, my alter ego. She is a side of me that few people have glimpsed. As I note in this book, Chita is sweet and kind; Dolores is a bat out of hell. She's the one who rises up, eyes flashing, smoke coming out of ears, when, as my daughter, Lisa, says, "Mom goes Puerto Rican." Not hard to imagine, right?

Like most actors and performers, I have lived a lot of my life in my imagination. In that sense, this book is a work of imagination, recalling and writing about people who blessed my life going back—way, way back—to the golden age of Broadway musicals. They still live within my heart as if it were yesterday and resurrecting them in these pages has been a singular pleasure. If time has dimmed the memory, then I have relied on the remembered emotions to fill in the gaps of fact. Writing this memoir has not been easy but it has been one of the most rewarding experiences of a life full of them.

Another reward is one that I could hardly have expected when this adventure began. In the course of researching my family history came an astonishing fact: the bloodlines of my mother's family included African American roots. As my siblings and I grew up, we were very much aware of our father's Puerto Rican heritage. He was Boricua, born on the island into the del Rivero clan. As far as the Anderson family was concerned, my mother, Katherine, and grandmother Sallie told us that we were of Scottish and Irish descent. That was true but only part of the story. A 1910 North Carolina census identified my maternal grandparents, Sarah "Sallie" Rand

and Robert Anderson, as "mulatto" then, a mixed-race designation often used for the children of once-enslaved people.

My mother and grandmother never spoke to my siblings and me of this ancestral path. Was my mother, who was born in 1905, even aware of it? How much did Grandma Sallie know of her mother, Susan Rand, who, according to government records, had possibly been born in 1840 in North Carolina? I wouldn't presume to judge as to why this was never divulged to us. It was likely their desire to spare us the indignities and limitations of an ugly racism as so many other mixed-raced families had done for their own children.

I am proud to embrace this newly discovered part of our family's history. To learn of it has been a blessing. I wish I'd known about it earlier; it would have deepened through blood my abiding affection for the many Black friends and colleagues you will read about in this memoir, especially Sammy Davis Jr. and Doris Jones, whom I always considered a second mother. Without Miss Jones as an early mentor, I don't think there would be a Chita Rivera. She not only recognized and nurtured my talents as a dancer but, like the greatest teachers, also taught me character and discipline.

As my life unfolded throughout the many interviews over the past two years, patterns emerged, memories were awakened, loves were rediscovered, and passions reignited. Time has allowed the "fits, fights, feuds, and egos" to be placed within a perspective that came with a whole lot of laughs and a whole lot of gratitude. In the course of a long career, I've never lost my sense of play. In some ways, even now, I'm still like that sixteen-year-old that stepped off the elevator holding on to Miss Jones for dear life, wide-eyed and ready for whatever the future had in store.

What came about surprised the hell out of me. Here's hoping it will surprise you, too.

1

ANITA'S GONNA HAVE HER DAY

West Side Story

Early in the summer of 1957, I approached the Osborne, the fancy apartments on the corner of Seventh Avenue and Fifty-Seventh Street, right across from Carnegie Hall. The doorman motioned me inside the foyer.

"Hi, I'm Chita Rivera," I said, hoping that my voice didn't betray any nervousness. "Mister Bernstein is expecting me."

That was Mr. Bernstein as in *Leonard Bernstein*—or as in *Lenny*, which is how I would eventually think of him. All I knew then was that he was the maestro—a star conductor, the TV host of *Omnibus*, a classical music series, and the Broadway composer of *On the Town*. And he had summoned me, Dolores Conchita Figueroa del Rivero, to his apartment.

"Ah, yes, Miss Rivera," said the doorman. "He said to go to his music studio. It's on the third floor. 3B."

The summons had come as something of a surprise. But when you're twenty-four, life is full of surprises. The surprises had started five years earlier when, on a whim, I'd accompanied a friend to an audition for the national touring company of *Call Me Madam* and I was cast in the chorus. I was only nineteen.

I grew up fast. After all, Elaine Stritch—blond, beautiful, brassy—was the lead in that production. I was planning a career in classical ballet and suddenly I caught the theater bug. Or it caught me. And I rode it into *Guys and Dolls*, *Can-Can*, *Seventh Heaven*, and *Mr. Wonderful*. Now I was in the middle of auditions for a new musical that had been the buzz of Broadway for months: *West Side Story*. Every actor in New York was longing to be part of it since *Variety* had announced that the great Jerome Robbins was working on a show with the writer Arthur Laurents, Lenny Bernstein, and a young lyricist named Stephen Sondheim.

Living on the Upper West Side at the time with my brother Julio, I read everything I could about the show in the dog-eared, coffee-stained copies of *Variety* that were passed around our group of scrappy, poor, and ambitious chorus kids. The musical was a loose retelling of *Romeo and Juliet*, and Laurents had updated the book, creating a plot ripped from the headlines of the day: gang warfare on the West Side of Manhattan. He had named his gangs the Sharks, who were Puerto Rican, and the Jets, who were white.

When auditions for *West Side Story* were finally announced, I was pretty confident that my ballet training would give me a literal leg up on the show's dance requirements. Maybe, just maybe, that would get me into it. But I was nervous when the callback came for the singing audition. Could I carry a tune? In those days, dancers danced. Singers sang. This show would be different.

To make matters worse, the singer who came right before me in the auditions at the Chester Hale studios was Anita Ellis, whose brother, Larry Kert, was up for a major role. She had a powerhouse voice and knocked her song out of the park. I had to follow *that*?

"Chita Rivera, we're ready for you," the stage manager said.

I walked into the studio and handed sheet music to the pianist. He took one look and said, "That's brave." I peered out to the table of judges at the end of the long room, which included Robbins, Bernstein, Laurents, and that young kid Stephen Sondheim, not much older than us, who'd written the lyrics.

"And what will you sing for us today?" asked the maestro.

I replied, "'My Man's Gone Now.' By Gershwin. Y'know, *Porgy and Bess*?"

"We know," came a voice from the back of the room.

I couldn't tell who said it. Auditions are always an out-of-body experience. And, Mother of God, so was this one!

You may well wonder at this point, "What was Chita thinking?" What in my naïve little brain possessed me to choose as my audition song Gershwin's lament sung by a grieving *widow*?

Blame Sammy.

Sammy was the pianist in a bar in Chicago where we gypsies (as we chorus kids were called), on the road with *Call Me Madam*, would gather after performances. We'd drink, flirt, and sing our heads off. I always hung back, too timid to solo, until one night, as I was about to sneak out, one of the chorus members grabbed me.

"Oh, no you don't, Chita," he said, blocking my way. "We know that you've been studying with Sammy. You've got to sing or you can't go home."

Weeks earlier, Sammy had heard me singing along with the rest of the group around the piano and said, "Chita, you can sing. If you want, I'll give you lessons while you're in town."

I could sing? Really? This was news to me. But I was always looking to improve myself. I jumped at the offer for the two weeks remaining in the Chicago engagement. It was Sammy who taught me to sing "My Man's Gone Now." It was nothing like my usual audition songs, light comic numbers such as "Take Back Your Mink." But when *West Side Story* came up, I thought, why not? The show was about something dark and soulful. And so was *Porgy and Bess*.

Now, my choice was being put to the test in front of one of the most accomplished groups in musical theater. I made a sign of the cross, whispered a brief prayer, and said to myself, "Okay, Chita, you're in it now!"

My man's gone now
Ain't no use a listenin'

I heard some muffled laughter and stopped.

"Do you want me to go on?" I said.

"Thank you, Chita."

I grabbed my dance bag and was on my way out the door when the stage manager stopped me. "Hey, wait a minute," he said. "Lenny would like to see you tomorrow at 10 a.m. At his place, the Osborne, Fifty-Seventh and Seventh. It's right across from Carnegie Hall."

I knew exactly where that was. I had by this time been to jazz classes at the rehearsal rooms at Carnegie Hall with Peter Gennaro, a wonderful choreographer and teacher. I'd already worked with Peter on *Seventh Heaven* and loved being able to study with him, going through routines with a roomful of other young women in tights. Their attention was as much on Peter as it was on the guy playing bongos in the corner of the room, Marlon Brando. The Wild One was wildly flirtatious with everyone, and the girls were beside themselves. I paid him no mind. I was too shy and scared. Maybe at a later time, Dolores—which was my first given name but better known to me as my sensual, dark, and renegade alter ego—would have returned his sultry stare. But not then. Not when my career depended on absorbing everything the city had to offer, including a dazzling array of mentoring talent.

The door of 3B opened and there he was, Mr. Leonard Bernstein, handsome and welcoming with his thick mane of black hair and beautifully dressed in a white shirt under a gray cardigan and navy blue pleated pants.

"I liked your 'My Man's Gone Now,'" he said smiling. "I admired your audacity. I think you just might be right for the role." We both laughed. But in my mind, I was stuck on the word "role." Role? What role? I'd have been glad just to be cast as one of the dancers in the show.

He took me by my hand and led me into the room, which had windows facing Carnegie Hall and which was dominated by a large black grand piano. Stubbing out his cigarette, he motioned for me to join him at the piano, on which was some music, sketched out in pencil. Then, his long fingers crashed down on the piano keys and the hair on the back of my neck rose. I had never heard music like that before in my life. Nor, I was sure, had the world. I was listening to the opening chords to "A Boy Like That," the first notes I would hear from a show that would change Broadway, and America—and me. All I knew then was that Mr. Bernstein was pouring his heart out singing of Maria's betrayal.

A boy like that who'd kill your brother
Forget that boy and find another

The music blew my mind! The rhythm hit me in the face! When I came back to earth, I wanted to be part of that rhythm. I wanted to live in the world of that music. It made me want, so badly, to fly.

✳

In the course of that extraordinary morning, I had a master class in dramatic singing from the master himself. I was nervous as hell and had butterflies in my stomach, so all I kept thinking was, "Please, Chita, don't throw up on Leonard Bernstein!" After one of my feeble attempts, he said, "Chita, your boyfriend's just been killed. You've just found out that your best friend, Maria, has slept with the boy who stabbed him. Give it a little heat!"

With patience and generosity, he pulled the role of Anita out of me. My confidence grew as the hour wore on, stirred by the fierce beauty of the music and the lean, smart lyrics. Together we went over Anita's songs and, more important, the turbulent emotions within them. Mr. Bernstein enjoyed playing the part—all the parts, for that matter—and he conveyed them with passion and purpose.

I drank it all in. When I came down from the heights and it was time to gather up my dance bag, I felt that I was saying goodbye to Anita as much as to the composer of *West Side Story*.

Let me correct that. I was saying "hello" to Anita. *¡Hola, Anita, mi hermana!* It dawned on me for the first time, after six or seven auditions, that my ambition just to land in the chorus was aiming too low. I was actually being considered for the role of Anita, the lover of the Sharks' leader, Bernardo, and best friend to his sister, Maria. Holy shit! Was a little bit of Dolores peeking through? Maybe. Because if you then happened to be walking on Seventh Avenue in front of the Osborne as I left the building, you would have seen a young woman in a light summer dress with a dance bag slung over her shoulder, levitating a foot off the ground and thinking to herself, "That song is mine! That role is mine!"

✳

As it turned out, the role *was* mine after a few more nerve-racking auditions. Thanks to my ballet training and to Peter's classes, I had aced the dance audition. And now, thanks to Lenny, I had passed the singing audition. (Could I now call Mr. Bernstein *Lenny*? Well, maybe. But only to myself and to you.) I couldn't wait to tell my brother Julio, who since I'd arrived in New York had shared every triumph and lamented every disappointment of my career. Getting the role of Anita was especially sweet because *West Side Story* was so close in blood and temperament to who we were as a people, as a family.

"Let's call Armando and tell him, Chita," said Julio, referring to my other brother. "Hang the expense!"

Armando was then serving in the Air Force in Germany and toll calls were costly. But I didn't hesitate. I loved my sisters, Lola and Carmen, but Julio and Armando were closest to me in age and capers. Growing up, the three of us had put on shows in the basement of our house in Washington, DC, collecting pennies from the neighborhood kids for admission. Through the crackling, transatlantic wires of the phone, I could hear Armando yell for joy.

In quick succession, the roles were handed out: Carol Lawrence was cast as Maria; Larry Kert as Tony, the former Jet who captures her heart; and Kenny LeRoy was Bernardo, her brother and my lover. Mickey Calin won the role of Tony's friend, Riff, leader of the Jets. Eight dancers and eight singers rounded out the major roles, and we were a cast of nearly forty altogether. Larry was among the last to be chosen so he joined us late as we were celebrating in a bar near the Winter Garden Theatre.

"I got it! I got it!" he yelled as he danced through the place. "And it's just my luck that I'll walk out of here and get hit by a bus!"

Rehearsals were intense, grueling, and always stimulating. Did I mention it was Jerry Robbins who was directing and choreographing? The usual four-week period was extended to eight weeks at Jerry's insistence, and once we got scripts and started running through the score, we realized this would be unlike any show to ever hit Broadway. What was expected of us was also unique. Jerry was strict, disciplined, and quick to temper. You always hear about how mean and nasty he could be. Evil, in fact. If that was what it took for his genius, so it was. But he was never that way with me. He was difficult, sure. Demanding? Absolutely. He was asking us to do things that we never, ever thought we could do. And yet we ended up doing them. The toughest part was making some of the most challenging and complicated choreography look easy. But we were eager to do it because, well, dancers? Dancers always want to please.

There were newspaper clippings of the latest gang warfare on the bulletin board in the halls where we were rehearsing. We read the stories and thought, "We're doing a musical about us." Okay, we were more about leg warmers than switchblades. But we felt a kinship with the characters who were near us in age and who, like us, were hot-blooded, hormonal, and competitive.

That was particularly true for those of us who were playing Sharks. I was one of the few in the cast with Puerto Rican blood. My father, Pedro Julio Figueroa del Rivero, was Boricua, island born. I was only seven when he died, but my mother, Katherine, told us stories about how this handsome man, dashing in his white suit, played the clarinet and saxophone in the big bands. I felt I was honoring him by bringing all I could to Anita. The congas, which were always going during rehearsals of *West Side Story*, were beating out rhythms that lay deep in my DNA. I felt it in my bones, and when the songs, with their fusion of Latin, jazz, and classical, put flesh on those bones, I was transported into a Spanish-inflected immigrant world that was familiar to me but that had never before reached the stage. It was gritty and real but elevated to artistic heights by the music and choreography.

Jerry demanded that we completely immerse ourselves in our respective worlds, and it was his particular talent to give us the freedom to find our place in those worlds. During scene rehearsals, it was very odd for us to hear him say, "Do what you feel!" Dancers are so used to doing exactly what we're told to do. But it was the mid-1950s, and the Lee Strasberg approach, known as "the Method," was just flexing its muscles as an acting style. In fact, I'd heard that Montgomery Clift, who'd studied at Strasberg's Actors Studio, was the one who'd suggested to Arthur Laurents that he write a musical about New York gangs. Arthur and the team had also first thought to cast James Dean, another famous actor from that school, as Tony in *West Side Story*.

I didn't know much about the Method. It hadn't penetrated into

musicals as much as it had in plays. But Jerry expected us to know everything about our individual characters—where they lived, their families,
their entire life story. One day, after rehearsal on a hot summer day, he
asked me to join him in the hallway for a chat. It was like being summoned
by the Pope.

"Who is Anita?" he asked.

"She's a rock," I replied as the sweat dried on my go-to rehearsal outfit
of black leotard, tights, and skirt. "She's proud, a leader, brave. She'd step
in front of the enemy to protect her own."

Jerry went on. "What's her relationship to Maria?"

"She's like a mother to Maria. She wants her to be happy but feels the
need to keep her away from danger. She's a fixer. Anita just wants everything to be okay."

Slyly, Jerry then asked, "In rehearsal, Anita turned her back on
Francisca. Why did she do that?"

I did some quick thinking. "Well, she pissed me off!"

"How?"

"Because Francisca doesn't believe in America, and I do."

"When you think of Anita, what color comes to mind?"

"Purple." I continued, "Anita is a tease. She's coquettish. I like her
sensuality."

"You've got *that* down," said Jerry. "But Chita, you're missing something."

I wasn't sure what he was getting at.

"Anita's a killer," he said, "when she has to be."

My relationship with Jerry was one of respect, trust, and even warmth.
As warm as you could be with someone so single-minded. I, along with
everybody else, knew that if we didn't measure up, we could get fired. He
did have his favorites in the company—as well as his targets. One of
Jerry's pets was an Italian guy with a gorgeous head of black hair and an
even more beautiful dance technique. That guy, Tony Mordente, played

A-Rab, one of the Jets, and he was a show-off and flirt. He caught my eye. I caught his—and kept it. You'll be hearing more about him later.

I have to admit that I was one of Jerry's favorites as well. Perhaps that was why I felt emboldened on one occasion to come to the rescue of one of the cast members. I could read Jerry's moods pretty well by then. From the beginning, I was always able to pick up on the temperature in a room. So when I saw Jerry starting to do a slow-boil, I looked over to see who he was looking at: Mickey Calin, who played Riff, making time with the girls. As Jerry passed me on his way to chew out Mickey—something he did often—I impulsively whispered, "Jerry, don't." To my amazement, he stopped. He stared at me, not quite sure what he had heard. Finally, he said, "Chita, you're a witch!" We both laughed. To this day, I'm not sure why I did it. Maybe it was Dolores, who hates a bully, coming through. And why didn't he just yell at me, too? He probably thought I was, in that moment, more Anita, the instinctive protector, than Chita, who always kept her nose to the grindstone. That's how much the roles grew on us in time.

Jerry expected our immersion into the world of *West Side Story* to be complete and unbroken. The members of the gangs were strictly forbidden to socialize with each other. Not even during breaks or at lunchtime. It would sharpen our hostility, not to mention give us a competitive edge when we got to the dance at the gym. It was another story after 6 p.m. when rehearsals ended. But until then we were pretty keen about staying in character.

I was paired with Kenny LeRoy, who played Bernardo. I liked him. With his long sideburns and curly black hair, he was the epitome of a leader—tough, assured, and strong. Someone Anita could certainly get her kicks with. And someone whose buttons you didn't push.

Carol Lawrence learned that the hard way.

Immersing herself in the role of Maria, Carol decided that she wanted to do something to bring the boys playing the Sharks closer together. So she gathered some black felt materials and cut out silhouettes of sharks that she gave to each of the gang members to put in their boots. Carol and I shared a dressing room during rehearsals, so I was present when Kenny came in and lit into her.

"I'm the leader of the gang! *I* make all the decisions!" he told her. "Now, you go out and collect those sharks you handed out and toss them in the trash." That was my Bernardo. Hot.

During dance rehearsals, Jerry, a perfectionist, worked us relentlessly. He took his background in classical ballet, fused it with hip and frenetic street energy, and created drama. I suspected that he and Peter Gennaro, his co-choreographer, had haunted the dance halls of Spanish Harlem before they started choreographing *West Side Story*. Jerry was never just about the steps. It was always about *feeling*. The mambo became an erotic pas de deux; the cha-cha, lively and playful.

Nothing was more exciting to us than working on "The Dance at the Gym." The music was galvanizing. When I heard it for the first time with the full orchestra, I became teary. So did the cast. It was the most beautiful combination of book, lyrics, and music we'd ever heard. Each day, we were like racing thoroughbreds at the gate, hyped up and raring to break out. Never more so than when we started working on that number. What Jerry emphasized above all else was clarity. No fuss, no clutter, no distraction. He dealt in the essence of dance, conveying emotion to an audience through incredibly complex and detailed steps. "Let me *see* you!" he often shouted. And by that, he meant, "Show me who you are as a person, as a character." Style, yes, but more important, *substance*. And even more, *awareness*.

In communicating that to us, no one was more crucial to Jerry than Peter. While he choreographed the Jets, Peter was in charge of the Sharks. They made a great team, although they were like night and day. Jerry was very analytical in his approach to dance. Peter was all instinct. Jerry was serious, always dressed in black, and you didn't dare fool around when you were with him. Peter was light, Southern, sweet, funny, and kind. He spoke with a lisp, which invited us smart-ass kids to mimic him: *Shweethearts, it's on the sheventh, not the eighth.* I had gotten to know Peter earlier when he choreographed *"Sheventh" Heaven* and also through taking his jazz dance classes. I loved and admired him. Working with him was pure joy.

Peter had grown up in New Orleans, where he not only picked up on the Black rhythms of the streets but also learned dance from the Black kitchen staff in his Italian family's restaurant. His movements were hip, jazzy, and improvisational, and he translated all that into the sensual signature of "America." Peter could invent a combination on the spot, do it again ever so slightly, and then do it yet again. To my mind, each one was as good as the next, but he was looking for the best fit and he worked—and worked us—until he found it. Peter also had the fastest feet on Broadway, and my ballet training helped me keep up with him. Ballet also allowed me to learn the dances much more quickly. It wasn't unusual for Peter to say, "That was good. But let's try it faster." Or, "You get the gig if you can jig!" And "jig" we did.

"America."

You're probably asking yourself, "Did Chita have a problem with the lyrics to 'America'"? In the decades since, some people have felt the original 1957 lyrics to be denigrating to Puerto Ricans (they were toned down some for the movie version): *Puerto Rico, you ugly island— / Island of tropic diseases.*

I'm very proud of my Puerto Rican heritage. But I saw nothing wrong with Anita and the women joking around by comparing their new home with the one they'd left behind. Most of the Sharks were from families who had recently moved to the United States. They were enthralled with the new possibilities it presented for their lives in the teeming tenements. In the mid-1950s, there weren't many stories about Latinos on film or in theater, and *West Side Story* opened the door for a lot of us. It was revolutionary, telling our story with raw honesty and tenderness. For one of the first times on Broadway, the show channeled the hopes and challenges for a Latino culture that Anita loved and defended. So, smoke on your pipe and put that in!

Peter first worked on "America" with both the boys and girls in the number. As was always the case, he then showed it to Jerry. After he presented "America," we were excused while the two men conferred. When we regrouped the next time to rehearse; the boys had been cut, and it became a number for only the girls. That was an inspired move. It made a statement about the central role of women in the musical. We were empowered by the change, and it showed just how perceptive and smart Jerry was as a storyteller. Later, when the movie was made, they reinserted the boys into the number, and it became cloudy and weaker.

Jerry ruled the roost in the rehearsal rooms. The producers, Hal Prince and Bobby Griffith, and the rest of the creative team were allowed in only at specific times. All of them deferred to Jerry. All, except one. Lenny was the only one who could overshadow him. When he entered the room, the waters parted. Not that he demanded it. He was much too casual in manner. That just made Lenny, this shining creature, more attractive to a bunch of dancers falling all over themselves. It was a privilege to watch him at the piano, with a cigarette in one hand and a pencil in the other, sketchi..g out a score on staff paper. I might be exaggerating, but just a little, to say that there was an erotic charge between the company and Lenny when he came in to teach us his glorious score.

And the "Quintet"! Every character is singing with anticipation of what turns out to be the most momentous night of their battle-scarred lives. Lenny just drew it out of us, eyes closed, coaxing, imploring, putting the fine points on the surging music. There he was standing on a chair, stomping his feet and flailing his arms. He got so lost in his score that he went straight through the chair. He totally disappeared into the orchestra pit. A moment of shock was followed with a burst of laughter. The rehearsal stopped cold until we could extricate him from the chair. Everybody simply fell in love with Lenny. He was not only this world-class maestro and New

York social lion. But he could also delight young kids with Prokofiev's *Peter and the Wolf.* Lenny, larger than life and brimming with it.

Among the quietest on the creative team was Arthur Laurents, who had yet to gain his reputation as the smartest, meanest, and loudest guy in the room. Since he was nearing age forty at the time, we considered him one of the old guys, along with Lenny and Jerry. They were all of thirty-eight. Harold Prince, the coproducer, wasn't even thirty, but he seemed like a veteran even then. The cast was never privy to the discussions among the creators. They would go off into other rooms, have their conferences, and then the next thing we knew we were handed new pages or new songs. They did occasionally pull us aside and offer some advice. In secret, of course. If Jerry had found out, he would have blown his stack. In comparison, chewing out Mickey would have looked like child's play.

One afternoon, Arthur took me aside. I thought his book for *West Side Story* was spare, honest, and smart; it was easy for me to believe the words. But I was just feeling my way through rehearsals when he asked for a private chat. We had been rehearsing the scene after the rumble in which Bernardo is killed by Tony. Anita is returning with her dead lover's jacket to the tenement where Maria lives with her family. She is bereft and numb and steeling herself to tell Maria that her brother has been killed. Stage directions called for me to place the jacket on a hook upstage and then knock on the door of Maria's room where she has just made love with Tony.

"Chita, take your time with Bernardo's jacket before you place it on the hook," advised Arthur. "Feel the jacket. Feel *him* in the jacket. Smell the fragrance of his tonic, that tonic he always put too much on." That was a superb little clue into where I was supposed to be emotionally. It got me through the scene and also provided a foundation for whatever happened onstage during performances. Such as a door getting stuck.

At one matinee, after I had hung up the jacket, I then knocked on the door of Maria's bedroom.

"Maria? Maria?" I said. "Maria, it's Anita. Why are you locked in?"

The problem? I was locked out. For real. I knew I couldn't break character. The audience could tell that the door was stuck, but if they laughed, we would never be able to recover one of the tensest moments in the musical. That's when, stunned by Maria's honesty ("I Have a Love"), Anita agrees to help her and Tony. Faced with a jammed door, I added another "Maria" and improvised a line, "Please, Maria. I have something to tell you." Still, the door wouldn't budge. In that moment I knew I would have to maintain my tearful state as I moved downstage and walked clear around the proscenium to get into Maria's bedroom. It worked. I kept my composure, and so did the audience. Those tense moments, when anything can happen because it's live, can be hair-raising for an actor.

Arthur's note also inspired me to devise a private ritual between Kenny and me each night after the curtain came down on the first act. The rumble had just ended with the bodies of Riff and Bernardo lying prostrate in death. Shielded from the audience by the fallen curtain, I came in from the wings and walked through the darkened stage, over the body of Mickey's Riff, and toward Kenny. Silently, I took his hand and lifted him up off the floor and we walked back to our dressing rooms together. We repeated this night after night. Theater is so much about ritual, whether it's seen or not. It's sacred in that way. And *West Side Story* imbued in us a respect for what was holy about it.

Each day was a new discovery about the roles and, in the process, about ourselves. That could be painful. It was Gerald Freedman, Jerry's directorial assistant, who opened a door to Anita that I never wanted open. While Jerry and Peter worked on the dances, Gerry worked on the book scenes with those of us playing leads. One day we were rehearsing the scene leading up to "A Boy Like That." Lenny had stoked the heat during that first master class on the song. But Gerry thought something was missing.

"That was great, Chita, but let's explore it more," said Gerry. "You've got brothers, right? Armando and Julio?"

I laughed. "I know what you're trying to do," I said, shaking my head.

I wasn't ready to go *there*. I didn't want to think of my brothers as gang members who might be killed in a rumble. Was he really asking me to imagine my brothers in place of Bernardo and Riff, who lay dead on a playground? That was just too "method." I had never worked that way before, and I wasn't sure that I wanted to. I feared I didn't have it in me.

"Can't I just dance the role?" I joked. That I could handle.

"Why don't you try it?" said Gerry. "Start singing and think of your brothers. Let's see where it goes."

That was just the problem. I was afraid of where it might go.

"Chita, you're stalling. Let's go," said Gerry.

I started to sing and thought of Armando and Julio, imagined the expression on my mother's face as I told her what had happened to them. I began to cry and stopped.

"I can't do this!"

"Keep going, keep going!" said Gerry. For the first time in my career, I felt ripped apart, exposed. As I sang, I started to back away from Gerry, farther and farther. By the end of the song, I was actually at the exit door of the room. As I retreated, someone was coming forward. Something broke in me that afternoon. A part of me was being born. Gutted. Sad. Angry. Defiant.

Anita, yes.

But also Dolores.

I had learned how to be a killer—when I had to be.

That energy came in handy when Jerry gathered the Jets and me to rehearse what I had been dreading: the "taunting scene" in which Anita is almost raped. She has been told by Maria to go to Doc's drugstore with a message for Tony. There she encounters the Jets, who begin grabbing at her clothes and calling her "lyin' Spic," "Bernardo's pig," "garlic mouth," and other insults.

Jerry allowed us to find our own momentum at first. He mapped out the drugstore and our relative positions in it. Then he said, "Feel free to start moving when you want to." There was a tense silence, and then the boys began to encircle me, calling me names. I felt like trapped prey. By the time I reached the door trying to get away, I was hysterical.

Since it was a tough scene, we rehearsed it sparingly. But once in performance, I was grateful for the challenge. It made me summon acting muscles I didn't even know I had—and some real muscle as well. If somebody grabbed my skirt, I kicked, shoved, and scratched them in the face if I had to.

Some nights that scene hurt more than others. Anita's degradation seeped into me personally, and I felt emotionally stripped. But what was important was to control my tears. If I sobbed, as I wanted to, then the moment would become about me and not about what was happening. Had there ever been a near rape scene in a Broadway musical before this? I wanted the audience to be more upset than I was. And I sensed they were.

After tryouts in Philadelphia and Washington, DC, where the response to *West Side Story* grew more and more enthusiastic as we neared New York— "America" stopped the show nightly—we finally arrived at our opening night at the Winter Garden: September 26, 1957. At the end, the curtain descended on the tableau of Maria cradling a fatally wounded Tony in her arms and the tender strains of "Somewhere" mingled with the quiet sobs of some in the audience. It really didn't matter what the critics wrote, though most of them were positive, but qualified; we knew that we had delivered something original and daring to Broadway.

My agent, Dick Seff, picked me up backstage to go to the opening night party at a hotel near the Winter Garden. We came downstairs from the dressing room after almost everybody had left the theater and I was surprised to see Jerry, the man who had commanded it all, standing alone onstage. Looking out at the empty theater, he looked sad. I turned to Dick.

"Please ask Jerry to come with us to the party." Jerry accepted the invite quickly, and off we went to join the cast, producers, and guests.

What I didn't realize at the time was that the creative team had endured such fights—about billing, credit, and other things—that nobody was talking to Jerry. We actors never knew about the drama surrounding the creative team. We were working so hard that we didn't have time for backstage gossip. A rarity, let me tell you. Once we arrived at the party, Jerry took leave of us, and we didn't see him for the rest of the night. That was Jerry. But if anybody had reason to be happy that night, it was the man who'd brought so much pleasure into so many lives.

West Side Story became a landmark musical, but the mythology around it was yet to come. *The Music Man* won the Tony Award for Best Musical over it that year. (More on *that* later.) Our first run lasted nearly two years but *West Side* wasn't for everyone. It didn't land on Broadway with a massive explosion. The true aficionados knew that they were seeing something amazing. But the regular audiences found it easier to respect us than to love us. Our show was dark, violent at times, and *real*. Each act ended with a death. Maybe it was just too much, too soon, too close to home. Hal Prince had often said, "I'm not interested in giving audiences what they want. I'm interested in giving them what they didn't know they wanted." And that realization takes time.

With *West Side Story* setting such a high bar in my career, I took myself a little more seriously for what was to come. (But not too seriously. Do that, and you become a bitch!) I am often asked, "How did it feel to be in *West Side Story*?" The simple answer? Ecstasy. I realized early on, even in rehearsals, that this show was a gift from God. I felt a tap on my shoulder and heard a voice, not unlike that of James Earl Jones, saying, "Chita, I'm now going to give you this present. Just do what you have to do—and be worthy of it."

Ever since then, I have tried my best to honor that promise. As Pedro Julio Figueroa del Rivero would say, *Gracias a Dios!*

This one was for you, Daddy.

Entr'acte

The Skirt Remembers

People often ask, "Chita, weren't you disappointed you didn't get to play Anita in the film of *West Side Story*?"

And I suppose I might answer "yes," except that when the movie came out in the fall of 1961, I was in a smash hit on Broadway: *Bye Bye Birdie*. Working on that musical, playing Rosie Alvarez opposite Dick Van Dyke's Albert, helped soothe the pain. I'd add that you really have to roll with the punches if you're going to be in this business. Helen Gallagher created the role of Nickie in *Sweet Charity* on the stage, but I played her in the Bob Fosse film. And yes, Janet Leigh played Rosie in the film of *Bye Bye Birdie*. Um, well, yeah. If you react at all, you have to laugh. I recall driving with Larry Kert past Hollywood's Grauman's Chinese Theatre, where the film of *West Side Story* premiered. Looking up at the marquee, Larry, who lost the film role of Tony to Richard Beymer, and I would "bawl" for a couple of seconds—and then go right back to what we were talking about.

However, when I first watched the movie of *West Side Story*, I have to admit that I did feel a pang of resentment. That was when Rita Moreno, as Anita, first made her appearance on the screen. I could feel Dolores welling up in me: "How dare she! That is *my* dress! That is *my* earring!"

Okay, you're probably saying to yourself, "Really, Chita? Over a dress?"

Yes. Really. Because it was so much more than just a dress. It always is. When you talk about costumes for any show, but especially *West Side Story*, you are talking about *character*. And also about *genius*. In this case, the genius of Irene Sharaff, who designed the dress. And the genius of Barbara Matera, who created it.

When you're standing in front of three mirrors having a fitting, you have enormous respect for the person kneeling down at your feet, invariably with pins between their lips. When they murmur this and that, you listen because you are totally in their hands and because they are smarter than you. Their discerning eye appraises you at your most vulnerable, often without a stitch on. How does the fabric flow and fall off the body? How does it drape and fill out the silhouette? What is the fusion of actor, character, and fabric so it becomes greater than the sum of its parts?

By the time I went to Irene Sharaff's workroom for the fitting for Anita, I had already been exposed to a costume designer's excellence: Marcel Vertès dressed my Fifi, the hooker in *Seventh Heaven*. He'd made her adorable, accessible, and very sexy; and Bob Mackintosh had made the Capri pants and blouse for my flirtatious Rita Romano in *Mr. Wonderful*.

But I was on my way to meet with *the* Irene Sharaff. By that time, she was world famous for having won her first of many Oscars for *An American in Paris* and for designing the luxuriant pale pink silk ball gown for Gertrude Lawrence in *The King and I*. She was commanding and authoritative when I walked into the studio—a handsome woman with a prominent nose and facial expressions that were made all the sharper with her favored black eyeliner. The day we met, she wore her hair in a bun and was dressed in black, over which she wore a blue smock.

Jerry Robbins knew her from the dance world, since Irene had designed his *Afternoon of a Faun* after having sketched out costumes for the Ballet Russe de Monte Carlo, American Ballet Theatre, and the New York City Ballet. I wondered whether Jerry had told her about our conversation regarding Anita and that the color purple had popped into my head. He didn't have to. Irene's palette was dominated by her love of reds, pinks, and oranges, in varying shades.

"I think the Sharks should be in sexy shades of cherry red, and Anita in purple," she told me as I stood in front of the mirrors. Colorful bolts of fabric were everywhere in the studio. I was a bit taken aback by her forceful presence. Irene was talking to someone who'd never thought of herself as a fashionista in any sense of the word. Before I arrived on Broadway, I had been a tomboy in everyday skirts and blouses who'd then graduated to a basic uniform of dancewear for ballet classes.

For *West Side Story* I had three changes: a robe in the beginning, a blouse and skirt for the drugstore scene in which I was nearly raped, and before that . . . *the dress*, the one I wore to the dance at the gym. You can imagine my excitement when an assistant brought it out and I put it on for the first time.

"Wow!" I said. "Did Jerry tell you I liked purple?"

"No," she quipped. "Anita did."

I peered into the mirror and looking back at me was Anita in all her pride and "don't-mess-with-me" glory. The tight bodice extended over the hips, and the skirt flared out to an edge of three rows of mini-ruffles masking the skirt seam. The underskirt had a pleated ruffle, and the net petticoat had red piping at the edge of the hem. I felt like a million bucks. The costume flattered my assets and diminished my flaws. The dress felt like a second skin. I loved every square inch of the fabric.

I twirled, flipping the skirt around, the rhythms of Lenny's mambo dancing in my brain.

"Be careful, Chita," said Irene. "Don't waste it. Don't be shaking that thing all the time. Tease out the colors. Wait for the right moment in the show. When you flip that skirt, the audience should see a world, an emotion, a taunt."

I understood what she was talking about. My impulse was to throw it all out there right away: "See how fierce I look!" But Irene was, quite subtly, teaching me how to wear a dress for a maximum effect—an extremely valuable lesson that would continue to be useful throughout the rest of my career. What it came down to was this: Chita, never forget that the dress is a living thing with its own demands and personality.

Irene asked me to do some dance steps, intimate and small at first, then grand and flashy. She wanted to make sure that the dress would follow each move in just the right way, a choreography of body, fabric, and silhouette. Then an assistant brought out two hoop earrings. I placed them through the pierced openings in my ears. Irene eyed them critically from every angle.

As she walked around me, I boldly suggested, "What if I take one of them off?"

Irene paused for a moment. "Why?"

"Anita's kind of a pirate, don't you think?"

"Which one?" she asked.

"The left one," I said, taking it off. We both looked into the mirror. She smiled.

"There, that's Anita!" she said.

Decades later, in January 1980, I got a call from Jerry, asking me to come down to the Minskoff Theatre, where he was in the midst of rehearsals for a revival of *West Side Story*. Debbie Allen was taking on the role of Anita while Jossie de Guzman and Ken Marshall were playing Maria and Tony. Jerry explained that he had been teaching Debbie the steps to the mambo in the dance at the gym and had blanked on an eight-bar section of the piece.

How did I feel coming into the theater, hearing once again the fast and furious drumming of feet to Lenny's throbbing music? Well, when you originate something, especially in a *West Side Story*, you always feel proprietary toward it. The originators of any show deserve that respect. But the cast could not have been more welcoming, and Debbie was adorable and open for me to teach her the steps.

I could remember some of them but got confused at what might have been my movements for the previous couple of bars. I tried again. But I still hit a wall.

"Jerry, let me come back tomorrow," I said. "I've got to go home and get something."

That "something" was a black skirt hanging in my closet that I had worn in rehearsals for the original production. It still fit like a glove. And the next day, Anita was back in business. I knew the minute I put it on that the skirt would remember the steps. And it did. All of them. Jerry and I shared a good laugh over the fact that the skirt, like the ballet slippers in *The Red Shoes*, had a life all its own.

"Why don't you leave it here, just in case?" Jerry said. "It's got a better memory than the both of us."

The memory of that purple dress is certainly never far from my mind. There are constant reminders. At almost every Halloween or Gay Pride Day in New York City, I can be walking down Ninth Avenue in New York's Hell's Kitchen and what should be coming toward me but, well, *the dress*. This time on the body of a strapping six-footer with a black wig, purple heels, and prominent Adam's apple.

I look to see if he's got the accents right. Yup. Just one earring, unlike in the film when Rita wore two. (A mistake.) I think of these homages to Anita as a helluva compliment. As we pass, I give him a wink—"You go, girl!"—and I also want to tell him, "Don't waste it!"

✳

A P.S. on Irene Sharaff and her Tony and Oscar awards for *The King and I*. The star of the musical, Gertrude Lawrence, tragically died at age fifty-four, in the midst of the Broadway run. She was buried in the ball gown in which she had waltzed around the palace with Yul Brynner in "Shall We Dance?"—one of the most goose-bumpy moments in Broadway history. I can't say that I'd want to meet my Maker in the purple dress of *West Side Story*. But I do know that wearing it was a moment of pure heaven.

Entr'acte

Tony Mordente: A Not-So-Quiet Thing

There is a lovely ballad, "A Quiet Thing," from the musical *Flora the Red Menace*, by my friends John Kander and the late Fred Ebb. I often sing it in my cabaret act. When I do, I am taken back to the many loves of my life through its beautiful lyrics:

> *When it all comes true*
> *Just the way you'd planned*
> *It's funny but the bells don't ring*

For the most part, love has come into my life on tiptoes. That is, with the exception of the first time. It came *roaring* in. Loud. Passionate. Crazy. His name was Tony Mordente.

Remember that guy with the gorgeous head of black hair and sideburns I told you about? The one who was Jerry Robbins's pet because he was such a dazzling dancer? The one who was such a sexy flirt and show-off? That was Tony. From the moment we saw each other on the first day of rehearsals, there was a bolt of current running between the two of us. Which was kind of dangerous, since Jerry forbade the Sharks and Jets to socialize, and Tony was playing A-Rab, a Jet. We weren't even supposed to look at each other. For dancers, that's a tough rule to follow because we love to congregate, mix, and mingle. But like that moment in *West Side Story* when Tony and Maria come together in the dance at the gym, Tony M. and I would sneak glances at each other, and the rehearsal hall would fall away.

"Isn't he cute?" said my friend Frances Taylor when she saw me looking at Tony executing some difficult steps with ease. "And, Chita, he's straight."

"You don't say," I replied nonchalantly. "He's such a beautiful dancer. I can't stop admiring his technique."

"Uh-huh, his technique," said Frances with a smile. "Is that why his nickname is 'Buns'?"

Okay. I've always loved me a good, solid, *round* rear end on a man. But I was first hooked on Tony's talent. Honest. He was always among the first to learn the combination. And when he started to move, he soared. That won my heart. And Tony let it be known among his buddies in the cast that he admired my dancing. Good to hear.

After we exchanged a few surreptitious looks, Tony got the nerve to chat me up. He had a boyish charm filled with "youse" and "heys" and "woudjas." Such as "Wouldja like to join me for lunch at the Midtown Pharmacy?" You bet. That was followed with more invitations, which I was always happy to receive (and to reciprocate).

As Peter and Jerry continued to build the mating dances in *West Side Story*, Tony and I began a less-than-discreet courtship. Word got around the company fast that we were dating. We never heard anything about it from Jerry, but Tony's fellow Jets chided him for transgressing policy. That only added to his boisterous and cocky appeal. I'd be walking down the street after rehearsals, and this car would sidle up alongside me. It would be Tony in his boat of a car: a 1954 blue Oldsmobile con-vertible. That car epitomized him: Colorful. Noisy. And fast.

"I love Chita! Hey, everybody, I love this woman!" he'd yell to the throngs pushing their way through Times Square. And I would yell back, "'I love Tony! I love Tony!'"

Tony put me on a pedestal, calling me his "Spanish lady," explaining, "I mean, like your mother, Katherine. Just nice and ladylike and well-behaved. A good Catholic girl."

That last description kept us innocent—at least at first. This was the fifties. We didn't just jump into bed with each other. Although I saw nothing wrong with sleeping, chastely, with some of my male friends. It never went beyond that because, well, a lot of them were gay. But also because we dancers are good at sniffing each other out, so we pretty much knew who would make a move and who wouldn't. Tony made his moves, all right, but they were largely limited to necking and petting like two high school kids behind the gym. After rehearsals ended at 6 p.m., we were on our own, so we would head to Sid and Al's, or Downey's, where all the chorus kids hung out, or we'd have a bite at our favorite Italian restaurant.

Tony was the youngest of his family and, of course, spoiled. His mother, Rose, would take the bones out of his fish, lest her baby boy choke during the delicious feasts she prepared for the family. His father, also a Tony, was a Schaefer Beer truck driver. I often wondered what he made of his son's ambitions, first in ballet, where he excelled, and then in musical theater. This was long before *Billy Elliot* and athletic dancers, like Jacques d'Amboise, were part of the scene. Italian-American teens caroused in bars, not at the barre. Rose was supportive, as were Tony's brothers, Sonny and Sammy, and his sister, Catherine. But it took Tony Senior a few years to come around. Then he saw his son dance a Bluebird pas de deux from *The Sleeping Beauty* at the 92nd Street Y. That blew away whatever reservations Pop Mordente might have had.

I adored Tony's family, and they in turn adored me and mine. I think my love affair with all things Italian started then with Rose and Tony and the Mordentes. God spent a little more time over Italy than over other countries. He certainly gave that country special blessings: the opera, the food, the humor, the gorgeous people. The north, with its beauty, regality, and poetry; the south, with its olives, passion, and heat. Ah, right. The *heat*. There's the rub. Can there be a people more driven to jealousy than Italian men? Tony was no exception. He was extremely jealous. So was I. But he was an Olympian.

One time, we were walking down the street, and some guy in a truck looked me up and down. Tony went ballistic. "What you lookin' at, pal?" Some curse words flew and the next thing you know, this huge guy, muscles bulging, gets out of the truck and towers over Tony like Bluto from the Popeye comics. I thought he was going to kill him. But Tony didn't move an inch even though the guy's fist was probably bigger than his whole head.

Tony and I had a few breakups, an inevitability when you mix an Italian with a Puerto Rican, a Jet with a Shark. One evening, long into our relationship, we had a fight that was one for the books. We were in the bedroom of our apartment in Flushing, Queens, and I had just had some professional photos done. They were headshots, so in the style of the day, my shoulders were exposed.

"So what did you have on?" he said in a troubling tone of voice.

"What do you think I had on, Tony?" I replied, sarcastically.

"What's up with the bare shoulders?" he asked. "You look naked."

"Don't be silly! Of course I had clothes on!" I retorted. He was getting my Dolores up. "You're just a crazy, jealous fool!"

Tony came toward me, looking like he was about to throttle me.

"Don't you dare!" I yelled. I rose up to all of my five feet, three inches and threw my head back. "I am Dolores Conchita Figueroa del Rivero and I do not get choked!" Then I added, "And you better hope I do *not* choke!"

We both collapsed on the bed in laughter. After a while Tony said, "I may be laughing but I'm still mad!"

When I recently reminded him of the incident, he couldn't remember it. "I'd never raise a hand against you," he said. "Though you'd have probably deserved it."

Tony and I laughed more than we fought. About six months into our relationship, I said to him after a performance, "Let's go have dinner." He accepted right away, though he thought I was going to kill him for something or other. Instead, I popped a question. "Are you going to finally marry me?" As you probably know by now, I can be a pushy bitch when I want to be. But Tony and I loved each other. Deeply. We were soulmates. He thought it was a great idea. We toasted with a couple of glasses of red wine and then he said, "I'm just sorry I didn't get there first."

We were married in early January 1958 with friends, family, and all our *West Side Story* castmates in attendance. Jerry, God bless him, threw a reception for us at his town house on the Upper East Side of Manhattan. It was a joyous affair.

A month earlier, I had learned that I was pregnant. (Okay, I know what you're thinking. I was a good Catholic girl—most of the time. But that Dolores!) It wasn't planned but both Tony and I were thrilled at the prospect of becoming parents. "I'm gonna be a papa!" he shouted to the people on the street as we cruised along in the '54 Olds. They invariably yelled back, "Congratulations!" By now I was used to Tony issuing bulletins about our lives from the car. He never left his feelings unexpressed.

When we told Jerry and the rest of the cast, they responded warmly, as usual. They were happy for us. My understudy was even happier because it meant I would have to drop out of the cast. But I was in no hurry. Five months in, I still wasn't showing. I felt terrific. I wasn't throwing up, didn't have cramps; I was as tight and healthy as could be during performances. Even the most strenuous scene—when Anita goes to the drugstore and is nearly raped—was handled with great care. The Jets took some steam out of their performances on my behalf and placed Baby John on top of me as gently as they could.

When I was six months along, I invited my gynecologist to attend *West Side Story*. He nearly had a heart attack. "Chita, you gotta get the heck out of there. Now!" I gave my notice. That night, I literally "became" pregnant. My stomach swelled. I felt life stirring inside me. The baby in my womb stretched out her little arms and legs and relaxed. It was as if Lisa, my daughter-to-be, had heard the Stage Manager in the Sky say to her, in a voice not unlike James Earl Jones, "Places, please."

There has been no greater production in my life than the miracle that took place on July 30, 1958, when Lisa Angela Mordente, six pounds, twelve ounces, was born. I have nothing to compare it to so I can't say whether her birth was easy or hard. I just remember that, while in the hospital in Queens, I kept screaming in pain and then I'd quickly say, "I'm sorry. I'm sorry. I'm sorry." That's the dancer in me. We are always saying, "Sorry." The doctor finally said, "Shut up, Chita. You don't have to apologize. You're having a baby!"

And then suddenly, there she was, beautiful, with a full head of black hair and cocked fists ready to take on the world. Tony said, "She looks like Rocky Marciano." Her paternal grandparents called her "the Puerto Rican Express." But all I felt at that awesome moment was, "She isn't mine. She isn't Tony's. She is hers." I realized, whatever happened, Lisa was an individual soul who would move through life with her own dreams, ambitions, loves, and joys. We could instill values through example, pray for her to find her bliss, provide for her with food, clothing, shelter. And, most of all, protection. I vowed then and there, come hell or high water, that Tony and I would protect her with every fiber of our beings. I would throw my body in front of anything or anyone about to harm her. It wasn't lost on me that Lisa's birth was concurrent with the beautiful but tragic pageant of death played out in *West Side Story*.

We took our baby girl back to the two-bedroom apartment in Queens where we'd moved after we got married. I was not going back to the Broadway production of *West Side Story*. Much to my delight, the British producer Hugh "Binkie" Beaumont had decided to postpone his West End production until I would be ready to resume performances. I was thrilled to be making my London debut in *West Side Story*, and Tony would also be reprising A-Rab there.

With an engagement at the Manchester Opera House looming in November, to be followed a month later at Her Majesty's Theatre, my body snapped back in no time. Four weeks to be exact. Let me tell you, Dr. Showbiz is the best therapy for postpartum depression.

Tony always said that the time he saw me happiest was when I was on my way to rehearsals—and this was no exception. We departed New York for Manchester in October with three-month-old Lisa in tow. Upon our arrival in Manchester, we were introduced to a nanny with a very English name: Blenda Peacock.

I returned to the role of Anita with renewed verve and passion. Actors are always the sum total of their life experiences, and during the previous eighteen months I had experienced a sea change. When Lenny had summoned me to his studio, 3B at the Osborne, I was a young single woman, hungry for whatever luck and life had in store. Now that girl seemed awfully innocent and naïve. I had since become a wife and mother, and I was reentering the world of *West Side Story* with a new lode of emotions and feelings. The preciousness of life was no longer theoretical. I had held it, newly born, in my trembling hands.

Anita—and Chita—would never be the same again.

2

DOLORES FINDS HER BLISS

Dolores, what are you going to do about it?"

I looked up at my mother, Katherine, and my heart sank. She had a weary and exasperated expression on her face. She'd just returned from a long, hard day of work at her secretarial job at the Department of Defense. The last thing she wanted to have to deal with was the mess in the living room created by her hyperactive nine-year-old daughter. I made a funny face, trying to make her laugh. That almost always worked. Not this time.

"Dolores, what have I told you a thousand times?" she said.

"Not to jump on the furniture," I answered, looking at the bamboo coffee table that lay shattered at my feet. This was the result of my literally bouncing off the walls at our family home, a two-story brick building at 2134 Flagler Place, Washington, DC. I had misjudged the distance from the couch to the easy chair and crashed through the table. My younger brother, Armando, couldn't contain his glee. "Oh, boy, you're going to get in trouble," he said.

"So, what are you going to do about it?" my mother repeated, arms folded.

"Glue it back together?" I said.

Even as I said it, I knew *that* was not going to fly. As usual, I was relying on my mother to have the solution. That's what women do. They solve problems. And she did. My mother had a practical side next to none. (Having five rambunctious kids can do that for you.) She made me clean up the mess. Then the next day, she led me through our neighborhood to a place she'd picked out with a lot of care. The northwest quadrant of DC was mostly African American with a smattering of Latino families. It was just a few miles away from the United States Capitol, where the streets were full of military personnel buzzing this way and that. The country was moving out from under the Depression and into World War II. That scene barely intruded into our lives, even though my mother worked for the Defense Department. She never brought her work home—something I learned to do years later, thanks to her.

My brothers now remember air raid sirens that went off from time to time. There was talk of German U-boats coming to attack DC. I didn't take much notice of the sirens, to tell you the truth. My world then was so narrow. It consisted of family, school, and all the fun I could get away with. I was not only active during the day, I was active at night, too. I walked in my sleep. One night, I even managed to walk off the landing on the second floor and into bushes, which luckily broke my fall. This event coupled with the coffee table disaster convinced my mother that something had to be done.

We stood in front of the building that was our destination. The small sign announced "The Jones–Haywood School of Ballet." My mother led me up the steps to meet the attractive, slender African American woman who would change my life.

"Dolores, this is Miss Jones," my mother said. The woman took my extended hand and folded it in a warm, soft handshake.

She bent down and said, "Are you willing to work hard, Dolores? Harder than you've ever worked before?"

I nodded. This was the answer to my mother's question. Dance was what I was going "to do about it."

✳

As these memories come rushing back, I'm in awe about how some things in our lives seem inevitable. How a smashed coffee table can lead to a jeté in a ballet studio, which can in turn land you in the chorus of a Broadway show. It may have been that Katherine del Rivero, born Katherine Rosalia Anderson, harbored her own dreams of being a dancer, and she passed that ambition on to me. She moved through the world like a dancer. Mother had the poise, erect carriage, long legs, and slender torso of a ballerina. She almost certainly could have become one if fate had not led her in a different direction: a meeting with a handsome young musician named Pedro Julio Figueroa del Rivero, my father.

That happened eleven years before my birth on January 23, 1933. When they met, she was in her teens, the youngest of three daughters born to Robert Anderson and Sarah "Sallie" Anderson. My grandparents had left North Carolina for Washington, DC, around the turn of the twentieth century. It was a good move. Family lore had it that Robert found work as a courier delivering documents from the White House of President Teddy Roosevelt to various offices around the Capitol. My mother said that one of her earliest memories was rolling eggs on the lawn of the White House during the annual Easter celebration. I always imagined that she won the contest. If she did, she was too modest to admit it.

By the time my mother and I were walking up the steps of the ballet studio, her father had long passed, and my widowed grandmother, Sallie, was living with us at Flagler Place. From time to time, her sisters, my aunts Mabel and Lilly, joined our family. The adults were all women then because my mother, too, had been widowed early. Pedro Julio, my father, had died of cancer, just shy of his forty-first birthday, in 1940. I was seven at the time, the middle child with two older siblings—Carmen, then sixteen, Julio, eleven, who we called Hoolie—and two younger, Armando, six, and the baby Lolita, who was one. My mother, only thirty-five when my father died, met that blow the way she dealt with setbacks throughout her entire life—with fortitude. She kept the heartbreaks to herself.

My memories of Daddy are spotty but precious. What holds a treasured place in our family is a photo of him, debonair and suave, in a spotless white suit, tie, and Panama hat. He played the saxophone and clarinet in the United States Navy band and, later on, in the Harry James Orchestra. A sax player. No wonder mother fell head over heels for him. I never knew how they met. Those sorts of details were never shared with us kids. If we had the inclination to ask—and I'm not sure we did—the response was along the lines of, "We don't talk about those things."

It was left to my imagination to wonder about when and where they came together. Was it like Robert De Niro and Liza Minnelli in the movie *New York, New York*? A young woman being swept away by the swagger of the guy playing sax in the orchestra? Or did they meet over a cup of coffee on some rainy night at the counter of a diner? Maybe in Detroit where they lived for a while before I was born? In time, I began to wonder whether Katherine had a renegade spirit like me when she was young. After all, once I was on the road at the age of nineteen with *Call Me Madam*, I invented ways to escape my chaperones. Why wouldn't she have done the same to escape the eagle eye of her parents?

In between orchestra gigs, my father worked for the government in some capacity. I remember him coming home from the Capitol, carrying groceries that always included a bag of popcorn for his kids. He was as smart-looking as my mother, whom he called Kate. He always arrived at the dinner table dressed in a suit and tie. When company called at our home, he made sure that he was dressed in a sport coat to receive them. That formality was a signal to us kids to behave at the dinner table. Fat chance. That rule was almost impossible to obey, except for my oldest sibling, Carmen, who inherited my mother's calm demeanor. The rest of us kicked each other under the table when we weren't trying to dance on it. Even Carmen once blew her top at Hoolie and threw a knife at him, which stuck on his shoe. What can I tell you? We del Riveros are passionate people. But what do you expect? I'm sure we weren't the only Latino family with busted-up furniture.

My father's flawless manners had been drilled into him by his large family, led by his parents, Armando Modesto and Aurora Figueroa, whom he'd left behind in his hometown of Yabucoa, Puerto Rico. This was during the great migration from the island to the United States after Puerto Ricans were granted US citizenship in 1917. Along with several of his brothers, he'd come to the United States at nineteen. He soon landed gigs playing in bands, first in Detroit and then in DC.

I don't remember my father practicing around the house. But I do recall my mother dancing out of the kitchen when dinner was ready. They both had a wonderful sense of humor, which became a prerequisite of mine for any man I ever dated. My mother had the greatest laugh, which would start from the bottom of her feet and travel through her whole body. It must've been devastating to be so suddenly widowed and at such a young age. She never remarried, never even dated as far as I can remember. I've always thought of that as an indication of how much she revered my father's memory. The last glimpse I had of my father was when my mother drove the five of us to the hospital. Children then were not allowed into the place, so we stood outside. Helped by my mother, my father came to the window, looking gaunt. With a faint smile, he waved to us—and then he was gone.

I don't recall much about his passing and funeral. I probably blocked it out of my mind. My brother Armando told me that in those days it was traditional for the body to lie in an open casket in the middle of the home before burial, and that is how we said farewell. This explains, at least in part, the start of my lifelong fascination with death—one that would come to my mind when I was in musicals about mortality such as *Zorba*, *Kiss of the Spider Woman*, and *The Visit*.

✷

Before my father passed, I can recall him, brimming with vitality, behind the wheel of his 1930s Packard. We piled in it for family drives around the District's stately monuments, which we took for granted. Didn't every city have them? In spring, we picnicked among the cherry blossoms in the shadow of the Lincoln Memorial, and on sultry summer afternoons, we took off for the beach to escape the heat. My father seemed to worship the sun as much as I came to do. Were those trips to the Chesapeake his attempt to recapture his youth in the tropical climes of Puerto Rico? In my father's description of it, the island loomed in my imagination as a sensual paradise. I longed to go there. Especially when we were freezing our butts off in DC winters. But travel then was rare and expensive.

I finally got to fulfill that dream in the early 1960s when I flew from New York to Puerto Rico to do an act at the Club Tropicoro in San Juan. The plane dipped below the clouds, and I got my first glimpse of the tropical greenery and sand-colored buildings set in a sparkling blue ocean. I suddenly became very emotional. My father's family history, which had been beating beneath my blood for all those years, became much more real in that moment.

Even if it took me awhile to get to Puerto Rico, the island had come to me in the guise of my relatives. These, of course, included Uncle Luciano, my father's brother, and his wife, Aunt Rita. I lived with them in the Bronx on Intervale Avenue when I first went to New York to study at the School of American Ballet. But I met the most famous of my father's family, his cousin Ramón del Rivero, when he made his first visit to New York City in the winter of 1953. I was excited by the frenzy of the crowds greeting him. He was a famous Puerto Rican comedian, composer, and star of stage, movies, and television known as Diplo. He was inspired by the Cuban comedian Leopoldo Fernández to create an

Afro–Puerto Rican character and took the name for his alter ego from a friend of his youth.

Ramón was seductive and handsome in a goofy sort of way. He had elastic facial expressions, an agile body, and a deadpan manner, sort of like a clownish mix of Charlie Chaplin and Red Skelton. He invented multiple characters, including a drag persona, for such shows as *El Tremendo Hotel* and *La Taberna India*. He also produced and starred in wildly popular TV programs like *They Can Kill Me But I'll Enjoy It*. That title alone sounds very del Rivero. He was beloved, especially by Boricua, native *puertorriqueños*, who had to come to America. Through him, they were able to keep in touch with what they'd left behind. Uncle Luciano and Aunt Rita faithfully listened to his radio programs and laughed their heads off.

He insisted on being called Diplo rather than Ramón because his father, José Ortiz Alibrán, who was a lawyer, considered it improper to have a comedian in the family. An opera singer and a priest? That was okay. But he drew the line at comedy. I imagine my great-uncle reconsidered that as Diplo's reputation grew. He was acclaimed as an entertainer but also as a humanitarian. In 1953, he initiated what is considered the world's first walkathon. He led a group on an eighty-mile hike from San Juan to Ponce to raise money to combat cancer. He himself would die of a congenital aneurysm only three years later, at the age of forty-seven. As his open casket was carried from the church to the cemetery, fifty thousand mourners flooded the streets to say farewell. In 1965, a fifteen-foot bronze statue was erected to honor his memory in his hometown of Yabucoa, and Diplo Day was declared in 2009. It's fascinating now to watch videos on YouTube of his funeral, women in mantillas dabbing tears from their eyes and men in suits with bowed heads.

I can't say what sort of impact, if any, having such a famous comedian in our family had on my eventual career. I must've been impressed with the excitement he aroused. But then there was also a priest in our family, and that captivated me in a different way. Don't laugh, but for a brief moment—very brief—I wanted to become a nun. I was inspired by the Sisters of Mercy from our local parish, Saint Martin of Tours. Those were the days when nuns wore long black habits, rosaries clipped to their belts, and starched white wimples and veils. Every Sunday, the del Riveros attended Holy Mass, the women wearing hats and gloves and the kids in their finest. It was my first encounter with theater, since the words of the Latin Mass mingling with the smell of incense and burning candles made for a pretty good show—especially after the priest, in colorful vestments, and altar boys, in surplices made their way down the aisle. Forget the convent. I wanted to be an altar boy. They seemed to have more fun. Especially after my brother Armando nearly set the church on fire. It wasn't his fault. It was the combination of a fan, an unsteady flag, and a nearby row of candles. Then . . . holy smoke!

After my father died, Mother went to work to support us. The chore of herding all of us cats fell to our grandmother, Sallie. I remember her as a sweet and loving woman in a flowered house dress. Aunt Lily was more strict. With her hair neatly pulled back into a bun, she was old-fashioned and crusty, not at all like her younger sister, my mother. Grandma Sallie showed mercy, but Aunt Lily refused to cover for us when we misbehaved. Our begging fell on deaf ears. Exhibit A: The smashed coffee table. For the most part, we took our limitless energy outside, no matter the weather.

Our neighborhood was our own Junior Olympics. I jumped from stoop to stoop, climbed the huge pear tree in our backyard, was a holy terror on a bicycle, and competed with the boys in running races. I never played with dolls. Girly things didn't interest me. Even after a visit from my "lady friend," I was less attracted to romance and was more into speed. Nobody in the neighborhood could beat me. I was a "cheetah." Fast. And a monkey. Reckless. I spent most of my youth with perpetually skinned knees. I liked nothing more than climbing to the top of the pear tree, hiding, and then scaring the hell out of anybody who walked by.

I can't remember a time when I wasn't a thrill seeker. It began on Saturday evenings, when we turned the basement of our home into a movie house, which became a magnet for the neighborhood kids. My older brother, Hoolie, had bought a second-hand sixteen-millimeter projector and rigged up a theater by tacking a white sheet on the back wall behind the coal bin. He rented movies from a downtown store, put up a sign in our window announcing the attraction, and charged eleven cents per ticket. Hoolie was quite the capitalist. He had an infectious enthusiasm for movies next to none, and his taste ran from Frankenstein movies to vintage musical movies to sci-fi epics. One of our favorites was Carole Landis and Victor Mature in the 1940 film *One Million B.C.* Who could ever forget the sight of Tumak wrestling a baby Triceratops?

For your eleven cents, you would not only get a movie but also a show. We must have thought we were the Roxy Music Hall. Once I began my ballet classes at the Jones-Haywood School, I would grandly bestow on this audience of pipsqueaks my immense gifts. With a cue from Hoolie, my first director, I would come onto the stage to perform a pirouette, a penché arabesque, or pas de chat, whatever I had learned that day. Little Dolores thought she was hot stuff. The audience felt differently. I was booed. Roundly. But I didn't care. I knew none of them could do what I was doing. I'm glad my stage debut was less than auspicious. I could only go up from there. After I was done flinging my pearls before swine as a dancing girl, I was in charge of pulling the curtain to reveal Armando, all in black with a Frankenstein mask on his face. The boos of our audience of fifteen or twenty melted into pitched screams as the kids ran helter-skelter up the basement steps. Sometimes I'd yank the curtain so hard that it would come off its rungs. Then I'd join the screaming hordes pursued by Hoolie, who was ready to kick my ass. Repairs were done quickly—Hoolie wasn't called "Mr. Fixit" for nothing—the children returned to their seats, and the movie began, the scarier, the better.

To this day, Halloween is one of my favorite holidays. In October, my house is famous for being a haunted wonderland. It's a setting worthy of Edgar Allan Poe. Grotesque mannequins on the porch roar "Your soul is mine!" whenever the bell is rung, and other assorted attractions chill the bones. I love Halloween because people can dress up, act foolish, and lose their dignity. It's impossible to keep your inhibitions, much less your composure, when you're terrified. Your everyday "mask" falls off and your real personality comes through. As anyone who's ever been in a show with me can tell you, I'm a sucker for scaring people and asking for it in return. I'm sick and demented in that way.

I have to say that one of my favorite fan encounters came when I met Boris Karloff. In the 1960s, I was on Garry Moore's variety TV show with Caterina Valente and Carol Burnett. We sang "I Enjoy Being a Girl" dressed like rejects from *The Addams Family*. It was not a pretty sight. I was elated when Boris Karloff showed up to do a cameo in the same show. He tolerated my fandom like a gentleman. But I'm sure he didn't have a clue as to what he was doing with those crazy clowns. Still, if you ask me, Boris Karloff is the sexiest man alive. Or was. When he was alive, that is.

You might also blame my fear freakdom on *King Kong*, another of our favorite movies when we were kids. Today, I can't sit in the audience of a theater without fantasizing about the curtain opening and seeing a big ape roaring and pulling at chains. Just like King Kong did in the classic 1933 movie with Fay Wray. (The 1976 remake with Jessica Lange didn't come close to matching the original.) Watching King Kong atop the Empire State Building being attacked by fighter planes is my kind of melodrama. The last line—"Oh no, it wasn't the airplanes. It was beauty killed the beast"—always reduces me to a basket case.

More predictably, Hoolie and I shared a love of musicals, particularly the classic movies of Ginger Rogers and Fred Astaire. Although I admired Gene Kelly, I preferred Fred Astaire as a dancer, the way he smoothly built character through his head, heart, and feet. It was his effortlessness that got to me. Years later, when I was working on *Sweet Charity* and *Chicago*,

Bob Fosse shared with me his worship of Astaire as the perfect dancer. Bobby always said the only ambition he ever had in life was to become the next Fred Astaire. I wasn't exactly looking to be the next Ginger Rogers. I was more curious than ambitious. Each day was one of discovery, whether it was the education I was getting at Mott Elementary School and Banneker Junior High or just walking around the neighborhood.

If God had a plan for me, I certainly couldn't have ascertained it then. What kid could have? In hindsight, however, there is a moment that should have given me a clue. It had to do with the cases that lay under my mother's bed. In them were my father's clarinet and tenor sax, relics of a professional life that had been prematurely silenced. On occasion, I would go up to her bedroom and open the cases, dazzled by their gleam. Tentatively, I placed my lips to the reeds and blew, curious to hear what might come out. I just managed to produce more noise in an already noisy household. My mother coped with our raucous energy however she could. I understand now that even as she silently grieved, she had to be aware that her children were also dealing with the loss. How would growing up without a father, especially in their formative years, affect them?

As I mentioned earlier, women solve problems, and my mother's solution to the problem of me was to enroll me in ballet school before I destroyed the rest of the household furniture. She must've given it a lot of thought. After all, it involved some expenses in a household in which money was scarce. Directing my limitless energy into sports or gymnastics would have been cheaper. But mother chose the world of music and dance. Was that to bind me more closely not just to her dreams but to the dreams of my father?

I thought of that when in 2013 I was made Grand Marshal of the Puerto Rican Day Parade in New York City. It was a lovely June day as I rode on a car through the streets with my grandnieces, Alexis and Arielle. We enjoyed waving to the crowds lined along Fifth Avenue and Central Park, moving to the pulsating Latin rhythms coming from the marching bands. Listening to them, who could possibly sit still? In the band preceding our car, I saw a young sax player, dressed in white pants and a green jacket embroidered with a gold braid. I can't remember my father ever playing for me, and I never had the chance to dance for him. But in that moment, I felt joined to him, as I did when I first glimpsed Puerto Rico. That day, I saw all the del Riveros who'd come to America reflected in the throngs celebrating our heritage and culture. Like my uncle Luciano, many of them had listened on the radio to Ramón "Diplo" Rivero. Or watched his programs on their grainy television sets. The pageantry celebrated the resilience of a people and the sacrifices so many generations had made seeking a better life for their families.

One sacrifice, from among my mother's many, stood out. It was the day that she brought out the saxophone and clarinet from under the bed. I saw her come downstairs cradling them and then she went into the living room where a stranger was waiting to buy them. I can only imagine how emotional she must have been as she handed them over. I'm sure she paid any number of pressing bills with the cash she held in her hands from the sale. But I now wonder if she sold my father's saxophone and clarinet, at least in part, to pay for my dance classes. In any case, I feel that my life and career have been an effort to repay this investment in me born out of grief and love.

For the next several years, the Jones-Haywood School of Ballet felt like a second home to me. The place smelled of sweat and floor wax, with a line of mirrors on a broad wall, along which ran a ballet barre. On one end windows looked out on the tree-lined street, and in the middle of the room a staircase led up to Miss Jones's living quarters. She shared those with Claire Haywood, who had once been her student when she was teaching dance out of her parents' house in Roxbury, Massachusetts.

In 1940, Miss Haywood had persuaded Miss Jones to move to Washington, DC, with her. They had never seen a Black ballet dancer in a production and decided to change that. The following year, they opened the studio to give minorities, especially African Americans, the opportunities that until then had been virtually unavailable to them. Several decades later, after founding the Capitol Ballet Company, Miss Jones was compared to Rosa Parks in a review of a dance honoring the civil rights heroine. "Seeing it, one couldn't help but think of the parallels between Parks and Jones," wrote the *Washington Post* critic Alan M. Kriegsman. "Both had marched in where others had feared to tread, breaking barriers the rest of the world had come to regard as impenetrable."

Both Miss Jones and Miss Haywood were strict disciplinarians, insisting on courtesy and respect among their students. The first thing we learned was that dancing was difficult and demanding. "You practically have to be shaken into it," said Miss Jones. I pictured a dancer in a blender, but I didn't dare giggle. That would not have been tolerated, especially by Miss Haywood, who was forbidding. I gravitated toward Miss Jones, who was also tough but gentle when necessary. She moved through the room with such grace that from the beginning, my goal was to be able to dance like her. I also wanted to sound like her. She corrected our movements in a soft, Bostonian accent so that "can't" came out "cahnt." It made her criticism easier to take. And there was always a lot of it. When Miss Jones moved our bodies into position, there was nothing awkward or tortured about it. What was most important was naturalness combined with technical expertise.

You won't be surprised to learn that her first mission was to get me to focus. She never tamped down my energy but instead directed and contained it. "You have to calm down, Dolores," she said. "You have to learn to concentrate on the moment intensely as though nothing else mattered." We got away with nothing. No excuses were allowed. No matter how hard we tried, the inevitable assessment from Miss Jones was, "Let's take that again. I think you can do much better."

I soon began to look forward to the classes, four times a week for a few hours after school. I was no longer much of a tomboy—skinned knees do not look good on a ballet dancer—and I became more comfortable with my new surroundings. I remained athletic but I developed a feminine poise cultivated by Miss Jones and inspired by the beauty of the taped music in the room. The classical masterpieces of Tchaikovsky, Satie, and Ravel were all new to me. The large console radio at the del Riveros was usually tuned to the sounds of big bands or, more likely, to mysteries like *The Shadow*. ("Who knows what evil lurks in the hearts of men?") I found it easy to be carried away by the gorgeous music while endlessly repeating pliés, étendres, relevés, sautés, tournés, glissés, and élancés. The terms alone unfolded a whole new world beyond our little corner. Sometimes it took me a while to come back down to earth.

Someone else who took a long time to come back to earth—literally— was my classmate Louis Johnson. There were a lot of young women at the school but few boys. A few years older than I, Louis was born in North Carolina and moved with his mother and grandmother to DC when he was six. Through the local YMCA, he fell in love with the arts and gymnastics, learning to tap and perform with Miles Conti. He later joined an acrobatics group that played at neighboring army bases. When the YMCA had to be renovated, they ended up temporarily rehearsing at the Jones-Haywood School. Watching them work out, Miss Jones, who had a good eye for talent, couldn't help but notice this young Black kid who couldn't keep still even during breaks. She asked Louis if he wanted to take ballet classes, and he said "yes" but didn't have the dough. He started paying for classes by cleaning the studio, and the school eventually offered him a scholarship.

Built like the proverbial brick house, Louis was one of the most beautiful ballet dancers I'd ever seen. He had a natural grace, a stunning elevation, and a brilliant technique. He was short, so unlike the taller dancers, who had a languid style, he sprinted, bounced, and flew higher than any of us. Well, almost any of us. I did my best to match him move for move, and we made each other better. Miss Jones often called on Louis and me to demonstrate various techniques for the rest of the students. It didn't give us big heads. At least, I don't think it did. Being a braggart was out of the question at the Jones-Haywood School, though we were taught to command the stage. "Make people take notice of you," Miss Jones said. As recitals neared, they drilled into us the craft of performing. You can imagine just how much I was able to apply this fundamental training when my career on the stage began to take off.

One day, Miss Jones informed us that talent scouts would be arriving from the School of American Ballet in New York to observe classes. George Balanchine, who had cofounded SAB in 1934 with Lincoln Kirstein and Edward Warburg, admired and respected the Jones-Haywood technique. He had the notion he could recruit dancers from the school out of its talent pool.

"It's very important that you do your very best when they come here," Miss Jones told us. "It's all up to you."

I was fifteen at the time, Louis was eighteen, and we were both too naïve to understand the importance of this visit. A few weeks later, Miss Jones, flushed with excitement, took us aside and told us that we had been invited to go to New York to audition for placement in the school. If we passed the test, a scholarship was in the offing.

By the time I got home that night, Miss Jones had already informed my mother about the offer.

"Dolores, do you want to go to New York?" my mother asked me, as she went about preparing the family meal.

Too young to take in fully what lay ahead, I simply said, "Yes."

She then explained that Miss Jones would take Louis and me by train to Manhattan for the auditions the following month. If we got into the school, I could stay with Uncle Luciano and Aunt Rita, who had an apartment in the Bronx.

"Now wash your hands and face, and get ready for dinner," my mother said, matter-of-factly.

A few years before this my older brother, Hoolie, had left home to join the armed forces. Now there was a possibility I would be leaving the house in which I grew up as well. I started to get excited. New York! The School of American Ballet! It all sounded impressive. But what was my mother feeling at that moment? Pride? Loss? Questioning whether she was making the right decision to let me go? Was she wondering what her husband, my father, would have said about his daughter going to the Big City? Only now do I ask myself these questions. How I wish I had sat down at the kitchen table and had a heart-to-heart with my mother. But at fifteen, you don't have those thoughts. Sometimes it takes a lifetime to arrive at a point when you do.

3

BLOOD IN THE TOE SHOES

Miss Jones and I had just gotten off the rickety elevator on the fifth floor of the School of American Ballet when the door of a studio was flung open. A dancer came rushing out into the hallway.

"I can't do it! I can't! I can't! I can't!" she screamed, tears running down her face.

I was nervous to begin with, and this just about finished me off. Like a lot of the other girls at the school, she was tall, blond, and quite beautiful. If she couldn't do it—whatever "it" was—how in the heck was I ever going to pull off this audition?

I turned to Miss Jones. "What happened? Why is she crying?" I said.

She replied, "Just stay in your own lane. Look straight ahead and be yourself."

"Be myself?" I'd never felt shorter, darker, and more Puerto Rican in my life. The women around me seemed taller, thinner, and prettier than I was. I kept thinking that my younger sister, Lola, should be here instead. I had good feet, was flexible and athletic, and had a pretty strong technique. But like our mother, Lola had the makings of a wonderful ballerina. She had good carriage and long legs and torso. I kept telling myself, "Think tall, Chita. Focus." Yet at that moment, I felt like running out of the place screaming, "I can't! I can't! I can't!" But Miss Jones wasn't about to hear of *that*.

We went into a classroom where a teacher was waiting for us. He was of medium build with a high forehead and a full mouth. I was intimidated until he greeted Miss Jones warmly, speaking to her in a thick Russian accent. They spoke about the Jones-Haywood School for a bit as I stood there, my heart beating faster and faster as the minutes wore on. At last, he announced that we were to get to work on the audition. To my disappointment, Miss Jones then left, leaving me alone with him in the room lined with mirrors and a ballet barre. He asked me to begin a series of barre exercises. He watched intently and clapped his hands in time as I performed combinations in the center of the room. I didn't dare look into the mirror—and I didn't dare look at him—as I began to do pirouettes and extensions, as he had requested.

When he asked me to demonstrate fouetté turns, my anxiety began to lessen. Something about the instructor made me want to please him. I even started to enjoy myself. Just as I began to think that maybe I could pull off the audition, he suddenly yelled "Stop!" He motioned for me to join him on the bench. I was embarrassed, thinking I had done something wrong. But as I moved toward him, I looked down and saw blood seeping through my toe shoe. A blister had burst. He asked me to sit on the bench and place my leg on his thigh. "I think we should take care of that, young lady," he said in a gentle manner. He yelled to a staff member to bring him some antiseptic and a Band-Aid. As he daubed and dressed the wound, he asked me about myself and what I hoped to accomplish if I came to the school. I racked my brain to come up with a right answer. Finally, all I could muster was, "Miss Jones thinks I can do much better!"

"Doris is right," he said. "One hundred percent is never enough. You must give 200 percent." After he finished bandaging me up, I resumed the audition. I was so hyped up by that time I didn't feel an ounce of pain.

At the end, Miss Jones came into the room. She and the instructor spoke for a while, occasionally glancing toward me as I sat on the bench, taking in the strange new world I had just stepped into. Suddenly, what had begun as a lark became a goal. For the first time since we had boarded the train in DC, I wanted to get that scholarship, badly.

Finally, after the teacher left the room, Miss Jones, smiling broadly, came over to me. "I have good news, Dolores," she said. "Mr. Balanchine thinks you did very well."

✳

In the musical *The Phantom of the Opera*, Madame Giry, the ballet mistress, beats out the time with her stick and sternly glares at the corps de ballet in tutus. The teachers at the School of American Ballet were nothing like the stereotype. They were strict but much more eccentric and colorful. Several of them, like Mr. Balanchine—and he was always referred to as *Mister* Balanchine—had trained and matured in the schools and theaters of imperial Russia, mainly the Mariinsky in St. Petersburg. So the hallways were always filled with the sound of whispered Russian. Others were from England and the United States, but all were immersed in teaching us the elements of classical ballet. The school had been founded for the purpose of bringing those techniques to America and to train dancers for the New York City Ballet.

Along with Louis Johnson, who was also accepted, I was thrilled to get my slippered feet in the door. I was sixteen at the time, but a very young and naïve sixteen. You'd have thought that going to New York for the first time would have been overwhelming in itself. But I don't quite remember it that way. Before I left DC my mother had arranged for me to live in the Bronx with Uncle Luciano and Aunt Rita. After I arrived, I enrolled at Taft High School on East 172nd Street, so a good part of my days was taken up with the Latino energy on the bustling streets of the Bronx. The subways, bo-degas, and apartments, with their fire escapes and water towers, molded my first impressions of the Big City. Along with those first impressions was one that you can't unsee once you've seen it: a flasher opened his coat to me on the subway. It was no big thing—but a memorable initiation into the peculiar rites of a city I grew to love.

Dancers tend to have tunnel vision. So despite the attractions all around, the magnet for me in those early years were the two floors of SAB in a building at the corner of Fifty-Ninth Street and Madison Avenue. The place may have been a bit shabby on the outside, but inside its walls were classes in the rich style of imperial Russia. It didn't take me long to become comfortable there. Eager to learn, I ate everything up. I quickly adopted the "look"—black tights, skirt, slippers, and de rigueur for a ballet dancer, a ponytail. Years later, when fire alarms went off in my apartment building, I rushed back in to grab my hair extension ponytail. The small blaze was quickly extinguished, but my impulse was not too smart. Blame Dolores.

The teachers, especially the women, embodied beauty, elegance, and grace. There was Muriel Stuart, who'd grown up in England and had studied with both Anna Pavlova at the Russian Academy and Martha Graham in New York. Dorothie Littlefield was an American and a little plump. She was less intimidating than the others and a favorite of begin-ning students. I was closest to Madame Felia Doubrovska, who, like Mr. Balanchine, had come from Russia. She favored floral skirts tied at the waist with a silk scarf and would move through the room with authority, even though she held in her arms Lala, her pet Yorkie. She was strict with us but spoiled Lala, who liked to mark his territory. We had to be careful where we walked. Madame Felia scrutinized our développés and exten-sions for balance and smoothness, and her criticisms were soft-spoken but could be withering. Her husband, Pierre Vladimiroff, was also one of our teachers, and, like her, he emphasized that dancers were performers who owed a debt to the audience: their all. They both stressed precision, limbs in perfect symmetry, attitudes that were alert, animated, and regal. With eyes in the back of their heads, they let us get away with nothing.

This was especially true when it came to Anatole Oboukhoff, who loved to generate in us the two *F*'s: fear and fatigue. Just before class, we could hear him come roaring down the hallway. That allowed us time to stop our gossiping and take our places at the barre. His uniform of choice was black linen pants and a flowing white shirt. Impatiently, he guided us through our routines in fast tempos, shouting out commands, snapping his fingers, and getting up very close to our faces. When he did that, you could smell the strawberry Lifesavers that he popped in his mouth non-stop. If you were very good, he might even reward you with one. He liked repetitions—port de bras, enchaînements—to build up our strength. Just when you thought you couldn't go any further, Mr. Oboukhoff shouted, "Again! Again!" Then he would test you even more by pressing his fingers into you to see if he could catch you off-balance. Some girls couldn't take it and ran out babbling, never to return.

I was game. Even on that day in class when he pushed me under a piano. We had been repeating countless relevés—a rise to the toes from a flat foot—and he knelt down to press his hands around my ankle. He wanted to see how strong I was and how long I could stay in that position. I could feel myself start to wobble and worried that I might land right on top of him. Sure enough, I "sickled" (buckled) and was about to land on his head when he pushed me out of the way and under the piano. I crawled back, looked up at his disapproving face, and burst out laughing. Which made the other girls in the room start to giggle. Then I jumped up, regained my composure, and took up a relevé attitude. Mr. Oboukhoff stared at me for what seemed like an eternity, then reached into his pocket and put a Lifesaver in my hand, extended in position.

SAB was like boot camp, and I relished it. You were tested constantly. I expected that. The year before I had gotten a taste of what was in store when I saw *The Red Shoes*. My brother Hoolie showed a print of it in the basement movie theater in our house. I was fascinated by the film. I thought Moira Shearer was wonderful as Victoria Page, whose ballet slippers become magical. I became disturbed, however, when they turned against her. I didn't fully understand the film until I got to SAB and realized just how much sacrifice a career in dance demands.

In this new world, our Victoria Page was Maria Tallchief. The year I arrived at SAB, she'd just enjoyed tremendous success as the lead in Stravinsky's *The Firebird*, choreographed by Mr. Balanchine. The intensity of her performance revolutionized ballet and established her as a prima ballerina. Her performance became the talk of the school, and I longed to see it but couldn't afford to buy a ticket. The next best thing was to look through a peephole in the door of the rehearsal room as Mr. Balanchine worked with Maria and other dancers I admired. These included Nora Kaye, with her passion, and Tanaquil LeClercq, who had legs that seemed to go on forever. We students would gather outside the door and take turns peering in, humbled by what we saw. I wanted to be able to dance like that but despaired that I ever could. Being a prima ballerina or even a principal seemed beyond my grasp. Just getting to dance in the corps of the New York City Ballet was the extent of my ambition.

For the first couple of years at SAB, I held fast to that dream. That was all we students ever talked about. But in time, perhaps even without my knowing it, seeds were being planted that would lead me in a different direction. That started with Janet Collins, a teacher at the school. Since I had been placed at level B as a student, my curriculum did not include the class she taught. It was called "character" or "plastique" dance, and it was significantly different from the traditional techniques of my classes. Miss Collins was young, attractive, and African American, the only person of color on the faculty. She'd been born in New Orleans, raised in Los Angeles, and had studied with Katherine Dunham. After she won acclaim at the 92nd Street Y for works she had choreographed and designed, Mr. Balanchine invited her to replace Merce Cunningham as a guest instructor at SAB. She taught a smart blend of modern dance, ballet, and what she'd learned with Katherine Dunham. There weren't many males at the school, and a lot of them were concentrated within her class, including Louis Johnson. I liked to watch them go through their combinations, which were more strenuous and faster than ours. The jumps were higher, the energy hotter, the moves freer and boundary-busting. Louis excelled under Miss Collins's mentorship and soon established himself as a force in the school. I joined the boys whenever I could, just for the fun of it all. I was thrilled to learn that another kind of dance existed beyond classical ballet.

From the moment I started studying at the Jones-Haywood School, I had thought of little else other than ballet. Miss Collins's class was a revelation. As was another discovery: the Palladium. Around my third year at SAB, a group of dancers suggested I join them at the Palladium Ballroom, a large dance hall at Broadway and Fifty-Third. It was not far from the apartment of my brother Hoolie. After two years in the service, he had moved to Manhattan and been hired as a photographer for the Medical Film Guild. When I graduated from Taft High School, I moved in with him. The Palladium had recently started promoting Latin Nights with the orchestras of the Two Titos: Tito Puente and Tito Rodriguez. My first visit to the place was a real eye-opener. I loved it.

Hundreds of couples—Cubans, Puerto Ricans, Dominicans, and Panamanians—dressed to the nines and packed shoulder-to-shoulder were furiously dancing nonstop under the colored lights and the blaring music of the large orchestras. It was said that if you hadn't played the Palladium, then you still weren't an orchestra or a musician. It proved a rite of passage for me as well. I quickly became carried away with those nights at the Palladium. There were competitions, and they were almost always won by a young and sexy couple who were amazing to watch on the dance floor. Augie and Margo Rodriguez had recently married and were just beginning a career of concerts and television appearances that would make them famous as "ambassadors of mambo." Their style was to mix Latin dance with elements of ballet, jazz, modern dance, and sheer athleticism. Who could stand still while listening to the sensational music and watching the hip-swiveling crowd? I was soon out on the dance floor fusing my ballet training with the salsa, mambo, and rumba steps I was learning.

At SAB, I had become totally immersed in the timeless traditions of the imperial Russian ballet. At the Palladium, I was drunk on the sense of possibility in the room. The United States had just won a world war, and Latinos were expressing the optimism and promise of their adopted country, just as my father, Pedro Julio, had done when he arrived from Yabucoa. Inspired by Miss Collins and Margo and Augie, I could sense that my ballet training could expand to include the rhythms that had always been a part of my being.

Then one day, something else became a little more real to me: Broadway. I knew of it, of course. Hoolie was a fan. But we SAB students were kind of snobby when it came to musical theater. When we heard someone was going out for an audition, we turned up our noses: "Oh, she's going to be in a *musical*? Poor thing." But the chatter in the hallways of SAB suddenly took a turn. Miss Collins was going to make her Broadway debut in Cole Porter's *Out of This World*, staged by Agnes de Mille. There was no way we could disrespect either of them. Agnes de Mille had choreographed Aaron Copland's *Rodeo* and brought her ballet expertise to Broadway in *Oklahoma!*

By then, I had begun to wonder whether my temperament was suited to ballet. After my run-in with Mr. Oboukhoff, I enjoyed my status as the class clown. I had a hard time suppressing my slapstick gene, making funny faces that cracked up the students when the teachers' backs were turned. It was entertaining, but it had no place in the serious world of ballet. Even if I made it into the corps de ballet, I thought I'd be fired because I couldn't manage to keep a straight face. My classmates tended to agree. They couldn't picture me in a lineup either, dancing en pointe in *Swan Lake*. To get the impression that I wasn't a good fit for the ballet, all you had to do was look at them and then look at me. They were the picture of what was then called "All-American." That wasn't me. Come to think of it, I was probably the first and only Latina at SAB while I was there. Louis Johnson was one of only two Blacks at SAB, joined by Arthur Bell and, eventually, Arthur Mitchell. Ballet at that time was an almost exclusively white world. As much as I longed to learn to dance as well as Maria Tallchief or Nora Kaye, I must've known on some level that being a principal or soloist wasn't in my future. As it happened, it would take another twenty-five years before Evelyn Cisneros of the San Francisco Ballet made history as the first Hispanic prima ballerina.

In time, I would learn that my future belonged outside the ballet world. But the training I received at SAB would form the basis for my entire career. I learned to consider what I do as a vocation—a calling—that demands discipline, commitment, and passion. The teachers wouldn't tolerate sloppiness. They taught us to endure pain without complaint, to do what we were told without excuses. Miss Jones and the teachers at SAB prepared me not just for a career but for life. Years later, when a car accident shattered my leg, I had only to picture Miss Jones saying, "Dolores, you can get through this," to know that I would.

Among the many pictures on my mantle is a vintage one of a young man in a ballet costume, back ramrod straight, arms in perfect extension, and an expression of serious intent on his face. It is Anatole Oboukhoff. I can't look at that picture without being reminded of metronomes, whispered Russian in hallways, repetitions until you drop, and the smell of strawberry Lifesavers. Ballet was a life saver for me.

4

MAKE 'EM LAUGH

———————

On the Road with *Call Me Madam*

One day in early spring of 1952, I asked my friend Helen if she wanted to join me at the Horn & Hardart Automat on Park Avenue and Forty-Second Street. The self-service place was a favorite of SAB students, where we could sit with a cup of "free" lemonade we made from hot water and lemon slices. Or when we were feeling flush, we could slip a nickel into the slot of a shiny aluminum dispenser, slide back a small window, and grab a piece of pie.

"I can't, Chita," she said, shortening my middle name from Conchita, as all my friends now did. "I'm going to audition for a Broadway show this afternoon."

I may have been skeptical of musical theater in the past, but with my newfound appreciation for the art form, this news perked me up.

"Oh, really? A Broadway show, huh? Which one?" I asked.

"*Call Me Madam*," she said. "It's at the Imperial now but a national tour is going out in May. Gonna play some weeks in Washington, DC, and then across the country for a year. The pay should be pretty good."

I can't say for sure if the notion of going back to my hometown in a Broadway show was even an inkling in my mind at the time. When you've just turned nineteen and consider yourself a ballet dancer, the idea of touring the country as a hoofer in a Broadway show seems exotic, if not out of reach—until, suddenly, it doesn't.

"Do you mind if I tag along?" I said.

Just the year before I had attended *Gentlemen Prefer Blondes*, starring Carol Channing, at the Ziegfeld Theatre. "Attended" might be overstating it. In those days, I couldn't afford the two bucks for a cheap balcony seat, much less the five for an orchestra ticket. So, along with my pals, we'd mingle with theatergoers at the intermission of a show and then sneak in for the second act. I can never forget the moment that I saw Carol as gold digger Lorelei Lee, lighting up the stage. With her saucer-eyed expressions, she was a combo of craftiness and innocence. But what really got me was how her dogged strength brought men to heel. Now *that* was the kind of woman I wanted to be.

Tall and gangly, she didn't look to me like what a "star" should look like. I was used to seeing fragile beauties on the screen. In fact, Carol was unlike anything I'd ever seen before, and to top it off, she was daring to go to places that I didn't even know existed. It blew me away that a woman could hold a stage like that.

"I want to do what she does to an audience," I thought. "I don't know how she does it, but I want to learn how to do that kind of magic."

✳

Helen and I stepped onto the stage of the Imperial Theatre where *Call Me Madam* was playing, stashed our dance bags in the corner, and started warming up on the stage with hundreds of other girls. I could overhear them talking among themselves like old pros, checking out the competition, considering their chances, and wondering whether "Mr. Robbins," the choreographer of the show, was going to be making the final selections. Eight women would be chosen to join with eight men to make up the dance chorus. In time, they'd be supplemented with another sixteen performers who'd do the singing. Thirty-two in all, just for the chorus!

I was of course familiar with the name of Jerry Robbins, since by that time he had made a name for himself in the world of ballet with *Fancy Free*, which had been turned into the musical *On the Town*. But I was so clueless that I scarcely knew of Ethel Merman, then the star of *Call Me Madam*, much less George Abbott, the director. And if I'd looked around the room, I would have seen a young twenty-four-year-old assistant stage manager named Harold Prince.

When Bobby Griffith, the stage manager, asked us to line up, Helen moved toward the back of the theater. With no fear, a little daring, and a lot of naïveté, I claimed a space in the front row. My ballet training came in handy. The routines we were asked to do came easy. Watching the other girls put some extra spin in their dancing, I followed suit. It was exhilarating. As the afternoon wore on, I learned for the first time what "Thank you" meant in the audition process: "Goodbye, better luck next time." Miraculously, I didn't hear it through the dozens of cuts that included Helen. Instead, toward the end, I heard, "Conchita del Rivero, could we see you dance with Kip Carlisle, please."

A tall, cute guy with dark hair and blue eyes came over, introduced himself, and took me in his arms. This is getting better all the time, I thought. Of course, I had been partnered in ballet since starting classes with Miss Jones, mainly with the exuberant Louis Johnson. But dancing to Irving Berlin's "The Ocarina" with Kip was proving to be a far different experience than the Bluebird pas de deux from *The Sleeping Beauty*. As the song progressed, something very new was happening to me: ballet was slowly receding to the back of my mind. In this place, there wasn't anybody yelling, "Plié, assemblée, tour en l'air! Again!" Or pushing you under a piano when you cracked up your fellow students. Here you were rewarded for making people laugh. I felt at home.

Maybe that was why I wasn't all that surprised when Bobby, the stage manager, told me that I had the job. There are those moments in life when you feel in your bones that this is where you were always meant to be: for me, it was the theater. It felt welcoming. It felt right. It felt safe.

Now that I was cast, I thought it might be a good idea to find out what the show was about. *Call Me Madam* had already been playing for two years on Broadway. But what did I know then? Up to this point, my world in New York had been SAB dance classes and the subway that took me between them and home with Uncle Luciano and Aunt Rita in the Bronx. The show had been inspired by Perle Mesta, a real-life Washington, DC, hostess, whom Harry Truman had named ambassador to the small country of Luxembourg. Howard Lindsay, Russel Crouse, and Irving Berlin had written the role expressly for Merman to play ambassador to the fictional principality of Lichtenburg. A rich widow, she gets romantically mixed up with the handsome foreign minister Cosmo Constantine. It sure wasn't *Giselle*.

I gathered with the chosen dancers to hear Bobby explain what came next. "We'll rehearse for four weeks, opening in DC with Merman and the original cast. Then after three weeks there, you'll play another week with the replacement cast before hitting the road." The road? The word meant nothing to me. I only knew that I was going to go to work and collect a paycheck for doing something that I loved to do: dance.

Kip raised his hand. "Who's gonna replace The Merm?" he asked.

"Elaine Stritch," said Bobby. "You'll like her, kids. She's a kick."

∗

Of course, the first thing I did when I got the job was to call home. My excitement came through the crackle of the collect call I placed to my mother.

"Dolores, what's the matter?" she said, alarmed. In those days, long distance was expensive, and you called home only in an emergency.

I explained the sudden turn in my fortunes, the words tumbling out so fast that it was hard for her to catch up. Mother recognized how thrilled I was, and she in turn was happy for me. And concerned. She knew just how headstrong and independent I was. Going on tour with *Call Me Madam* meant a year away from home traveling across the country, staying in God-knows-what-kind of places, and in the company of people who were not necessarily as disciplined and focused as ballet dancers. These were *show people* her Dolores would be living among.

Mother wasn't about to take my word for it. She hopped on the train to New York and conferred with Carl Bernstein, the company manager (not *that* Carl Bernstein). He reassured her that I would be chaperoned under the watchful eye of Frances Clark and Owen Coll, an older couple who would be playing the duke and duchess in the production. Only after they had passed Mom's approval did she allow me to sign the contract. What she hadn't counted on was just how determined I could be in escaping any kind of supervision—and that the star of the production would take me under her wing. Bobby Griffith was right. But I didn't just like Elaine Stritch; I worshiped her. Which was exactly what Elaine needed from everyone all the time, as I was to find out.

I don't know why Elaine took a shine to me. Maybe because I was the youngest in the cast, though she herself was only twenty-seven at the time. She seemed so much older, but then, she was always being cast in roles beyond her years. It was almost as if, like Tallulah Bankhead, she could say, "I was born—then I was forty." Also, we were both Catholic, and in those days Catholics sought out other Catholics. I'd even heard that her uncle was a cardinal in the Church. When I met Elaine, she still had something of the convent girl from Michigan about her.

"Y'know, Chita, Catholicism isn't that different from show business," she once told me. "It's theatrical and it doesn't close on a Saturday night."

In those early days, Elaine noticed that I was watching her during rehearsals every chance that I got. And why not? She was then a glamorous, slim, and long-legged blonde, worlds away from what she'd later become: the popular, brassy, and bawdy entertainer who could turn the air blue and crack up an audience just by singing "Ohhhhh" in a song like "Broadway Baby" from *Follies*. Or blasting out a guttural primal scream as Joanne in "The Ladies Who Lunch" from *Company*. Her voice was much smoother then as well, not having yet been made smoky through too many cigarettes and long nights in saloons. I also was shocked to see that she never wore a bra during rehearsals. "They're too damn constricting," she said.

Having become famous in the New York columns for whom she dated—Marlon Brando, producer-director Jed Harris, and tycoon Conrad Hilton—Elaine was hell-bent on becoming a star and was unapologetic about it. She wanted the "whole cheese," as she once put it to me. "It's too fucking hard otherwise." That just made her more nervous about playing her first starring role in *Call Me Madam*. Even worse, she was stepping into the shoes of Ethel Merman, who was set to play the beginning of the national tour with us in DC. Comparisons were inevitable. The engagement itself was a big deal. Not only was the show a parody about Washington politics, but it was also the inaugural production of the newly renovated National Theatre.

Call Me Madam was a big deal for me, too. I was coming home. It had been a little over three years since I'd gotten on the train with Doris Jones and Louis Johnson to go to New York to audition for the School of American Ballet. And here I was making my stage debut in a hit Broadway show at the National. The theater was only a few miles from Flagler Place, but it might as well have been in another country. I was going to be able to invite my mother, Grandma Sallie, and my siblings to see me in a show. While my family didn't know an Ethel Merman from a Kate Smith, they were thrilled to see their first Broadway show. I couldn't have been prouder to introduce them to my new chorus mates. Stardom still seemed a galaxy away, so I never thought to introduce them to Ethel Merman.

To tell you the truth, I didn't *get* Merman. I knew that she had an adoring Broadway public and her name meant a lot at the box office. She had an impressive voice that could reach the balcony, and the grateful audience sent it bouncing right back. But I didn't find her warm and funny. Not like Stritch. Elaine was more subtle and amusing in the part. She was sexier, too, probably because she was starring opposite Kent Smith, as General Cosmo Constantine. Kent was handsome, debonair, and eighteen years older than Elaine. He had by that time been in a series of movies, including *Cat People* and *The Curse of the Cat People*—just the kind of flicks that my brother Hoolie would have screened in our basement on Flagler Place.

Once we were on the road, Elaine often invited me to her dressing room, most times just before Kent would arrive. That should have tipped me off that I was meant to be some sort of camouflage for them. They were clearly mad for each other, and Kent was married at the time, even if that relationship was on the rocks. I was vaguely uncomfortable about playing the role of decoy for their intimate get-togethers, though I was never sure just how intimate they were. Catholic girls practically invented guilt, but I knew by that time that stolen kisses could be hotter than those freely given.

Before I scooted out of the dressing room to leave Elaine and Kent on their own, there were glasses of champagne to be sipped. Bottles of bubbly were always chilling in buckets in the dressing room. In those days, everybody drank and it was tolerated, even by such a strict director as George Abbott. There's a story that when Elaine was rehearsing *Call Me Madam*, she was having a tough time with the song "You're Just in Love." She came to one rehearsal with a coffee cup filled with scotch. She kept blowing on the cup, pretending that it was too hot to drink.

"Hot coffee, Elaine?" said Mr. Abbott.

"Yes sir," she replied.

"Can I have a sip?" he said.

Elaine had to oblige. Mr. Abbott tasted it and handed back the cup. "Hmmm. Good coffee," is all he said. He probably knew it was a way for Elaine to steel her nerves. She admitted to me that she'd gotten through the opening night of *Call Me Madam* in DC with a rosary and a bottle of brandy. "At least it was Benedictine," she cracked.

Onstage, Elaine never showed an ounce of fear or nerves. Even that early in her career, she taught me how to command a stage, how to make your talents suit the role rather than the other way around. In her hands, Sally Adams became a sly, wise-cracking dame with feminine grit and flawless timing. Elaine demanded the attention of the audience, and once she got it, she never let them look anywhere else. Like Carol Channing, she got away with things that nobody else could by sheer force of personality. She was tough, and through that toughness she was funny. By pretending that she didn't care if you laughed or not, she soaked every bit of humor out of the role and then some. Which could make it rough on her costars.

Kent wasn't threatened by her. He liked their chemistry onstage. But David Daniel, who played Kenneth Gibson, Sally Adams's press attaché, had to put up with her stealing every scene. "You're Just in Love," the duet between Sally and Kenneth, which Elaine finally nailed, became a highlight of the show. Dressed in a nightgown for the scene, she flipped around her skirt of pink tulle so much that you could barely see David. She used her body like a natural athlete.

Elaine encouraged me to study, as she had, with Erwin Piscator and Lee Strasberg, the great gurus of the time. But I was having too much fun dancing to be concerned with method acting. Besides, dancing was acting, wasn't it? I had learned that from the moment I stepped foot in Doris Jones's dance school. And dancing in *Call Me Madam* was the most fun yet. I was amazed at how easily I assimilated into that world.

I'll never forget walking for the first time into the dressing rooms we shared in the basement of the National Theatre. There were all these gorgeous girls with their legs up on the makeup tables, putting on nylons, beading their eyelashes, daubing on their eyeliner, and looking over their shoulders to give me the once over. I felt like a little drowned rat next to them, but they soon welcomed "the kid" into their club. Since ballet dancers don't do makeup all that well, they taught me how to work it in front of the lined mirrors: Nivea cream, Max Factor powder, Chanel rouge, Nars semi-red lipstick, and Mehron pancake.

If I was worried that I might not measure up to the seasoned professionals who were at those tables, I needn't have. I was lucky that my dancing partner in *Call Me Madam* was Kip Carlisle. He was the bomb! And it didn't hurt in the least that he was cute. As a dancer, you're only as good as what you're doing and who you're doing it with or doing it to. And Kip helped me a lot.

✳

I soon learned that the chorus was all about the power of the group. If you were in it for yourself, you didn't last long. It was about looking out for one another. If you didn't, you could get killed. Or at least run over. From the very beginning, I never felt like I was alone out there. If you got lost—"Wait a minute, how did I get this far left?" or "Shit! I dropped an earring!"—you were never lost for long because the line would bring you right back to where you belonged. We were like a living, breathing chain, only as strong as its weakest link, bound together by a desire to make magic for the audience. Decades later, Gwen Verdon and I would be "two dancing as one" in *Chicago*. But then, in 1952, we were sixteen dancing as one.

What struck me most was the closeness of the company. We dancers made fun of the singers, and the singers made fun of us. They tried to dance, but couldn't, and we tried to sing, but couldn't. They had the most gorgeous voices, which, for me, was an aphrodisiac. I even dated one of the singers in the show. Keyed up after performances, we'd hit the local bars and sing around the piano until last call. At age nineteen, I was under the drinking age at the time but Owen Coll and Frances Clark didn't stand a chance. I wasn't about to let the group go to the Top of the Mark in San Francisco or Sammy's in Chicago without me. While my chaperones thought I was in my room reading Edna Ferber's bestseller *Giant*, I was sneaking out of my room with my partners in crime, Mary Alice Kubes and Rae Abruzzo.

After I was bounced out of one club because of my age, Rae suggested that I might look older if I dyed my black hair champagne blond and shaped it into a poodle cut. I was a little bit reluctant to cut off my ponytail—almost every ballet dancer had one in those days. But I came out of a beauty parlor in Chicago with a new hairdo that I thought made me look more sophisticated. It probably only made me look more like a poodle. I suppose I was as wild in those days as I had to be, which wasn't all that wild. Whenever I was about to get into any serious trouble—what Elaine called "bad girl shit"—thoughts of my mother would pull me back. God and Mother kept me on the straight and narrow.

Most of the time, we traveled in trains, bedding down in a series of Pullman cars rumbling through the American countryside. We'd pull down the partitions and have pajama parties, playing cards, knitting, and swapping stories, sort of like those scenes of the girl band in the movie *Some Like It Hot*. I loved playing the class clown. Dancers were the jokers; singers were the more serious type. The length of the tour, a year, allowed you to get to know people and yourself really well. If someone was selfish, I learned to ignore it. And when I couldn't ignore it, I learned to put any negativity in a place where I didn't let it affect me, personally or professionally. Having that length of time to be a part of an ensemble in close quarters provided invaluable lessons that I would recommend for anybody coming up in the business.

The national tour of *Call Me Madam* was a joyous time for me. I was, as the song goes, "walking on air." This period in Broadway history is often referred to as a golden age. That usually refers to great artists—like Irving Berlin, Cole Porter, Rodgers and Hammerstein, and Lerner and Loewe—creating musicals at the peak of their powers. But it was a golden age for performers too because there was so much *work* each season. So many *opportunities* to learn and practice our craft. And that's all we wanted from life. And the applause? That was just icing on the cake, a barometer that we were doing a good job. I was yet to learn what Elaine Stritch told me early on: "The audience, Chita, can be your best friend."

Another added bonus was what Sally Adams in *Call Me Madam* called, "Cabbage, lettuce, money!" For the first time in my life I was earning a bonanza—$250 a week. I liked having money. I liked spending it. On a poodle cut or anything else. But I knew that as soon as I could, I would buy my mother a mink stole. You know, one of those wraps that have the mink biting the tail of another mink. I will never forget the look on her face when I handed her the box from Saks Fifth Avenue—this woman who had sacrificed so much for her family throughout all the hard years since my father had died.

"Oh, Dolores," she said, "I can hardly wait until Sunday so I can show it off at Mass."

A photo of my beloved mother in the park wearing the stole—chic, elegant, and so very happy—is one of my most treasured belongings.

Call her Madam del Rivero.

5

A MOMENTOUS ENCOUNTER

Gwen Verdon and *Can-Can*

The year was 1954, I had turned twenty-one, and much to my surprise, I was in a smash hit on Broadway, *Can-Can*, written and directed by Abe Burrows and choreographed by Michael Kidd. In fact, this show would seed the beginning of my career, and the gardener would be none other than Gwen Verdon.

One afternoon between the matinee and evening performances of *Can-Can*, I was on my way to the chorus dressing room of the Shubert Theatre on the third floor when Dee Dee Wood, my friend and fellow castmate, caught up with me.

"Chita, Gwen is looking for you," she said.

"Gwen Verdon wants to see me? Why?" I said.

Dee Dee just shrugged her shoulders. Worried that I'd done something wrong, I hurried back down to the second floor where Gwen, the breakout star of *Can-Can*, had her dressing room. Even though I was six months into the run, I didn't really know her all that well. At that time, chorus kids rarely if ever socialized with the stars of a production and didn't talk to them unless they were summoned. What made Gwen's request even more puzzling was that I had earlier auditioned to understudy her in the featured role of Claudine. She was one of the laundresses who nightly danced the naughty can-can at the nightclub run by La Môme Pistache, played by the French star Lilo. To my disappointment, I didn't get the gig. Who was I kidding, anyway? How could I have had the charisma to step into Gwen's shoes if called upon? I could just imagine the groans when the stage manager announced, "Ladies and gentlemen, at this performance, the role of Claudine, usually played by Gwen Verdon, will be played by Conchita del Rivero." Conchita who? Maybe in time I could manage that. But not now.

The door to Gwen's dressing room was open, so she first saw me reflected in her makeup mirror, standing by the door. She was dressed in her striped costume, with red hair piled atop her head in an up-do and a velvet choker around her neck. She beckoned me to grab a chair and join her at the dressing table. As I sat down beside her, I was taken in by her luminous green eyes, flawless complexion, and wide mouth, which had broken out into a welcoming grin. The air was suffused with the smell of greasepaint mixed with her favorite perfume, and, to my mind, the confidence of an actress who was wowing the audience night after night.

Turning to me, Gwen said in that unmistakable, quivering voice, "Listen, Chita, I know you may be discouraged that you didn't get the understudy job. But let me tell you something. You don't need to understudy anybody. Be more confident. Go out and create your own roles. Forge your own path."

I felt my face getting flushed, as though a weather system was flowing through me. She had just blown open a door. But to where? I wasn't sure. I just knew that in that moment my life had changed. This advice wasn't coming from a parent, a teacher, or a peer. It was coming from someone who knew talent and knew the business. Before Gwen had come to Broadway, she'd been the assistant to the mercurial and difficult choreographer Jack Cole on the West Coast. That alone made us dancers idolize her. Then came the opening night of *Can-Can*, which had the critics competing to find the superlatives to describe her show-stopping performance.

Declaring her the "dance discovery of the season," Walter Kerr in the

New York Herald Tribune wrote: "Miss Verdon comes upon sex with a magnificent astonishment, rueful, dismayed, interested, and deeply pleased all at once. The abandon with which she takes over the later, 'Apache' business—sending chairs and males spinning with a flick of her ankle—is devastating."

Now, in her dressing room and faced with such a gift of encouragement, I could only mumble my thanks, resist the impulse to curtsy or kiss her hand, and float out of the room.

"So what did Gwen want?" Dee Dee asked as I sat down at the rows of mirrors lining one wall of the chorus dressing room.

"Oh, she just wanted to console me for losing out on the understudy role," I responded. What I should have said is, "Gwen told me to grow a pair."

✴

I had never wanted anything so much as being a part of *Can-Can*. While we were on the road with *Call Me Madam*, the buzz had reached us that Cole Porter had written a new show, a follow-up to his comeback success *Kiss Me, Kate*. It was about a nightclub in Montmartre in nineteenth-century Paris that drew the ire of the morality police because it featured ladies showing their bloomers in a scandalous dance called the can-can. Even more of a lure to us dancers was that Michael Kidd was going to be the choreographer. You had made the grade if you could master his athletic, high-kicking, and earthy dances.

I missed the auditions for *Can-Can* because I was still on the road with *Call Me Madam*. When I finally returned to New York in the late spring of 1953, the show was in its pre-Broadway tryout in Philadelphia. I thought that ship had sailed. But then word got around that one of the chorus dancers had to drop out because of illness, and Michael Kidd was holding auditions in New York to replace her. I couldn't get there fast enough. But

I was not alone. When I arrived at the rehearsal hall, hundreds of other dancers were there, also hoping for the chance to be the replacement.

Through the crowd of women in leotards warming up on the stage of the theater, I got my first glimpse of the man who'd by that time won Tony Awards for *Finian's Rainbow* and *Guys and Dolls*, the musical phenomenon that was then still playing on Broadway. Michael was lithe and muscular, with thick dark hair and sensual lips. He was shorter than I thought, maybe because he loomed so large in my imagination. With his rough and swarthy features, he didn't even look like a dancer. He looked more like the gangster he'd played in his youth in the Ballet Caravan production of *Filling Station*. Or like the Chaplinesque handyman he'd fashioned for himself in his own ballet, *On Stage!*, which he'd done before he was whisked off to Broadway.

Putting us through our paces, Michael was incredibly precise. He asked for pirouettes, step ball changes, tour jetés, and chaînés. Then just for fun, he ordered us to do double stomps and turkey trot steps—fast, robust steps that were so much a signature of his shows. After he'd winnowed down the group to about two dozen, he announced, "Okay, girls, now I want you to change into high heels for the next routines." There were some groans as we hurried over to our dance bags. But like most choreographers, he ignored our complaints. Pain and exhaustion were just part of the territory. Besides, Michael never asked dancers to do anything he couldn't do himself. By that time the Kidd legend had been polished by a story making the rounds. A few years earlier, he'd been rehearsing the number "Take Back Your Mink," from *Guys and Dolls*. Onna White, then a dancer in the chorus, raised her hand.

"Michael, we can't do this routine in heels. It just won't work."

Without missing a beat, Kidd said, "Onna, gimme your shoes."

He had small feet so he had no problem fitting into the high heels. Michael then proceeded to execute the entire routine, flawlessly. There were no further complaints. Or at least the dancers just talked among

themselves about it. Sprains and bruises were commonplace as we tried
to do what Michael did so easily. A few years later, Grover Dale said that
when he was in *Li'l Abner*, he and Tony Mordente couldn't wait to finish
yet another one of Michael's exhausting marathon dances. Then at the
end, as they gasped for breath, they would whisper to each other, "Fuck
you, Michael Kidd!"

✳

About an hour into the *Can-Can* replacement audition, the hopefuls had
been whittled from hundreds to two: another girl and me. At this point,
Michael took us each aside. It was part of his process to draw out the personalities of his dancers with a chat. If they were tense or uncomfortable
while talking to him, it was a sign that they weren't going to fit into the
ensemble.

I was nervous at first. Though he was only thirty-six at the time, he
seemed so much older. But Michael put me at ease with his sense of humor and blue-collar background. The child of Russian-Jewish immigrants
whose father was a barber, Michael had worked as everything—soda jerk,
jazz drummer, photographer, and newspaper copy boy. His real name was
Milton Greenwald, but he quickly earned the nickname "kid" because he
was small and skinny. At first, his ambition was to be a chemical engineer
until a friend took him to a modern dance performance. Shortly after that
he found himself in front of mirrors practicing what he'd just seen on the
stage. Eventually he started taking classes "just for fun." He liked the vigor
and camaraderie he found in the dance world as opposed to the sterile
environment of science. "No people. No laughs. Too lonely," he said.

Then one day, Michael was in the chemistry lab when someone asked
him, "What the heck is a pirouette, anyway?" So he did one. The only
problem was that he smashed into some expensive equipment and sent

hydrochloric acid flying everywhere. He recalled, "The prof suggested maybe I should take a leave of my studies before I killed somebody. When I told my parents I wanted to be a dancer, they thought I was crazy!"

I responded by telling him that I almost killed myself smashing into a coffee table before my mother sent me off to dance lessons with Doris Jones. "Maybe we're too dangerous to be around," he said. When I told him about the scholarship to the School of American Ballet, his expression brightened. "I went there too!" he said. "That's where I learned that dance has to be character-driven. Dance without emotion, without connecting with an audience, is not dance. Not to me." As we shared war stories of our dance teachers at SAB, I began to think that I had a pretty good shot at getting that replacement job.

The optimism didn't last long. My so-called charmed career came to a screeching halt when I endured the first crushing disappointment in the theater. (With many to follow, I might add.) I didn't get the part. I headed for the exit, humiliated, and made a beeline for Sid and Al's. At any given time, there'd be a heap of dance bags thrown in the corner of the restaurant. This was where all the chorus kids went to grab a glass of milk, a cup of coffee, or a double bourbon to celebrate snagging a role or to drown their sorrows when they didn't. Joining a table of friends, I asked for my usual vodka and tonic since I'd heard by that time that gin made women mean. While my friends commiserated with me, I suddenly saw Michael Kidd enter the restaurant and move toward our table.

Standing next to me, Michael said, "Chita, I had to come over and tell you that the only reason you didn't get the part is because you couldn't fit into the shoes and costumes of the girl leaving the show. The producers don't want to spend the money on a new outfit."

Wow! I thought. So that was it: you could get—or not get—a job based on factors far beyond your control. The size of your feet. Or your head. It's a basic lesson of show business, but it was a first for me. I felt the gloom lifting. I thanked Michael for telling me. He certainly didn't have to, but that was the kind of guy he was. What I didn't tell him was that I'd have cut off my toes like Cinderella's stepsisters to get into *Can-Can*.

Michael then said, "Listen, the minute I need to replace anybody in *Guys and Dolls*, the role's yours. That goes for when we need a new girl in *Can-Can* too." And then he added, "You're good, Chita. But you can be so much better." Note taken.

✳

Michael was true to his word, and a few weeks later, I was called to replace Onna White in *Guys and Dolls*. It was the first time I stepped onto a Broadway stage, but I don't recall marking that event in any way. I didn't—and still don't—differentiate between Broadway and the road. Maybe it was because my first role was in the national tour of *Call Me Madam*, and to me, audiences are audiences. They come into the theater, whether in New York City or Keokuk, Iowa, with the same hopes and expectations: to be entertained, and to tell the performers, as someone once said, "Move me, astonish me, break my heart."

What I could feel when I stepped onto the stage of the 46th Street Theatre, now the Richard Rodgers, were the ghosts of every performer who had ever graced the place. I'm one of those crazy people who can hear the faint sounds of actors, dancers, and singers of past shows, their steps echoing through the decades down to us. So when I went to see *Hamilton* at the Rodgers, there was no way I couldn't feel the presence of Vivian Blaine, who was achingly funny singing "Adelaide's Lament," and Isabel Bigley, beating her drum to summon those dice-tossing "sinners" played by Sam Levene, Robert Alda, and Stubby Kaye. I was a Hot Box Girl in *Guys and Dolls* for only a few months and enjoyed every minute of it.

I was put into a featured dance role in the number "Havana," which is when the story of Sky Masterson and Sarah Brown moves to Cuba.

As a Latina, I could put extra verve into the riotous sequence. There is just something in my blood that makes my hips move like a washer on high speed, and I wished that my father, Pedro Julio, who'd played with some Latin greats, could have seen me in the show. And, by the way, I had no problem dancing in those high heels. I've always loved high heels, on stage and off. I love the way the shoes sexily elongate a woman's legs. As Bette Midler once said, "Give a girl the right shoes and she can conquer the world." To this day, you'll never find me in flats or sneakers.

I also had a good time performing in the "Take Back Your Mink" burlesque in *Guys and Dolls* during which we started out in Alvin Colt's extravagant gowns and fake fur stoles and then stripped down to lacy black Teddys. We looked good! But as Michael always said, "Beauty onstage is nothing, girls. It's not enough to look good. You must *feel* good."

✴

In early 1954, after a few months in *Guys and Dolls*, I got the call to join the cast of *Can-Can* by replacing Ina Hahn, one of the laundresses who also played the Inchworm in the famous "Garden of Eden" ballet. I hate those furry things with dozens of legs, but that didn't stop me from wanting to be the best inchworm who ever crawled across the floor of the Shubert Theatre. The dances in *Can-Can* were far more strenuous than anything I'd done in *Guys and Dolls*, but I was determined to match up to a chorus that was made up of the best dancers anywhere. Just barely twenty-one, I was the youngest of the group, so their instinct was to help out "the kid" until I got my sea legs.

I began a habit of getting to the theater a good hour or even ninety minutes before performances in order to warm up on the stage. I loved being alone in the dimly lit theater, looking out at the rows of empty seats and hearing the muffled talk of the stagehands getting ready for the performance. In time, I would be joined by a beautiful, blue-eyed and blond creature, all legs and sexy bearing. It was Dee Dee Wood, who became one of my best friends. Dee Dee and I had both been students at the School of American Ballet, but it wasn't until *Can-Can* that we grew much closer.

In no time, I was calling her Deets and she was calling me Chita-Beeta. To the company, we were the White and the Dark of It. I thought of Dee Dee as my soul sister, even though we were as physically opposite as we could be. I loved her effortless glamor, which she downplayed in favor of just being "one of the boys" with me. We joked around a lot, something we shared with her boyfriend and soon-to-be husband, Marc Breaux. He was a handsome Cajun who, like all my friends from Louisiana, was fun-loving and free-spirited, especially after a lot of rounds of spirits. Dee Dee and Marc would eventually go on to assist Michael Kidd on *Li'l Abner*, before being lured to Hollywood to choreograph such films as *Mary Poppins* and *Chitty Chitty Bang Bang*, where they taught Dick Van Dyke his elastic and witty moves.

In *Can-Can*, Dee Dee was paired with Eddie Phillips, a fabulous, red-headed dancer, and I was paired with Socrates Birsky. He was also a wonderful and frisky dancer but who, on one occasion, had lousy aim. He was most dangerous when we were dancing the "Quadrille." It was a fast-paced number filled with high kicks, flips, tumbles, and cartwheels, made all the more difficult to execute because we were wearing long, heavy woolen skirts with petticoats underneath. At one point, I was in an arabesque with one leg up and Socrates was supposed to throw me so that I hit the floor in a split and slid off to the side of the stage. Instead, he threw me so that I was heading right toward a table. I ducked—or I might not be around today. By the way, those costumes were so hot that I can recall Beverly Tassoni, a dancer, sitting in second position in a number and fanning—not her face but her crotch. And talent is when you can do that and not seem lewd at all.

If we upped our game in *Can-Can*, it was not just because of Michael but also because we were sharing the stage with Gwen. As was my custom,

I stood in the wings and watched her every chance I got. Through a swift, agile body and voice with an endearing warble, Gwen's Claudine could convey every flavor in the book: sultry allure, innocence, clownishness, vulnerability, and strength. When Gwen hit position, a Mack truck couldn't move her. Once she grabbed your attention, she wouldn't let it go, reaching all the way to the back of the theater. She did this vocally and physically, for sure. But also in spirit. She poured her soul into her performance, remaining true to each and every moment, rock solid and light as air. Gwen couldn't be fake if she tried. She took Michael's motto to heart: "Dancers are actors without words." Every gesture had to count.

The fusion of ballet and theatricality was a revelation to me but also instantly familiar. When I was at the School of American Ballet, I wanted to do so much more than we were told. I wanted to go beyond what was shown to us in order to tell stories. The ballet dancers who most appealed to me, Nora Kaye and Maria Tallchief, excelled in doing that. It was little wonder that Michael chose to cast Nora in his first and only ballet, *On Stage!* In *Can-Can*, I recognized that there was a way to make dance tell a story with blasts of verve and humor. Being in this show was like getting a hit of pure oxygen day after day for the better part of a year. To my mind, the best kind of high.

Michael had said, "If you can make the audience respond to the dancer as a real person doing something believable within the theatrical framework, then you've done your job." It was a liberating experience for us to watch Gwen do just that because it opened up all sorts of possibilities.

In their own way, both Michael and Gwen had told me, "Do something that can come only from you, Chita." From that moment on, I swore it would become a personal mantra.

What would come after *Can-Can* would make me live out that promise. And to paraphrase Willy Loman in *Death of a Salesman*, I'd be out there on a shoestring and a prayer.

Entr'acte

A Roman Candle

About midway through my run in *Can-Can*, I had a fevered and romantic encounter with the president of Armenia. Well, at least that was what I nicknamed him, though I can't for the life of me tell you why. Let's just say Greg Roman was an imposing guy, even though he was only a few years older than me. Imposing? Correction. He was one of the most gorgeous men I had ever laid eyes on. His real name was Ishkhan Giragosian, but by then he'd been rechristened Greg Roman by the agent and producer Paul Gregory. Through his agent, Greg had landed his first acting role ever—a small part in the Broadway production of Herman Wouk's *The Caine Mutiny Court-Martial*, which starred Henry Fonda, John Hodiak, and Lloyd Nolan.

That all-male drama opened on Broadway in January 1954 at the Plymouth Theatre, conveniently located just an alley away from the Shubert Theatre, where a number of pretty ladies were kicking up their heels in *Can-Can*. It wasn't too long before the boys were "raising Cain" with the girls—including a boy named Jim Bumgarner, who later morphed into the star James Garner, and Richard Norris, who was Greg's roommate at the Belvedere Hotel on West Forty-Eighth Street.

One evening, Richard, who was concerned that his roommate spent most of his free time holed up in the room, persuaded Greg to join him at a meeting called by Actors' Equity at City Center. My friend Dee Dee and I had come to that same gathering, which was at 11:30 p.m., after the finish of our shows. As we walked into the packed theater, I locked eyes with a handsome, muscle-bound man with dark hair, a strong jaw, and a smoldering look. He took my breath away. After Dee Dee and I were seated on the aisle, I looked up to see Richard—who never missed an opportunity to play mischievous matchmaker—with the same guy.

"Chita, I want you to meet Ishkhan Giragosian, who is a Persian weed collector," he said. Neither Greg nor I knew what to make of that billing. I don't think Richard meant "weed" to be taken in the same way as we do today. But we were both grateful for the introduction and wasted no time in getting together. Dee Dee's verdict was immediate: "What a hump!"

If I were to draw for you a picture of just how, well, hormonal, that time in our lives was, I couldn't do better than the world evoked by Stephen Sondheim in the song "Waiting for the Girls Upstairs," from *Follies*. In it, Steve describes stage door Johnnies waiting for giggling showgirls dressing to go out on the town, ". . . clicking heels on steel and cement."

On our first date, after we'd finished our respective shows, Greg took me on the Staten Island ferry. Costing only a nickel for a round trip, it was the greatest bargain in the world. As we motored past the Statue of Liberty, we got to know each other. Greg was the son of Armenian immigrants who'd settled in Toronto. As he grew up, he took an interest in body-building and was even a runner-up to the title of Mr. Ontario, before he headed to Los Angeles to pursue a career as an actor. He'd read in an industry magazine that Paul Gregory was actor Zachary Scott's agent. So he took a bus from Santa Monica to Gregory's office on total impulse. Smart move. It led him to a Broadway debut—and into my arms on the ferry.

When we got back to Lower Manhattan, we discovered that the subways had closed down for the night. So we walked, hand-in-hand, the five miles from Battery Park to my apartment on West Fifty-Fifth, where I was living with my brother Hoolie. Later, Greg told me that Richard was waiting up for him when he returned so he could get all the "juicy" details. When Greg told him about our walk back, Richard exploded.

"Wait, you made Chita walk five miles after she'd been busting her butt dancing for hours in *Can-Can*?" Richard said. "You should have splurged on a cab, you idiot! You'll be lucky if she ever sees you again!"

I didn't mind the walk at all. I think I would've walked all the way to Armenia to be with Greg. And we didn't just walk. We *floated*. Mainly, after our shows, we floated right up Eighth Avenue, turned right on West Forty-Eighth, and scurried up to room 1119 in the Belvedere Hotel. There, night after night, Greg introduced me to the mysteries of life, love, and sex. On warm nights, we would drag a mattress up to the roof and look up at the moon and the stars made dim by the lights of Broadway.

On another occasion, Greg and Richard snuck through the stage door and stood on the side during a performance of *Can-Can* so they could see me in the show. David Colyer, the assistant stage manager, caught them and gave them hell. "How gauche to do such a thing!" he said to the boys before kicking them out. Greg said he turned to Richard and asked, "What the hell does 'gauche' mean?" It wasn't an adjective I'd ever apply to Greg. Others come to mind: "Sweet." "Attentive." And, "toe-curling, heart-pounding hot."

✳

After *The Caine Mutiny Court-Martial* closed, Greg and I continued to see each other, sometimes with Dee Dee and Marc Breaux, and on occasion with James Garner and Lynn Bernay, a beautiful dancer who was also in *Can-Can*. One of the things I loved about Greg was that for the first time, I was dating a *dramatic* actor. I felt an even greater degree of belonging in the theater as I dove into this new realm. There was something riveting when the boys talked about Lee Strasberg and Stella Adler, the Actors Studio and the Group Theatre, Marlon Brando and James Dean.

Greg eventually returned to California and we drifted apart. But decades later, in 1996, I was appearing in the national tour of *Kiss of the Spider Woman* at the Ahmanson Theatre in Los Angeles. At the end of one performance, during the curtain call, I noticed a man emerging from the audience with a bouquet of three dozen red roses. It was Greg. As he handed me the flowers, I whispered, "Come backstage!"

Greg came to my dressing room looking, as the song goes, "better than a body has a right to." We chatted and made arrangements to go out for dinner. As soon as he made his exit, I turned to my indispensable assistant, Rosie, and sent her to buy suspenders, stockings, a garter belt, and a crisp white man's shirt. My makeover was fast and furious. When I heard a knock at the door of my hotel suite, I greeted my special guest in an outfit that would have been at home among the murderesses of *Chicago*. I was dressed to kill. "Come in," I said, trying to sound as though I lounged around my rooms like that all the time. Our reunion didn't disappoint.

People often ask me whether there's anybody I think of in particular while I'm singing love songs in my cabaret act. Quite frankly, the answer is that I'm there to sing in service of the songwriters whose themes are timeless and universal. But I know that I can always add an extra layer if I play in my mind certain images of past lovers, say, in a hotel room or on a rooftop. I conjure up the sly, knowing smile and the all-enveloping warmth of memorable close encounters. That's how it was with Greg, my handsome Armenian president.

6

FROM INCHWORM TO MARILYN MONROE

Shoestring Revue

Y ou know you're not really right for this part," said the stage manager. "But since you're here, get in line." He handed me some
pages of a script I was to read for the creative team of a new show,
Shoestring Revue.

A glance around the audition room confirmed I had no business being
there. Standing next to me waiting their turn were leggy, busty blondes in
body-revealing dresses with slashes of red lipstick highlighting their pretty
faces. And here was I, short, dark, dressed in a black skirt and leotards, and
with a nose like "a chicken's butt," or so said my brothers, teasingly. But I
wasn't daunted. Dania Krupska, my friend from *Can-Can*, had told me
about the show that she had been hired to choreograph.

"It's going to be a revue with dance, comedy skits, and new songs," she
explained. It was to open at the President Theatre Off-Broadway in late
February 1955, just months after *Can-Can* closed. The pay wasn't great:
$50 a week on a show whose entire capitalization was $18,000.

"But I don't know if I can be funny onstage," I protested.

"Yeah, but you can dance and I'm looking for a dancer," Dania
responded. "It could be fun. The producer's a guy named Ben Bagley.

He's only twenty-one. What a piece of work! But he seems to know what he's doing. What do you have to lose?"

I read the pages that were handed to me and laughed aloud, drawing stares from the other girls. The script was by Michael Stewart, who was thirty years old and five years away from writing *Bye Bye Birdie*. He'd put his comic chops into crafting a sketch called "Epic, or I'll Be Glad When You're Dead, You Roskolnikov You." It imagined the film producer Mike Todd trying to persuade Marilyn Monroe to star in his movie, based on Tolstoy's *War and Peace* and to be shot in Yugoslavia.

"Yugoslavia?" exclaims Marilyn. "That's near Europe!"

Marilyn tells Todd that he's too late. His archenemy David O. Solznikoff has already offered her the starring role in a movie of Dostoyevsky's *Brothers Karamazov*. To which Todd replies, "Dostoevsky! Tolstoy! What difference does it make? They're both Slavs."

"Who cares how they eat!" says Marilyn.

I loved the material. I wanted to be a part of it. To my mind, it would be one of the first, if not the first, impression of Marilyn Monroe in a show. But I was a twenty-two-year-old Latina who had just a couple of chorus credits to her name. Could I play this very white, very sexy, blond bombshell? Skepticism was understandable. Hell, I was skeptical myself, even apologetic that I hadn't tried to look more like her. But I was game to try anything—even if I was being jostled by a line of hot-to-trot beauties. They thought the best way to impress the director, Christopher Hewett, was to pucker the mouth, breathily whisper the lines, push out their boobs, and shake their hips.

As I waited my turn, Dania came by with a man she introduced as Alvin Colt, the designer of the show's costumes. "Come with us," she said, as they led me into a side room. There, Alvin told me to change into white shorts and a tight sweater while he stuffed tissues into my bra. Then he plopped a blond wig on my head.

"We're going to get you this part," he said. "All you have to do is say Michael's lines, and you'll be just fine. They'll know what to do with you."

I looked in the mirror. What peered back—a blond Latina in shorts and with big boobs—made me laugh. I thought I looked more like Mae West than Marilyn. I wiggled: *Come up and see me sometime.* Maybe I could throw in a little Dietrich: *Falling in love again, never wanted to . . .* But I took Alvin's advice. When the lines are that smart, you're more than halfway there. The rest is up to you. Finally, I decided to channel Marilyn by way of Carol Channing's Lorelei Lee. Sexy. Funny. But with a vein of steel. Maybe I could do this after all.

✳

Much to my surprise, I got the offer to be in *Shoestring*. For a moment, I was like the dog that caught the car. Could I really be funny? Do improvisations? It meant stepping out of the comfort zone of the Broadway dance chorus and into a group of bright young comics in a small theater Off-Broadway with dressing rooms in the toilets. We were all different shapes and sizes. Among the cast was Arte Johnson, Dody Goodman, Dorothy Greener, and a formidable, gimlet-eyed Amazon with a basso profundo: Beatrice Arthur.

Beady, as I came to know her, was eleven years older than me, nearly thirty-three, and married to Gene Saks. He was then an actor but would one day become Neil Simon's go-to director for his stage and film productions. I was immediately drawn to Beady. She was a "boss lady"; she'd once been a member of the US Marine Corps Women's Reserve before she got the acting bug. Quirky and complicated, she hated wearing shoes so she was barefoot every chance she got and had a phobia of birds and chewing gum. Beady was never mean, but she could be blunt. Despite her forbidding presence, she was generous and took me under her wing. It wasn't long before I was known as the Little of It and she, even barefoot, as the Big of It.

We got those nicknames from our producer, Ben Bagley. He was thin, small, and frantic and wore glasses in order to make people think that he was older. He also had protruding ears that earned him the nickname Dumbo. Ben was odd and caustic and proud of it, telling us that a passerby had once remarked to his grandmother, "What a sweet child!" To which she answered, "It would take a detective to find any sweetness in this child." Ben boasted that he was "incurably insane."

Shoestring reflected Ben's erratic personality. I quickly learned that in a revue you were "slapped around" a bit, thrown to the wolves here and there. I didn't mind because along with his eccentric taste, Ben had a stunning ability to recognize talent. In addition to the cast, his eagle eye had spotted songwriters Lee Adams, Charles Strouse, Sheldon Harnick, and Ronny Graham, all of whom would go on to create major theatrical hits. Into the potpourri of *Shoestring* they had put in musical skits that included "Medea" as envisioned by Walt Disney (Dorothy sang about bluebirds before hacking up her children), global warming arriving in Manhattan ("There are oysters in the Cloisters"), a parody of *Reader's Digest* headlines ("The Eleventh Baby Is the Easiest"), and a torch song to end all torch songs called "Garbage": *Your cruelty to me done hit me like a hammer / You done destroyed my heart, my soul, / And, most of all, my grammar!*

This song featured Beady standing under a lamppost "for fifteen years . . . brooding and wet with tears" and complaining about her lousy sanitation lover. While she sang, Arthur Partington, my partner from *Can-Can*, and I danced a "dream ballet" tango. As the song ended, I dove into a garbage bag.

It was divine! After Beady took out the garbage—me—I came back to play Marilyn and Lady Godiva in the revue, which, at this point in my career, was a course in Comedy Acting 101. All the same, I hadn't come to *Shoestring* completely unprepared. I had been weaned on making a fool of myself at home and had been the class clown at the School of American Ballet. By then, sponge that I was (and still am), I had already learned a lot from watching Carol Channing, Elaine Stritch, and Gwen Verdon. But *Shoestring* made me stretch more than I ever had before, particularly in playing Marilyn. I felt vulnerable, which worked for the character. For the first time, I wasn't protected by a line of dancers on a huge Broadway stage. The revue was in a 350-seat Off-Broadway theater with not much distance between performer and audience.

Lucky for me, I had joined a parade of clowns who encouraged each other to be fearless in trying out material. They eagerly went up to the edge and right over—and I went with them. We had each other's backs. There was Dody, whose voice was once described as "a Tweetie Pie cartoon bird strangling on peanut butter"; Arte Johnson, sweet, kidlike, and totally goofy; and Dorothy Greener, a tiny dynamo who had a lunatic gleam in her eye and who never got the recognition she deserved. However, I was most influenced by Beady.

Beady was as bold and brash as all New York. Her confidence, bass voice, and comic command were irresistible, yet her training at the Actors Studio gave her a refined sensitivity. Offstage she was all business. But onstage? She had a dry, ironic sense of humor and expert timing. It started with "the look," a haughty and firm stare, which alone drew attention. Then she would purse her lips and pause just before delivering a line that always knocked everybody out. Beady could get away with stuff that nobody else could—the mark of a genius.

Recognizing just how green I was, she once said, "Cheet, when you're out there, you gotta be an exposed nerve." Referring to her hero, Sid Caesar, she added: "It comes down to belief, truth, nothing else matters. To get laughs, you gotta be deadly serious. Take your time. Don't give in too easily. And screw 'em if they don't laugh."

Good advice, especially when it came to Marilyn. At the first performance of *Shoestring*, I had no idea whether anybody would laugh at the skit. I knew that after I was cast, the writers had tailored the role as neatly as Alvin Colt had designed my tight, beaded gown and blond wig. I stood trembling as Maxwell Grant, playing Mike Todd, described to Marilyn the film he was producing. At one point, he stopped when he saw that my mouth was twitching like the goddess he was pursuing for his movie. "Were you going to say something?" he asked. After a pause, I responded, "No, it just looks that way." The audience laughed. A huge sigh of relief then went ricocheting though my entire body. And that got another laugh.

✳

Playing Marilyn was not the only transformation of mine that owed thanks to *Shoestring*. A few weeks before we were to open, Arthur Partington and I were sitting at a restaurant on West Forty-Eighth Street across the street from the theater.

"Ben told me that I should change my name," I said, chowing down on my usual tuna on white with mayonnaise.

"What's the matter with Conchita del Rivero?" he asked.

"He said it was too long to put on the posters," I responded. "What do you think of the name Chita O'Hara?"

Everybody was calling me Chita by that time and I liked the sound of all those vowels. Besides, my mother, Katherine, had Scottish and Irish blood, and I thought of it as a tribute to her. My notions of the ideal female onscreen were Bette Davis, Joan Crawford, Ida Lupino, and, especially, Maureen O'Hara. She could beat the hell out of John Wayne without breaking into a sweat.

Arthur agreed. "Sounds pretty good to me," he said. But I quickly found out that it didn't sound as good to my friends. When I answered my phone "Chita O'Hara," I heard more than a few "clicks" on the other end. People thought I was nuts.

"Girl, you are so not the O'Hara type," said Dee Dee. "I've heard of the Black Irish but, Chita O'Hara? Really?"

She had a point. Was I afraid that I'd lose jobs because my name sounded too "ethnic"? Maybe. After trying out more names, I thought what the hell? Chita del Rivero. That's me. That's the lady in the mirror. Then I thought, why not drop the "del" and sub an "a" for the "o"? Chita Rivera. It sounded snappier, easier to pronounce, more melodious. It could fit on a marquee—*if* that ever came to be. And the name still respected my family background. If I was going to lose some parts because directors or agents thought my name sounded too south of the border, well, that was *their* problem.

Flying on the confidence we gave each other and ready to make fools of ourselves, *Shoestring* opened on February 28, 1955, to rave reviews. Walter Kerr of the *New York Herald Tribune*, no pushover of a critic, wrote: "'Shoestring Revue' has one little virtue that a lot of great shows don't have: It's funny. It's funny almost before you've got your coat off and stays funny." Another critic wrote that I had a "sultry south-of-the-border aspect" that captivated the audience in a calypso number about sinners through the ages, a "nearly libelous" impersonation of Marilyn Monroe, and a skit about mink that had me parading around as Lady Godiva.

✳

The run of *Shoestring* was extended, and at one point, Dorothy, Beady, and I were invited to go to Chicago to perform our numbers at an industrial show for Oldsmobile. (These early-morning shows were commercials for products at company conventions.) I was so relieved that I was able to measure up next to such exceptional talent. I clipped the notices and sent them to my mother. She loved everything that I did, critics or no critics.

One night after the show, Beady told me that someone was waiting to see me. I walked out and was met by a young guy with a round face, who was neatly attired in a three-piece suit and wearing dark-rimmed glasses. He looked like someone from the CIA. He was in fact an agent, but one from MCA, the talent agency, where he was a fledgling to David Hocker, who headed the musical theater division. Looking not much older than me, he introduced himself.

"Hi, I'm Dick Seff. Your Marilyn was great and 'Garbage' was terrific. How did you manage to dive into that bag?"

"The bag opened and Dania said to dive in, so I dove right in," I said.

Dick laughed. "You're an original, Chita. You've got great timing, and those legs of yours can do impossible things. I think you've got quite a future in this business. Who's representing you?"

I replied, naïvely, "What do you mean?"

"I mean, do you have an agent?" he said.

Nobody had ever asked me that before. Someone would actually take care of me? Look for jobs and all that stuff? Dick told me that while his boss looked after their big clients, like Ethel Merman, Rosalind Russell, and Rex Harrison, he was looking to build up his own portfolio. That was how he'd found himself making the perilous journey backstage, managing broken steps and a dark hallway, to a central space outside the toilet. He offered to take me on as a client. I quickly agreed. I liked him. He was genuine and great fun to be around. A few weeks after I signed with him, I learned that I was in good company. His portfolio soon included John Kander, Fred Ebb, and Ron Field, who were just then beginning their careers. Years later, I would work with them several times, and we would all go on to Tony-winning successes.

I stayed with *Shoestring* only briefly because I got a gig in a new show, *Seventh Heaven*, starring Ricardo Montalban and Gloria DeHaven. But those few months were life-changing. I'd gone into *Shoestring* barely knowing what a revue was and came out of it a comedian with a new name, some good notices, and a smart young agent, who would remain with me for decades. To paraphrase E. B. White, if you go to New York, you must be willing to be lucky. I *was* prepared. But a large part of that means going through open doors even if you're scared. My luck was to be learning from some of the best comic talents of the day, especially Beady. To this day,

I think of her as "a comic scientist." She was that precise. I wasn't surprised that she later transformed the sitcom into an art form in *Maude*. By the way, Norman Lear, who produced that groundbreaking comedy, first saw Beady in *Shoestring*. That's just how perceptive the "incurably insane" Ben Bagley was in spotting talent.

Which goes to show that you never know who may be out there in the audience. I learned early on that the more you get around, the more chances you might have to be noticed. If I hadn't learned from Carol Channing not to be bound by type—Anita Loos had first written Lorelei Lee as a petite brunette—I might never have had the guts to compete with that lineup of busty blondes. Here's the thing: When you're an actor and a dancer, you almost always have feelings of not being enough. What takes the edge off is being accepted by artists whom you admire. The cast of *Shoestring* did that for me. I became surer of myself. I could hear my own voice better. I had flexed new muscles. If you can go from being an inchworm to being Marilyn Monroe, that's progress. And take it from me, there's no greater thrill than making people laugh. All this would not have happened if Dania Krupska hadn't opened the door for me and if I hadn't been willing to make a fool of myself.

Jump into a garbage bag?

"Say yes!"

Entr'acte

Chita-Rita and Other Revues

After *Shoestring*, I never returned to Off-Broadway, but I did another couple of revues: a 1972 production of *Jacques Brel Is Alive and Well and Living in Paris*, and *Jerry's Girls*, which I did on Broadway in 1985. I never considered *Jerry's Girls* to be a revue, though. Not with songs like "I Don't Want to Know," which is a whole show in itself.

I love the revue format, and one of my favorites is Gerard Alessandrini's *Forbidden Broadway*, which hilariously mocks us show people. When I heard that he was going to include "Chita-Rita," a spoof about the "rivalry" between me and Rita Moreno, I got a little nervous. Ever since Rita had re-created my role of Anita and won the Oscar for the film of *West Side Story*, both of us have been saddled with the confusion that comes from being identified by the same iconic role. This is not to mention that our names sound similar. Same number of syllables and vowels. The similarity would come up again when I played a character called Rita Romano in *Mr. Wonderful* in 1956. But it never really bothered me until people started to confuse us with each other. Now when people say to me, "I loved you in the movie of *West Side Story,*" I straighten them out and then politely say, "I was the *original* Anita."

When the *Forbidden Broadway* skit came up, people kept asking me, "Are you going to see the show?" Whenever celebrities get spoofed, they either avoid the show like the plague or they run toward it. Rita's reaction? "No comment." Mine was different. Like a cat, I'm curious. I didn't think I had to come out on top; I just didn't want to come out on the bottom. From what I can remember, I came out relatively unscathed. In fact, I laughed my head off. *Forbidden Broadway* always features some of the most talented actors around, and this was no exception. Donna English and Jeanne Montano came out in the same outfit, purple dress with red petticoat, just like Anita in *West Side Story.* They alternately sang:

Chita:
Chita Rivera is not Rita
Rita Moreno is not Chita
Chita is Chita and not Rita
I would prefer you forgot Rita!

Rita:
My name is Rita and not Chita
Though I look like you a lot, Chita
When people smoke too much pot, Chita
They think you're me and I'm not Rita!

Both:
So if you want to keep who's who straight
Here's how to settle the great debate
I am the one you should emulate
She is the bird who should migrate!

I thought it was an honor to be included in the satire. I love jokes, especially if the joke is on me. If you're going to be in the business—hell, if you're just going to get through life—you have to be able to laugh at yourself. And I have a lot of chances for that!

Entr'acte

Seventh Heaven

Both Beady and I left *Shoestring* to be in Victor Young's *Seventh Heaven*, a musical melodrama about star-crossed lovers, a soldier and a young woman of "easy virtue," during World War I. The show, which starred Gloria DeHaven and Ricardo Montalban, really didn't work, but since it was set in the racy Montmartre of Paris, you just had to have a madam, played by Beady, and a trio of hookers, Camille, Colette, and Fifi, played by Gerrianne Raphael, Patricia Hammerlee, and *moi*. Since the costumes were designed by Marcel Vertès, who won an Oscar for the film *Moulin Rouge*, we were the most gorgeous street-walkers in Broadway history.

The best part of *Seventh Heaven* was working with a short, lithe stroke of lightning called Peter Gennaro, one of the three dancers who introduced "Steam Heat," Bob Fosse's iconic number in *The Pajama Game*. I'd met Peter in *Guys and Dolls* and, impressed with his torrid moves, took his jazz dance classes. The actress Grace Kelly, who also took his classes, was a friend of Gant Gaither, the coproducer of *Seventh*

Heaven. She recommended Peter to him and that led to his debut as the show's choreographer.

It was an inspired choice and meant the dances would be fast, furious, and sexy as hell. "Yeah," Peter would say, "it's kind of wild. But that's the wild I want it to be."

Peter knew of my early background and so devised a five-minute "White and Gold Ballet" for the show, which I danced with Scott Merrill, a handsome hunk and damn good dancer. When it came to the struts and bumps of my lady of the night, however, I fumbled at first. I found Peter's modern jazz contractions odd and a little more than suggestive. Since he had partnered and then married a ballet dancer, Jean Kinsella, he was the perfect bridge between the two worlds. He noticed that I had a hard time getting the "bump," a point of sale for any hooker. I found it vulgar. But Peter was the first one to show me a release and contraction with feet turned in, not out. That managed to shape my body in a totally different way than the ballet's five positions.

"Chita, you're a ballet dancer, but like me, you have fast feet, quick hips, and a feeling for the music," he told me. "You get the rhythms. Let them carry you. Trust it. You can't make a vulgar move."

Following Peter's advice, I got my first good notices for dancing thanks to him. Critic Frank Quinn wrote, "Chita Rivera is a gal of flashy, bold personality . . . who struts and slinks like a panther. She does a howl of a routine with her calypso can-can."

What I learned from Peter then, and later in *West Side Story*, continued to bless my career, particularly when I worked with Bob Fosse, the guy who put Peter, along with Buzz Miller and Carol Haney, on the map in *The Pajama Game*. Fosse's pelvic thrusts were tighter, more subtle, and more erotic. But Peter's lessons gave me the freedom to explore sexuality without being overridden by the watchful "figures" on my shoulder: God on one, my mother on the other.

Another memory connected to *Seventh Heaven* was the sweetness of Ricardo Montalban and the insecurity of his costar, Gloria DeHaven. At one point, Gloria, stricken with the flu, had to sit out a few of the performances. Pat Hammerlee and I cheered Gerrianne, our Camille, when she went on to play La Môme Pistache. Meanwhile, I made a point of taking chicken soup to Gloria, who was holed up in her hotel. Only thirty years old, she was something of a big name at the time, so I was surprised that she milked me for information about Gerrianne's performance.

"How's the girl?" she asked, sniffling and dabbing her nose with a hanky. She was particularly curious about how her understudy had sung "Where Is That Someone for Me?" and "It's a Dream," her two ballads. Actually, Gerrianne had sung them more lyrically and with a stronger voice. But I wasn't about to tell Gloria that. It was the first time that I witnessed firsthand the insecurity that comes from stardom; that was why Lilo was so intent in cutting down Gwen Verdon's part in *Can-Can*. I was flustered as to how to answer Gloria's questions until I summoned what I thought was an ego-saving response.

"Well, Gloria, she certainly isn't you!"

7

THE YEAR OF SAMMY

Mr. Wonderful

O n my dressing room table at home, among the crystal heart and the many framed photos of dear friends and family, there is one that stands out. I am in profile, my head is bowed, and I am kissing the slender, ebony fingers of a man—Sammy Davis Jr., a friend and one-time lover. His face, framed in his trademark dark-rimmed glasses, is calm, which was almost never the case with him. Like so much that went between us, the kiss is sweet, a sign of respect for his talent and for what that talent cost him.

However, before I met Sammy in the winter of 1956, my approach toward him was decidedly different. In fact, when I heard he was coming to Broadway in a new show called *Mr. Wonderful*, I was unimpressed.

"What's he doing on Broadway? He's a nightclub singer!" I said to my friend D.D. Ryan, then working as an assistant to a young photographer named Richard Avedon. My nose was almost as high as the puff of smoke emanating from the Camel cigarette billboard under which we were then walking at Forty-Fourth and Broadway.

"I wouldn't be so hoity-toity, Miss Chita Rivera," she responded defensively. D.D.'s husband, John Ryan, was the stage manager for *Mr.*

Wonderful. "You weren't exactly playing Lady Macbeth in your last show. A streetwalker, as I recall."

"A lady of the boulevard," I corrected her, defending Fifi in *Seventh Heaven*. "Not just anybody can do eight shows a week with the snap of a finger. Club acts are on for, what, an hour? For a coupl'a weeks at a time? He'll be toast in a month."

"We shall see," said D.D. "Jule Styne is producing but not writing the music, and he's no dummy," she said of the composer who had yet to write such iconic musicals as *Gypsy* and *Bells Are Ringing*.

She continued. "Don't underestimate him, Chita. He has a big hit with 'Hey There,' and his gigs are selling out like crazy. Johnny says that the advance is huge, bigger than *My Fair Lady*." That show was opening a week after *Mr. Wonderful*.

What piqued my interest was that D.D. said John had told her that there was a role perfect for me. "You should try out for the show," she said. With a mischievous grin, she added, "And, Chita, she has her own number: 'I'm Available.'"

"Don't tell me, she's a hooker, right?" I said.

"A lady of the boulevard," she said.

＊

On the first day of rehearsal, the room was buzzing with the usual giddy anticipation. But it was the most colorful and diverse cast I'd ever been in. Not the usual Broadway types. At Sammy's insistence, *Mr. Wonderful* was a wholly integrated show, still a rarity on Broadway in those days.

"I don't want just one colored girl or guy in a sea of white," he said to the producers, who, in addition to Jule Styne, included George Gilbert. Sammy had also demanded a story that hewed close to who and what he was: a Black entertainer who'd fought his way to the top of the nightclub world. Thus he was playing Charlie Welch, who'd escaped the scars of

American racism by relocating to Paris. There, Fred, an agent played by comedian Jack Carter, discovers him and brings him back to the States where he becomes a great success. Olga James, a gorgeous young actress with a voice to match, played Ethel, Charlie's love interest.

I'd read the script by Joe Stein and Will Glickman. It was pretty flimsy. Like every actor, I'd typically flipped through to see *my* part. As D.D. had described, Rita Romano was something of a tart. It was a convention at the time to have a gum-cracking sexpot move across the stage at various times throughout the show telling a story about some guy who's trying to bamboozle her into bed.

"He sez to me, 'Yada, yada, yada.' And you know what I sez to him? I told him to go to hell!" At least for the first time in my career, I had a solo number: "I'm Available."

Jack Donohue, a big, friendly guy who was directing and choreographing, explained that the ensemble would rehearse the first act for the standard three weeks before a pre-Broadway tryout in Philadelphia. The original score would be by Jerry Bock, William Holofcener, and George Weiss. The second act would largely be Sammy's nightclub act, choreographed by him and backed by his father, Sam Senior, and "Uncle" Will Mastin. The three of them had started in vaudeville as the Will Mastin Trio. Sammy had been introduced into the act at the age of three and had quickly migrated to being the star attraction.

"And what are we supposed to do during the second act?" I asked Jack.

"You lucky guys will play the audience," he responded.

Albert Popwell, who played what was listed as a "bop musician," sidled up to me. "Don't roll your eyes too much, Chita, they'll pop out of your head." Whatever was going to happen, this show was going to be a blast, with guys like Albert in the cast. Fresh from playing in *House of Flowers*, he was tall, loose-limbed, and funny. He was a daredevil of a dancer. He thought nothing of doing pratfalls in the middle of the street, horrifying drivers who had to brake suddenly to avoid him.

Just then Sammy came—no, *bopped*—into the room, and the whole place braked. He was neatly dressed in tight jeans and a turtleneck sweater. A small diamond ring glistened on his finger. This was a decade before the Nehru jackets, acres of bling, oversized sunglasses, and tight shirts open to the waist. He was short, dark, and rail thin. One gust of wind and he'd be flying over the Broadway Theatre, I thought.

He gathered us around him. Gesturing to Jule Styne, he said, "When this man here started talking to me about coming to Broadway, I told him, 'Keep talking. But keep your distance, baby, or you may get a kiss on the lips.' Broadway has always been a dream for me! You cats probably already know this, but nothing beats it for stature and dignity. We're gonna work hard and we're gonna party hard. And if you help me, we're gonna knock this town on its ass."

Sammy made no bones about the fact that he'd come to Broadway hat in hand. But he also knew that if anybody could bring together the worlds of nightclubs and theater, Blacks and whites, jazz and pop, he could. Donohue would choreograph us, but Sammy would do his own dancing and choose his songs from out of his own repertoire. "I have to do my music and my dancing my way," he had told Jule Styne.

The cast whooped and hollered. But I was still skeptical. Do the music and dancing *his* way? That was not what I'd been taught. You did what you were told in the theater and ballet worlds. *There are sharper minds at work than yours, Mr. Sammy Davis Jr.* And then rehearsals started. And my reservations began to evaporate into thin air.

Sammy leaped and bounded across the rehearsal room to the music. Yet in a flash he could pull it all back and his movements became small and intense. Everything he did came from his soul. His silky voice hit every note with singular style, wringing out every ounce of emotion. He could do everything and anything—sing, dance, act, tap, mimic, and make you laugh. The sheer exuberance of it all was mesmerizing. His greatest gift was a simple one: he delivered joy.

I came to learn just how ironic that was, given how much crap he'd had to deal with even then, at the age of thirty. After all, it wasn't long before this that he'd almost been killed in the early morning hours of November 19, 1954, when his Cadillac had smashed into another car near San Bernardino, California. The cone-shaped steering wheel had gouged an eye beyond repair. Converting to Judaism, and being a golf enthusiast, he'd since been cracking jokes that his handicap was being "a one-eyed, colored Jew."

His glass eye looked so real that one day, during a break in rehearsals, Albert, who we called "Poppy," and I were debating which eye had been injured.

"I think it's the right eye," I said.

"Right eye, stage left, you mean, which is the left eye," said Poppy.

"No, right eye, front of house, which is the right eye," I retorted.

Sammy overheard us and pointed to his left eye. "This one," he said. Then he added, "But you cats better behave cuz I have eyes in the back of my head to make up for it." Then he pointed to me and said, "I'm onto you!"

Embarrassed, I laughed. Onto me? I wasn't quite sure what he meant. Was that bad or good? During rehearsals, Sammy made a point of watching my scenes even though he wasn't in them. I didn't think the material was that big of a deal. I just exchanged some silly repartee, leading up to the song "I'm Available." But Sammy laughed as much at my takes as Rita as I laughed at his comic asides as Charlie Welch.

One evening, he caught up with me outside the rehearsal hall. "Hey, Chita, wait up, I want to talk to you," he said.

"What for?" I said. I sounded annoyed, which was exactly opposite the case. I was flattered. Sammy read my expression wrong. That often happened since I have always been told that my "resting face" looks serious, even angry. Poppy was forever telling me to smile more so I didn't look like a bitch.

"Some advice, Chita. Don't sell yourself short," said Sammy. "You're more ambitious than you think you are. And your talent is equal to your ambition. Go for it! There's nothing wrong with ambition."

He had a point. At that time, and even now, women—not just actresses but women everywhere—were taught *not* to be ambitious. It wasn't good manners.

He continued. "You're a natural clown, like me. We're both fools, baby. But we're clowns who know how to make it work for us."

I took this all in. There is something inspiring about people who believe in you more than you believe in yourself. I had heard it from Gwen Verdon during the run of *Can-Can*. And now from Sammy Davis Jr. I idolized Gwen and I admired Sammy. Hearing it made me flush with both pride and anxiety. I thought of myself then as just a working dancer, living in a basement apartment with my friend, Mary Alice Kubes. Could I possibly live up to what they saw in me?

"By the way," Sammy added. "If you want to catch a drink with me sometime, I'm available."

I didn't know much about Sammy's love life except that he was single. D.D. told me that he was attracted to white women. (Years later, in 1960, his marriage to May Britt, a Swedish actress, would cause an international furor.) When I confided to her of his come-on to me and my growing attraction to him, she wasn't surprised.

D.D. said, "When I went to see Sammy for the first time in a nightclub, I saw a short, skinny guy who wasn't what you'd call a looker. By the end of the act, I was totally over the moon. And that was true of almost every woman in the room. Talent is an aphrodisiac."

I was a big flirt and definitely titillated. But I didn't take Sammy up on his offer, at least not for the time being. He was Big Time and I was a featured player. It was enough for me to join the cast parties he threw in his suite at the Gorham Hotel on West Fifty-Fifth Street. The producers had put him there for the year-long run of the show. He wasn't kidding when he said that we'd party as hard as we worked. Penthouse B, with its overstuffed furniture and long terrace, quickly became the show's canteen. There was little distance between the stars and the rest of the cast. The Will Mastin Trio had spent many years as the opening act for main attractions, warming up the audience for them. Yet the stars would never allow the underlings to party with them. And Sammy would be damned before he let that happen with the cast of *Mr. Wonderful*.

At those gatherings, Sammy acted as the Lord of the Revels behind the bar at the end of the narrow room. He drank Kahlúa out of a silver goblet like his hero, Frank Sinatra. He spent money like water, calling up platters of food from the local delis and keeping a never-ending supply of top-shelf liquor on hand. He was generous to a fault and eager to be loved—even if he thought he had to buy it. There were stories about how, on his way to the theater, he would walk down Fifth Avenue and spend thousands on gifts at Tiffany's, Sulka, or Saks Fifth Avenue.

I looked up to him, competed with the rest of the cast for his attention, and hung on every word of his stories. How at the age of seven, he stole the film *Rufus Jones for President* from the great Ethel Waters. "Of course, I played Rufus Jones," he said, adding that Ethel never worked with kids again until *The Member of the Wedding*. He regaled us with life on the road with his dad and his Uncle Will, who we learned wasn't related to him by blood. "They don't call it T.O.B.A. for nothin'," Sammy said, teaching us the acronym for a circuit known as "Tough on Black Asses." These were the series of towns where Black-themed shows would tour. "If you can survive that, you can survive anything, including Broadway."

We played games, listened to records—Sinatra, Ella Fitzgerald, Louis Armstrong, and Nat King Cole were particular favorites. At one point, I decided to put on a record by a young kid who was just then breaking through: Elvis Presley.

Sammy said, "That boy's got style, Chita, but he just learned it from Big Mama Thornton and all those Black rhythm-and-blues singers down South. Give them a little credit. You gonna go into music, know your pop history. You gonna be an artist, know your art history. You gonna be in theater, know your Broadway history."

Sammy was obsessed with Shakespeare, and he handed out booklets for us to act out scenes from the Bard. His imitation of Laurence Olivier was right on the button. From Elvis to Olivier, Sammy absorbed everything around him and used it to his advantage if he could. And I was absorbing everything that I could from Sammy.

Sammy shared his life with us at those Gorham parties, but he was careful to keep the "bad shit" under wraps. It was only later, once we had begun our affair, that I learned the burdens he'd been shouldering as a black-as-ebony target for people looking to feel superior. Even as the clubs became more exclusive for the Will Mastin Trio, it still meant the endless struggle to find room and board across the tracks in the Black section of town.

During his stint in the army, he'd been urinated on by some nasty white boys. They pinned him down while they painted racist slogans on his body. Sammy quickly learned that he could survive the ugly onslaughts by entertaining his fellow soldiers, dazzling them so they could no longer see color, at least temporarily. He knew that if he could beat them at their own game, he could come out on top. Sammy was always looking for ways to be hurt less, or at least differently, by racism.

This was all a revelation to me at a time when the civil rights movement was beginning to take on speed. Call me oblivious, but I hadn't really seen color before the year of *Mr. Wonderful*. Early on, I had lived in a Black section of Washington, DC, with a smattering of Latino families, like my own. In the mid-1950s, there were separate water fountains downtown for whites and people of color and the theaters had only recently been desegregated. I had taken classes from Doris Jones and Claire Haywood, who were both Black and whose school had been founded to give minorities an opportunity to enter the world of ballet. And I had won a scholarship to the School of American Ballet along with Louis Johnson, who was Black and would go on to become a star with the Alvin Ailey American Dance Theater and the Dance Theatre of Harlem. Broadway, too, was an equalizer of sorts, though I realized just how many more hurdles Black actors and dancers faced than a light-skinned Latina.

But now, thanks to Sammy, I was quickly learning that the saga of Charlie Welch in *Mr. Wonderful*, supposedly loosely based on his life, had been sanitized beyond recognition and would be sanitized even more before we reached Broadway. The true story would have been much too brutal for audiences to face. After all, the producers had hired Sammy to deliver joy.

✳

The Philadelphia reviews for *Mr. Wonderful* were bad.

"They liked Sammy and Olga—and Chita got some nice mentions, but that's about it," George Gilbert, the producer, announced to us the day after. "We're going to make some changes, so be prepared to receive new pages while we're here."

When a show is in trouble on a pre-Broadway tryout, everybody tends to run for cover. There are so many possibilities as to what's wrong about it that it's kind of like the proverbial rearranging of the deck chairs on the *Titanic*.

There was a general consensus among the creators that the "iceberg" was the racial element. Charlie Welch's anxiety coming back to a racist United States from France was turning off the audience. The decision was made to change the venue from Paris to New Jersey and to make Charlie into a lounge singer who was just too timid to go for the big time in New York.

"Well, that just takes the piss out of the show," I said to Poppy. "As if Sammy was ever timid about facing success. He hungers for more of it! It just doesn't make any sense. I hope Sammy makes them stick to the story."

Jeri Gray, who played the Cigarette Girl in the show, snorted at my comments.

"Girl, what do you know?" she said in her husky voice. "The Man always thinks he knows better. Sammy's been around long enough to know that. He's not gonna buck 'em. He's got too much riding on this show. Now, dere it is!"

I loved Jeri. Black, tough, and outspoken, she was unlike anybody I had ever met. She was blessed with a great figure, but she was certainly not your typical musical theater type. In fact, *Mr. Wonderful* was her Broadway debut, and it would be her last. That was too bad. The theater could have used more like her. She had been born Jeruth Persson in Harlem, played the Apollo Theater, and then gone west to Las Vegas, where I gathered Sammy had befriended her. I could picture him saying to her, "Jeri, we're going to Broadway. C'mon. I'll put you in the show." He'd said that to more than a few who were in the cast out of his strong sense of obligation and loyalty. He always treated them like a million bucks. Next to Poppy, Jeri, who spoke in a scratchy voice, made me laugh the most. I was always seeking her out.

One day, I decided to pick her up on my way to rehearsals. She was staying at the Alvin Hotel, across from Decca Records, where all the jazz musicians lived and partied. Charlie "Bird" Parker had an apartment there. I came up to her door in my ballet clothes, all innocent and naïve, and rang the bell. A big burly guy opened the door and the smell of marijuana smoke nearly knocked me over. He gestured for me to come into the darkened room, which was full of other men sitting around, listening to music, and sharing joints. Just as one of the guys was about to offer me a toke, Jeri came bursting out of the bedroom.

"You give her one of those and I'll kill you!" she said to my would-be joint benefactor.

Jeri quickly hustled me out of the room.

"What are you doin' here, girl?" she asked in her smoky voice.

"I thought we'd walk to the theater together," I said, still curious, not to mention a bit shaken, by my first glimpse of a renegade world of jazz, sex, and drugs.

"I ain't rehearsin' today, hon," she said, walking me down the hallway. "Now, you get along. And don't come back, ya hear? Now, dere it is."

It was the year of Sammy, I was twenty-three, and I was getting quite an education.

✳

Chastened by the Philly reviews, we were anxious and nervous on the opening night of *Mr. Wonderful*, March 22, 1956, at the Broadway Theatre. We had every reason to be. Brooks Atkinson at the *New York Times* wrote that it was "a spectacular, noisy endorsement of mediocrity," and the other critics were not much kinder, attacking its limp story line. Sammy emerged relatively unscathed in the reviews, but the next day, the mood was funereal. As we prepared for a second night audience, we knew the enthusiasm would be tempered by the reviews. Even the columnists were writing our obituary. "If you want to see *Mr. Wonderful*," one wrote, "we suggest you get over to the Broadway Theatre this week. It won't be around very long."

Then Sammy appeared. Although it was nearly showtime, he wasn't dressed in the shabby outfit of Charlie Welch in the first act. He came in dressed to the nines, angry and defiant. He looked every inch a star and proceeded to prove just how he'd gotten that far. In no uncertain terms, he had told the producers that from here on in, he was going to be calling the shots. He gathered us all around him and pledged to fight to keep the show running.

He said, "I signed for a year and by God, I will play out my contract. I will go on every talk show, do every interview, cut ribbons at every store, and host every charity event I have to. But I need your help. I need you to play like every night is opening night. Fresh. Full out. Like we're the biggest hit on Broadway. And we will be."

We were all in, of course. And Sammy kept his word. His perseverance in keeping the show running was something to behold—and to learn from. The critics were not so easily defied in those days. Nor are they today. Until that evening, I'd always thought that taking your losses in stride was just part of the business. Acknowledge failure and move on. But that was not Sammy's style. Nothing excited him more than going up against the Man, whether bigots or hard-to-please critics. Sammy had a constant need to prove worthy of the public's affection, to prove worthy of being a star. His energy was infectious.

Ticket sales improved, and at every performance, the entire cast sat at tables to watch Charlie Welch weave his magic in the second act of *Mr. Wonderful*. Sammy never did anything twice in that hour-plus of songs and patter, even insisting on changing his clothes "so the kids won't be bored." How could we be? An up-tempo number would be followed by a soulful ballad followed by a tap dance. Even a time step would be embellished with a twist.

It was during this year-long run on Broadway that Sammy developed and perfected the club style he'd carry throughout his life. His comic timing was impeccable: the mimicry, the self-mockery, and the laugh that would start with his eyes closed, a guttural catch in his voice, and then the trademark stagger around the stage as he recovered. At any given moment, he would spontaneously begin playing the drums, the trumpet, the piano, or whatever struck his fancy. The audience loved it, especially when on special nights celebrities like Shelley Winters, Humphrey Bogart, Lauren Bacall, or Milton Berle would join us onstage for the second act.

The after-show parties at the Gorham continued as well. Sammy hated to be alone, and so his ever-growing entourage included D.D. and John Ryan, George Gilbert, the columnist Burt Boyar and his wife, Jane, and his musical director George Rhodes and his wife, Shirley Ann Vest. As the night wore on, he'd use every excuse to keep us there: another round of Kahlúa, another game of Monopoly, another spate of storytelling around the bar. One evening, as people were filing out, I began to collect my things to leave as well.

"You going already?"

"Sammy, it's three o'clock in the morning."

"C'mon, dance with me," he said, pulling me in close.

"But there's no music," I protested. As he pressed into me, I thought, "Wow, our bodies fit pretty well."

"Chita, you and I have a lot in common—"

"I know, I know, we're both Puerto Rican," I said. He had told us that his mother, Elvera Sanchez—who had divorced Sam Senior when Sammy was only three—was of Boricua heritage. However, I later learned that she was of Afro-Cuban descent.

I saw that the room had emptied out. I wriggled out of his arms and started to leave.

"Why don't you stay?" he asked.

I stopped and turned back to him. "Stay?" I said. "You mean, like *stay*?"

"Dat's what da man said." Sammy looked boyish and vulnerable. It wasn't hard to imagine him at the age of five, dancing for nickels on a Harlem street corner. There was something deeply touching about him.

At moments like these, I have two voices in my head. Uh, make that three. God; my mother, Katherine; and Chita. Well, make that four. There's also *Dolores*. And she was saying: "Okay, maybe your heart isn't going *boing*! But admit it, Chita, this is a man you adore, as much for his talent as for his sweetness. Go for it!"

I stayed.

But what Dolores didn't reckon with was whether I could ever fill the neediness of the little boy within him.

✳

In the mid-1950s, interracial marriage was still banned in many states; antimiscegenation laws weren't prohibited until 1967. I was Latina, but I registered as white. My affair with Sammy wasn't a big deal for me in that regard. At the time, I was more concerned that he was the star of the show and becoming more famous by the minute. I told my brother Hoolie about the affair and he was happy for me. And it quickly got around to the cast as well, who were all going through their own version of matchmaking. That's just a perennial sideshow of any Broadway musical. Still, Poppy had a lot to say.

"Chita, better watch out, hon!" he said.

"What do you mean?" I retorted.

"What I mean, child, is it can be dangerous out there for a white woman and a colored man."

"What can they do to us, Poppy? Besides I'm a Latina."

"What planet you from? This is America!" said Poppy. "People who hate don't go around askin' questions."

At first, Sammy and I stayed on "safe ground": the Gorham. That meant not only Sammy's Penthouse B but also the suite with kitchenette occupied by Sam Senior and his second wife, Rita Wade Davis. Small, pretty, and quick to smile, she was known as Pee Wee. It would be hard to ever utter the word "relaxed" in the same sentence with Sammy—it was always go-go-go with him—but he was happiest and most at home when we ate supper in his father's suite. I grew enormously fond of Sam Senior, who was friendly and open. Pee Wee, who cooked up some delicious soul food for us, was just as adorable and doted on both "my boys." They took me in like family. If Sammy liked me, that was enough for them.

Uncle Will Mastin joined us for those dinners, and he was as withdrawn as the others were talkative. The three of them had been together since 1928, and a lifetime exposure to the wiles and betrayals in the business had hardened Will. It led him to cast a skeptical eye on everything and everybody he encountered. He didn't really give a crap about the perks or celebrity of what they were doing. He just wanted to make sure the trio got their fair share out of the cash register. In fact, he was getting more than that since Sammy had become the breadwinner of the Mastin Trio. Even as his star rose, Sammy insisted on splitting the proceeds three ways and would continue to do so until he was forty-five, when he went out on his own.

During the run of *Mr. Wonderful*, Sam Senior and I became very close. He confided in me more and more about his worries as his son's career took off. Success brought as many problems as it solved. The weekly take for Sammy was $6,000, down from the $12,000 per week he had gotten from his nightclub gigs. I also knew from Sam that his son's free-spending ways had put him in hock to Chicago mobsters. Both the wise guys and his agents were pressing him to give up Broadway and return to the more lucrative club circuit. But Sammy was determined to play out his contract on Broadway as long as audiences kept coming. And thanks to his limitless publicity efforts, they were.

Part of that meant us going out on the town regularly with the Ryans, the Rhodeses, and Jane and Burt Boyar. Although Burt wasn't as powerful as Walter Winchell or Ed Sullivan, a mention from him guaranteed a spurt at the box office. The elegant and popular supper clubs that we frequented were carefully chosen by Sammy. He had a sixth sense of which of them might yank away the welcome mat, even if the reservation was in the name of the star of a Broadway hit. A few years earlier, the Stork Club had been at the center of a controversy when Josephine Baker, the celebrated Black singer and dancer, stormed out because of the slow service—an unmistakable snub. Sammy generally conceded the unspoken policies, but it bothered him nonetheless.

On the other hand, Ed Wynne and Frank Harris, who had worked for

Sherman Billingsley, owner of the Stork, opened the Harwyn Club, which quickly became a popular destination with the likes of Joan Crawford, Grace Kelly, Tony Curtis, and Janet Leigh seated at the banquettes. Wynne attended *Mr. Wonderful* and had sent a special invitation to Sammy to be his guest at the midtown club. That became one of our regular haunts. The Davis entourage was always given VIP treatment there, along with such other places as Chandler's, Tony's Caprice, and Danny's Hideaway, a popular steakhouse on East Forty-Fifth Street.

Even though the people seated around the banquettes earned more in a week than I did in a year, I wasn't in awe. I didn't know from money, and I didn't care. What I cared about was being a dancer, doing a good job, earning my own living, and spending time with people I liked. This world was definitely a step up from hanging out with the gang at Sid and Al's. It was a heady time. But I felt comfortable wherever we ended up. As Dolores might have said, "I could get used to this."

One day, just before a matinee performance of *Mr. Wonderful*, Jeri came into the dressing room, reading a newspaper. She called over to me.

"Hey, you're in Burt Boyar's column." She read: "Chita Rivera is Sammy Davis Jr.'s 'Mr. Wonderful' offstage, too."

I was both excited and scared. Since I had started on Broadway, I'd rated a few mentions in reviews, including for *Mr. Wonderful*. I had cut those out and sent them to my mother. But this was different. They weren't referring to me as a character. They were referring to me as, well, *me*, a woman who was dating Sammy Davis Jr. A Pandora's box of publicity had just been opened. I was learning what every celebrity knows: once that box is opened: you can't stuff everything back in it.

Jeri, who like Sammy was intuitive as hell, saw the expression on my face. "C'mon, baby, enjoy your time in the sun. Even if you play the long game, it'll be short enough. Now, dere it is!"

Jeri was right, of course. But I didn't clip the column and send it to my mother.

While Sammy enjoyed the VIP treatment at places like the Harwyn Club, as prestigious as it was, he could never let go of the places that he felt might not welcome him. Even an imagined slight could send him into a tizzy. One night we arrived at Sardi's, where a huge party was in progress in the main dining room. We were shown a table in the back, which didn't sit well with Sammy. He thought that we had been seated in Siberia. Others at the table made light of it, insisting that wherever Sammy sat was the VIP area. I could sense his unhappiness.

"Do you want to leave?" I said. As a middle child, I was always trying to fix things. Not always possible when it came to Sammy.

"No, that would bring too much attention," he replied. "We'll have our drinks and then go."

On another occasion, we were hanging around Penthouse B at the Gorham when the Boyars came back from their nightly rounds at the latest hotspots. Sammy had been restless all that evening. His financial obligations had been weighing heavily on him. He felt he needed some new distraction, so he decided to test the waters.

"Hey, Burt, when are you going to take me to the El Morocco?"

Burt paused. A long silence. Then he said, "Why not tonight?"

Sammy thought for a while. And then a curious expression crossed his face: he knew what he was about to set in motion.

"Chita, how would you like go to the El Morocco?" he asked. His voice was more tense than enthusiastic. I had never been to the zebra-striped supper club, which then was the Valhalla of New York nightlife.

"I think it would be fun," I said. "Should I go home and change?"

"Stay just as you are," said Sammy. But he suggested to Burt that he call the El Morocco to let them know that he was bringing guests. To be more specific, that he was bringing a guest named *Sammy Davis Jr.*

Burt dialed the El Morocco. After someone answered, Burt took the phone into the bedroom, but we could hear him becoming more exasperated as the call went on.

When Burt reemerged, Sammy already knew. "Don't tell me," he said. "They're 'fully committed.'"

We stayed in that night, but nothing could lift the gloom, no matter how many Kahlúas passed over the bar. The others drifted off into the night, leaving Sammy and me in the hotel room. No matter how much I tried to fix it, Sammy remained perturbed. Nothing ever rolled off his back. The scar tissue was too deep. Keeping up all those balls he so deftly juggled was becoming too hard. He was at war with himself, with the world, with his obligations, with life.

Then Sammy picked up a Black newspaper, the *Amsterdam News*. Since he had become a big star, Sammy's immersion into white café society had not gone unnoticed in the Black press. He threw the paper over to me. There was a caricature of two guys reading a newspaper with the caption, "Sammy doesn't come up here, cattin'. He be wanting to be downtown and white."

Sammy said vehemently, "I don't want to be Black, I don't want to be white, I just want to live in a world where that doesn't make a damn bit of difference. Why can't they just let me live my life? What do they want from me?"

Then Sammy, trembling with rage, took out his glass eye and held it in his fingers. I stood there, stunned.

"Here! Here! Is this what they want?!" he yelled. He tossed the eye into an ashtray. There was dead silence.

I moved to embrace him. His entire body tensed. He turned away in embarrassment.

"Just go," he said quietly.

"Sammy—"

"Chita. Please. Go."

I ran out of the room, down the hall, and into the elevator. By the time I walked out into the pouring rain, the shock had worn off and I burst into tears.

✳

Our affair ended shortly after. In the weeks following the hotel room incident, we were sheepish around each other. I had seen Sammy at his most pressured and vulnerable, and the images were seared into my mind. I realized then that I was in over my head. I could not meet the emotional demands of this wounded man; we lived in two different worlds. Besides, I just wasn't brave enough. Instinctively, I knew I had to get out of the way so he could find someone who was. I hoped he would.

Sam Senior and Pee Wee said that they missed me at the laugh-filled dinners in their suite. And I missed them. Sam had hoped I would marry his son. I later learned that Sammy felt the same way, though I don't think I was aware that the relationship had gone that far. Marry Sammy Davis Jr.? What a different turn my life would have taken. But I have always believed that we are as much guided by God, or the stars, or whatever you take as gospel, as we are by our own choices, misguided or not.

Mr. Wonderful closed on February 23, 1957, after a year's run. Sammy had fulfilled his obligation, and Broadway had added luster to a stardom that would grow only brighter in the years to come. After the closing, I went to audition for a show, once called *Gangway*, which became this thing called *West Side Story*.

In the succeeding years, Sammy and I bumped into each other from time to time, and it was always a joy to be with him. Ironically, shortly after our affair ended, he would become good friends with my later-to-be-husband, Tony Mordente. Sammy would also become very close to our daughter, Lisa. From the moment they met, she was devoted to him and he to her. When I lived in Los Angeles, Sammy would come by to pick up Lisa and take her to Disneyland along with his three kids, whom he had with May Britt, the Swedish actress. As Lisa grew older and became aware of our previous affair, Sammy would often tell her, "You know, you could have been mine!" He once autographed a picture to her: "You *should* have been mine!"

In 1990, when Sammy was dying of throat cancer at the age of sixty-four, he saw very few people. Tony, Lisa, and I were honored to be among them at the Beverly Hills home he shared with his beloved wife, Altovise. I was happy that after all the brickbats and death threats Sammy had to endure during his marriage to May Britt, he had found this gracious and beautiful woman to share the last twenty years of his life. During that time, I hated the way that Sammy had become a mascot for the Rat Pack—the way they'd belittle him with racist innuendo. I believed he didn't have to take it; he was more talented than any of them.

A Franciscan priest once told me, "We become who we are through other people."

How did that twenty-three-year-old become Chita Rivera through Sammy Davis Jr.? I saw how bravely he fought throughout his life, always redeeming it when he took the stage. It was the only place where he felt safe, where he could fully express himself, where he could more fully be a man. He shared with me a history of Black entertainment that I had been totally unaware of. I learned of the cost and terrible beauty of all he had to endure—only to bring happiness to people. I know I'm living today on the genius of all the creative people I have met in the course of my career, and that year was no exception. Sammy, Sam Senior, Will, Jeri, Poppy, and all those who got knocked down and came right back up because, as Sammy might say, "That's the only place to be, baby!"

In 1989, a benefit for the United Negro College Fund celebrated Sammy Davis Jr.'s sixtieth anniversary in show business. He had only a year to live as he sat in a box with Altovise and watched while Michael Jackson, Whitney Houston, Bill Cosby, Eddie Murphy, and many others paid homage to a man they described as the "greatest living entertainer." At the conclusion of the program, Gregory Hines, who had been inspired by Sammy, did a superb tap routine. He then invited Sammy to come to the stage to do a number with him. Sammy, bent with age and crippled by cancer, rose from his seat and moved slowly to the stage. When the spotlight hit him, he steadily gained strength until he blew Gregory Hines away to a rousing ovation. As the applause subsided, Greg knelt down and kissed Sammy's feet.

Now, as I look at the picture of me kissing Sammy's hand, I recall that he was once asked how he wanted to be remembered. He said in two ways:

Sammy Davis Jr., "Entertainer."

Sammy Davis Jr., "He tried."

8

"HELLO, GOWER! HELLO, DICK!"

Bye Bye Birdie

Gower Champion was being tactful but direct. We were in the dining room of the Gorham Hotel, early in 1960, and he was sizing me up. He was looking to see whether I could play the character of Rosie, a starring role, in the first big Broadway musical he was directing and choreographing, a show called *Bye Bye Birdie*.

"Look, Chita, I thought you were very good in *West Side Story*," he said, looking dapper in a yellow cardigan and slender in the tightest houndstooth pants I'd ever seen. "But if I was being considered to play a role unlike any I'd ever played, you'd be curious if I could do it. So what I'd like to know is, can you be light and vulnerable?"

Me, "light and vulnerable"? Sure! But there was a more specific question hanging over the lunch.

"Mr. Champion—"

"Please, call me Gower," he said.

"Okay, Gower," I replied. Then I added, joking, "And you can call me Dolores Conchita Figueroa del Rivero Montestuco Florentina Carnemacaral del Fuente."

He laughed. "Is that really your name?" he said.

"Honest to God, my full birth name, but I never use it," I replied. "And with a name like that, isn't what you're really wondering is, 'Can she play anything other than a Latin tomato?'"

Gower grinned, showing the whitest, straightest teeth right out of Hollywood.

I figured that my Puerto Rican ethnicity might be the elephant in the room. Ed Padula, the producer of *Bye Bye Birdie*, had told me as much when he set up the lunch. Months earlier, while I was performing in *West Side Story* in London, he had asked Gower, who was then in the UK himself, to check out my performance. Gower had sent Ed a wire back: "Chita's great but she'll turn our Rosie into a Spanish omelet!"

Spanish omelet, Latin tomato, sexy spitfire. Call me naïve, but it had never occurred to me that I couldn't play just about anything that was handed to me. Hell, I'd already played Fifi, the French streetwalker; Rita Romano, the Italian chorine; and even Marilyn Monroe, the blond siren of show business. Three years later, I'd play Linda "I Enjoy Being a Girl" Low in *Flower Drum Song*. Typecasting was something forced on us from the outside. Producers, directors, and casting agents were used to playing it safe, and in 1960 there weren't a lot of Latino stars making a splash. Desi Arnaz's Ricky Ricardo was something of a lone wolf out there, and Lucille Ball had gone to the mat to get him cast in her popular TV series. Perhaps my momentary gambit to become "Chita O'Hara" had been a concession to that kind of thinking. But my impulse was always to make a joke of stereotyping. That was kind of why I thought my mouthful of a name could be an icebreaker with Gower.

For a moment I thought it might have backfired. But then Gower said, "Why don't you take a week and prepare something to show me what you can do. That is, if you want the role."

✳

Did I ever! I fell in love with Rosie and the musical the minute I heard about it from my agent, Dick Seff. *Bye Bye Birdie* was a satire, cooked up by writer Michael Stewart, on the mania Elvis Presley was then arousing among teenage girls (and their mothers). I wasn't a fan of Elvis myself. His gyrations made me laugh. I thought of him as a pale imitation of the real thing: the cool, sexy, Black guys, like Little Richard, rocking out in the clubs of Harlem, Chicago, and Memphis. Michael Stewart had been inspired by Elvis's induction into the army to create a comedy in which teen idol Conrad Birdie gives one last kiss to an all-American girl, Kim MacAfee, of Sweet Apple, Ohio. That publicity ploy is engineered by Rosie Alvarez to get Albert Peterson, her boyfriend and Birdie's manager, back into solvency. Then he just might marry her and settle down, finally escaping the apron strings of his overbearing Jewish mother. By the way, my character was originally called Rosie Grant. It was Latinized when I was cast.

I know the plot sounds corny. But that was the point. One last kiss to the white-bread Eisenhower years. What appealed to me about *Bye Bye Birdie* was just how much it was the flip side of *West Side Story*. The raw gangs rumbling on the streets of New York had changed into the giggling teenagers gossiping on phones about who was going steady with whom. After Carol Haney turned down the role of Rosie, Dick called to tell me that Michael, along with the songwriting team of Charles Strouse and Lee Adams, were interested in playing the score for me. All of us had worked together on *Shoestring Revue* five years earlier. Lee and Michael had written the Marilyn skit that had brought me my first major notices. Additionally, I'd met Ed, our producer, when I did *Seventh Heaven*. He'd been assistant to the director. I was learning that Broadway could sometimes seem as small a town as Sweet Apple, Ohio.

Michael, who would go on to write such smash hits as *Carnival!*, *Hello, Dolly!*, and *Barnum*, was a short, wiry dynamo, fast and funny. Ed Padula called him a cross between Peter Pan and Dorian Gray, with the determination of a "feather-boaed constrictor." Charles was as intense and ambitious as Lee was laid back, and they too would go on to write more hits, including *Applause* for Lauren Bacall and *Golden Boy* for Sammy Davis Jr. On our way up to Charles's apartment, Dick cautioned me to play it cool. I was to adopt my best poker face so that at the end of the evening, he could tell them, "We'll have to think about it."

"That way, I can get you a better deal," he said.

We settled into the living room with drinks, and Michael gave me a synopsis of his witty script. Then he handed the floor over to Charles and Lee. Once they started in on the songs, "A Lot of Livin' to Do" and "Put on a Happy Face," I couldn't contain myself any longer. I jumped off the couch and said, "I've gotta do this show!" Dick slapped his forehead, but our youthful energy—I was twenty-seven, they were all in their thirties—could've levitated the building. We came back down to earth when Ed said that I had one more hurdle to clear—Gower.

I knew who he was, of course. Very good looking. Very tall. Very Hollywood. And very Technicolor. He and Marge, his bubbly blond wife, had formed a dance team, the Champions, who'd graced television and films, scoring big in the 1951 remake of *Show Boat*. At twenty-nine, Gower had won his first Tony Award staging Carol Channing, my idol, in the Broadway revue *Lend an Ear*, and he had a few other minor shows under his belt. He was coaxed by Ed to come back East to direct and choreograph *Bye Bye Birdie*. That was why I found myself lunching with him at the Gorham—the same place where I and the cast of *Mr. Wonderful* had played games with Sammy in his suite.

Another good luck sign was that my audition for Gower was on the stage of the Winter Garden Theatre, where *West Side Story* had played. Charles and I had worked on presenting a couple of songs: "Little Girl Blue," to show my vulnerable side, and "I'm Available," from *Mr.*

Wonderful, to show that I could "make 'em laugh." I arrived at the Winter Garden wearing a simple navy blue dress with a white peter-pan collar and sporting a new hairdo.

While Ed, Gower, and Elliot Lawrence, the show's music director, sat in the middle of the orchestra, I nervously went up on the stage, sat on a stool, and began to sing Richard Rodgers and Larry Hart's best slit-your-wrist song:

> *Sit there and count your fingers*
> *What can you do?*
> *Old girl, you're through . . .*

I never got to the next stanza. Gower bolted out of his seat and came down the aisle.

"That's enough, Conchita Whatever-Your-Name-Is!" he said. "You're our Rosie."

I made a beeline to the pay phone in the lobby to share the good news with my mother and my brother Hoolie. Ed and the boys caught up with me and we went back into the theater to watch the auditions for the role of Hugo, Kim's hapless boyfriend. The young men auditioning were cookie-cutter types until a baby-faced twenty-year-old came into the light and sang a sweet tune of longing. I was so moved by his effortless innocence and goofy charm that I turned to Gower and said, "If you don't hire this boy, I'm leaving." I didn't have to speak up. This kid's special appeal was so evident that he got the role. And it wasn't surprising when eight years later, Michael J. Pollard was Oscar-nominated for his film debut in *Bonnie and Clyde*. Soon after, our cast was filled out with Susan Watson as Kim, Dick Gautier as Conrad, Kay Medford as Albert's meddling mother, and two stunning choices: Paul Lynde, as Kim's basket case of a father, and Dick Van Dyke, as Albert, a major mama's boy and, lucky me, Rosie's romantic interest.

＊

The charming song "Put on a Happy Face" was first written for Rosie but was taken away from me and given to Dick Van Dyke midway through the show's development. Was I miffed? Not really. I had plenty of other songs and a couple of show-stopping dances. Besides, it was the perfect song for Dick, and the reassignment gave his character a boost with the audience. He sang it beautifully to a lovelorn teenager and showed off a physical limberness that was all his own. Of my costars, Dick put a happy face on me more times than any other.

Ed had seen Dick in *The Boys Against the Girls*, a short-lived Broadway comedy revue, and touted him to the team. "I didn't think much of the revue, but boy oh boy, this guy's a natural," he told them. Once we started rehearsals, I had to agree. Not only was Dick funny, he was also cute, with his dark hair, wide dimpled smile, and startling blue eyes. Having come out of a small town in Missouri, he had that polite reserve that made you want to tease him. I remember his wife, Margie, coming to an early rehearsal when Dick and I were going over a scene in which we had to kiss. We were both very shy about it.

Wait. Let me correct that. Chita was shy about it. Dolores, my alter ego, was anything but: "Kiss him, girl. Kiss him! You know you want to!" Those sorts of things can be a perk of acting. But you can't get carried away.

When Dick was cast, he confessed to Gower, "I should tell you that I can't dance." Gower wasn't fazed. "Leave that to me," he replied. Leaving dance in Gower's hands was a no-brainer. He could make a turnip look like Fred Astaire, not that Dick needed that much coaching. When Gower arrived in New York, he brought Hollywood with him. His approach to dance was cinematic, a West Coast style that could be both specific and widescreen, simple and complex. He cast his dancers very carefully, looking for colorful traits to which he could direct the audience's attention.

Gower often said, "I want the audience to look *where* I want them to look and *when* I want them to look."

He devised the theatrical equivalent of a movie close-up and then could pull back when he wanted to envision the whole picture. Decades later, the 2002 Tony-winning musical *Hairspray* owed a lot to Gower's opening of *Bye Bye Birdie.* I'm thinking of the scene that featured the chorus kids, each in a Technicolor square, singing "The Telephone Hour."

One afternoon, as we returned from a break, Gower was smiling like a boy with a new toy.

"Come with me, Chita," he said. "I've got something to show you."

Michael had written a scene in which Rosie, furious that Albert has hired a blond sexpot, Gloria Rasputin, storms out and stumbles into a meeting of the Sweet Apple Shriners. Gower wanted to show me how he was going to stage the scene. He led me by the hand into the theater, and we stood together facing upstage where he had arranged a table at which sat seven chorus boys in fezzes. As the pianist played sinuous Middle Eastern music and we watched the guys, Gower instructed me on how I would turn the meeting into a free-for-all. He had my body flipping, twisting, twirling, and sliding across the table and onto the laps of the boys. Then I slid upside down, legs akimbo, under the table. The dizzy seven-minute number had the boys popping up and down like a whack-a-mole game, leaving up to the imagination exactly what I was doing to them. As Gower and I stood there, I saw my part in the puzzle, astonished at the mathematical precision with which he'd mapped it out. You could take the central dancer out of the equation and it still made sense. "The Shriners' Ballet" was a Keystone cops silent comedy with a little bit of the Marx Brothers thrown in. The number became a classic, establishing Gower as one of the most inventive choreographers to hit Broadway.

We rehearsed *Birdie* downtown at the Anderson Theatre in what used to be the center of Jewish theater just below Fourteenth Street. Dick and I took our lunch break at Luchow's, a vintage restaurant where the old waiters would ignore what you ordered and bring you what they thought you ought to have. Dick would crack me up at lunch, imitating the stage doorman at the theater. He was this scary-looking codger whom I dubbed Kharis, the mummy in all those 1940s movies that my brother Hoolie showed in our basement on Flagler.

Dick was so comical that there were times during rehearsals when I couldn't even look at him for fear of breaking up. Gower, who was all business with his legal pad and pencils sharpened to a fine point, hated interruptions like that. One day it proved too much. We were working on a scene in which Rosie says to Albert, "You go your way and I'll go my way. East and West on the Lincoln Highway." Michael's script was full of off-the-wall lines like that. Dick scrunched up his face and looked at me with this quizzical expression: *What does that even mean?* Suddenly we were laughing so hard that we couldn't stop. (It's known in the theater as "corpsing.") The minute we managed to collect ourselves, we started giggling all over again. Finally, Gower, exasperated, said, "Just go home!" At least he didn't shove me into a piano like Mr. Oboukhoff had at the School of American Ballet.

✳

When we moved from New York to Philly for our out-of-town tryout, the advance for *Bye Bye Birdie* was a paltry $200. Nobody gave us a chance of success. Kay Medford's agent had cynically told her, "Take the job. You'll get paid for five weeks of rehearsal. The show'll never get out of Philly." The lack of faith didn't dampen our spirits. If anything, it made us work harder. During the run, I was asked whether I would screen test for the role of Anita in the film version of *West Side Story*. I suppose I could've asked Dick, my agent, to get me out of my contract. But I said "No." I was surprised at how easily the answer came to me. I was happy. Tony had been hired as Gower's assistant and had also been cast as Conrad Birdie's understudy. So we were working together, and our Lisa, now two years old, was often in the wings or in our dressing room in her stroller. And I loved the company. That included Kay, who was a terror as Albert's crazy mother, putting her head in the oven whenever he didn't do what she wanted; and Dick Gautier, with his hilarious imitation of Elvis.

Birdie was such a good time that you'd think there'd be no need for Dolores to rear her angry head. But you'd be wrong. She was poked out of her lair by Gower after a performance in Philly. It was our usual practice to gather onstage after the theater had cleared to receive "notes." These were Gower's comments on anything any of us might be doing wrong or how the show could be improved. Dick and I sat together, pencil and notepad in hand. I smoked in those days; it took me away from biting my nails and helped me figure out a scene. I made a habit of matching the color of my cigarette holder to my dress. I thought it looked great. I actually liked the holders more than the cigarettes. Thankfully, I quit the half-a-pack habit early on.

Once we were all assembled, Gower declared, "With the exception of Paul and Kay, that was the worst performance I have ever seen." That didn't sit well with Dolores. I thought it was totally unfair and insulting to Dick and me. I could feel my face turning red. I slammed down my pencil and jumped up off the floor. "We don't have to take this! I'm leaving! C'mon, Dick!" He was startled by my reaction and just sort of mumbled, "Uh, uh, uh, uh . . ." Dick hated conflict. Years later, Rose Marie, who costarred with him on *The Dick Van Dyke Show*, dubbed him the "Six-Foot Tower of Jell-O." I ran down to my dressing room, slammed the door shut, and locked it. I had every intention of calling Dick Seff and telling him to get me out of the show.

Gower came to my door and knocked. I let him in—eventually. He apologized.

"Sorry, Chita," he said. "I thought by including you and Dick, my note would land more forcefully on the kids. You and Dick get along so well with them. We're under a lot of pressure, there's never enough time, and I wanted to shock them."

Thank God, Gower didn't take me seriously about quitting. What in the hell would I have done? I had just turned down the screen test for *West Side Story*, and I had no prospects in line. What a fool! Looking back, I probably learned on *Birdie* the importance of picking your battles carefully. That meant keeping Dolores at bay—not always an easy job, especially when I think somebody is being a bully. As it happened, Paul Lynde came into my line of fire for that very reason.

Paul, who garnered raves in *Birdie*, was one of the most inventive comedians I've ever encountered. In anybody else's hands, the role of Harry MacAfee, Kim's conservative father, would have been a typical second-banana turn. But Paul was a force of nature, mugging shamelessly, ad-libbing mean asides to the MacAfee children, and stealing every scene with his well-timed sarcasm. His hysterically funny performance not only shaped the part but also made him a star. He later became a huge favorite in films and television in shows like *Hollywood Squares*. Paul was talented, no question. But he was also smug, arrogant, and nasty. His fangs became even sharper when he was drunk. One day, he made the mistake of attacking my family, which turned me into a fire-breathing dragon.

Tony had taken a brief sabbatical from the show to play another gig, and his understudy stepped in to take his role. Paul had gotten used to playing opposite the replacement so Tony's return to the show threw Paul's performance at a matinee a little off-kilter. Once the show was finished, he went ballistic on my husband, viciously insulting him in front of the entire company. When I heard about it, I went flying down to Paul's dressing room. I flung the door open to see him sitting at his makeup table, holding court with some of the chorus boys. They took one look at me and scattered.

Shaking with rage, I pointed my finger at Paul and yelled, "If you ever, ever talk to Tony, or anybody else in this company, like that again, I will rip your head off!"

Paul turned pale and just looked at me with his mouth open. I probably looked like such a gorgon that Kharis the mummy would have run back into his crypt. I turned on my heels and left. I'm sure Paul called me all sorts of names behind my back, but he stayed out of my way from then on. Like many comedians, he lived with nerves exposed, always on edge, fearful of the day when he might not get the laughs he expected. Comedians tend to pay a high price for their special gifts. But that was no excuse. If you bring down the morale of the company, then watch out for Dolores. My daughter, Lisa, calls it "when Mom goes Puerto Rican."

The character of Rosie had originally been conceived by Michael Stewart as Polish so that Albert's antagonistic mother, Mae, would never be at a loss for ethnic jokes to hurl at her prospective daughter-in-law. When I was cast, Michael turned her into Spanish Rose. Hence the song "Spanish Rose," with its clicking castanets, tacos, tangos, and tequila. I wasn't crazy about this song, which satirized Mae's racism. It's what minorities have to put up with all the time, this sense that we aren't as "American" as whites. Asian Americans are forever being asked "Where are you really from?" even though their family might be five or six generations in this country. The first stanza of the song mocked Mae's insistence that I was some predatory "tamale" right off the boat when the truth of the matter was that Rosie hailed from Allentown, Pennsylvania.

My first instinct when I'm asked to focus on my ethnicity is to turn the tables, as I had with Gower on our first meeting. Or to spice it up with humor. When I was given the song "Spanish Rose," I decided to fight fire with fire, singing it with the same brio as I had mocked Marilyn Monroe in *Shoestring Revue* and had sung "America" in *West Side Story*. I even threw in an imitation of Señor Wences, the popular Spanish ventriloquist who was a frequent guest on *The Ed Sullivan Show*. My resentment of the song evaporated once I got a handle on it. I didn't know it then, but what I was doing was getting control of the stereotype—what minorities have had to do in show business throughout history. Coupled with Gower's witty and sly choreography, "Spanish Rose" became another highlight of the show.

Buoyed by strong notices, *Birdie* was an immediate hit in Philadelphia. By the time we left, the advance in New York, riding on the buzz, had grown to $200,000, a rarity for an original musical by relative unknowns. Opening night was even more exhilarating. At the after-party, the show's publicist brought in the papers bearing stellar reviews and welcoming the first rock 'n' roll musical to hit Broadway. Typical was John Chapman, writing in the *Daily News*: "The funniest, most captivating, and most expert musical comedy one could hope to see in several seasons of show going." "The Shriners' Ballet" was praised in every one of the notices. Chapman wrote of me in that ballet, "The lady is as exhilarating as the idea is impudent. She succeeds in enticing every dazed male on the premises."

I was particularly amused when Kenneth Tynan wrote in the *New Yorker*, "Miss Rivera, who looks like a cross between Marlene Dietrich and a Latin-American soubrette, performs smartly throughout, but her high point is a number called 'Spanish Rose,' in which she parodies Hispanophilia in all its aspects, from *cante hondo* to 'La Cucaracha.'" Another reviewer predicted Dick's future: "Lanky Dick Van Dyke is brilliant trying to cheer up a moon-faced sad girl with footwork that would do credit to Disney's animators." Needless to say, Dick went on from *Birdie* to star in one of the most popular sitcoms of all time. He also brought his inimitable charm to such films as *Mary Poppins,* in which he actually danced with animated characters, as well as *Chitty Chitty Bang Bang.*

✳

Several decades later, in 2006, Dick and I were reunited when he made a surprise guest appearance in my Broadway musical *Chita Rivera: The*

Dancer's Life. His dark hair had turned snow white and we both had some mileage behind us. But as we sang a duet of "Rosie" in the show, we picked up as though the intervening years had been mere speed bumps. He wasn't tooling me around the stage on a baggage cart as we had done in the original show. But we both knew that Albert and Rosie and their relationship would always be ours—and so did the audience.

People often ask me if I feel ownership of the roles I have created on-stage, including Anita, Rosie, Velma, Claire, you name it. Hell, ya! The character may be filmed without me, revivals of the shows may come and go with new names playing the part, and there may even be movie remakes, such as *West Side Story*. To the actors inheriting these parts, I say, "Blessings. More power to you!"

But no matter who steps into Rosie's shoes, she'll always be mine. There's no reason to let go of her. Why would I? I know her—right down to the marrow. She still lives in me, and if I could, I would play her today. It was a thrilling time in our lives, when the creators and I first brought her to life. Somebody pushed you to the limit, and you had to respond.

As always, a new Chita emerged by the end of the run of *Birdie*. Someone who picked her battles more carefully. Someone who knew that when something feels right, go for it. Someone who has a Dolores within her to take on the bullies but who needs to keep her in check, so that it's always about the show and not ego.

To paraphrase Shakespeare, "A rose by any other name is still a rose." But when I think of *Bye Bye Birdie*, I imagine that a rose by any other name is . . . Dolores Conchita Figueroa del Rivero Montestuco Florentina Carnemacaral del Fuente.

Smoke on your pipe and put that in!

9

LONDON, JUDY, THE BEATLES, AND THE LESSONS OF FAME

Tony Mordente has always said that he became an adult when we went to London, first in 1958 for *West Side Story* and then again in 1961 for *Bye Bye Birdie*. I can't say that I came of age in England. I was twenty-five and already a wife and mother when Tony and I and three-month-old Lisa boarded a jet at Idlewild for the transatlantic flight. But it was in London that I learned to handle the public attention that was coming my way after two Broadway successes.

I hesitate to use the word "star." I never thought of myself as one until many decades later when I won critical acclaim and a second Tony Award for *Kiss of the Spider Woman*. For years, Fred Ebb said to me, "Chita, you have to learn to be a star and you'll be treated like one." I wasn't that interested, to tell you the truth. This may stem, at least in part, from lessons I learned in those early years in London. Lessons that came from a group of English actors, like Julie Andrews, Laurence Olivier, and Judi Dench, as well as a surprising involvement with Judy Garland and the Beatles.

Not that there was anything wrong with being fawned over as we were as a company when we arrived in England to put on *West Side Story*. In fact, we embraced it: the guys who couldn't get enough of the "birds" who were all too available to them; the girls who loved the double-decker buses that took us to Harrods and the shops in Knightsbridge. Both Tony and

I fell in love with England. Even with the pea soup fog. At times, it was so thick the cabs, driven by cockneys who were impossible to understand, inched along the road. The heaters devoured our sixpences and yet still couldn't ward off the chill. There were the elegant teas at the Savoy and the steaks at the pubs, costing all of eight shillings and sixpence ($1.15). How could we not be fascinated by a place that had given the world the queen, Jack the Ripper, and Marmite?

The welcome was pleasant, mainly because of Hugh "Binkie" Beaumont, our producer for both *West Side Story* and *Birdie*. I was particularly grateful because he chose to postpone the production of *West Side Story* until I gave birth to Lisa and had recovered well enough to travel. He even provided a nanny, Blenda Peacock, a woman as starchy as her uniform. Binkie, a wily businessman, was a powerhouse in British theater and was particularly close with Noel Coward and John Gielgud, whom he presented in prestigious productions. I got a healthy introduction to the famous "stiff-upper-lip" of the Brits when Binkie told me that his boyfriend, the playwright John Perry, had left Gielgud for him, and yet he and John remained good friends. A class act.

Just before *West Side* opened its pre–West End engagement in Manchester, Binkie gathered the company to warn us that British audiences were far more restrained than American ones. So imagine our surprise when in Manchester and London, they were unrestrained in their enthusiasm; the ovation that greeted "America" was so huge that we couldn't go on. At the end, the air was filled with "bravos." They liked what we did, but they also appreciated how different we were. To them, my Anita was exotic, unlike anything they'd ever seen before.

Even more gratifying was the kind reception from the English theater community. I was particularly taken by a pretty twenty-four-year-old Judi Dench, who joined us in our warm-ups before performances. She was a magnetic presence, as was Julie Andrews and her husband at the time, Tony Walton. Julie, of course, was already a major star, having captivated audiences in *The Boyfriend* and *My Fair Lady*. But you wouldn't know it from her "just-call-me-Jules" friendliness. We quickly became friends. Far from the images of the "practically perfect" nanny in *Mary Poppins* and the uncertain novice in *The Sound of Music*, she was bawdy and down-to-earth.

The Brits could relate to *West Side* (more so than *Birdie*) because they had their own gangs, which were called Teddy Boys. Just before we opened, there had been the Notting Hill race riots in which white gangs attacked West Indian youths. The reviews for *West Side*, which were raves, pointed out the similarities between the Teds and the Sharks and the Jets. Despite the show's parallels to England's own racial problems, we settled down to a long run.

Birdie didn't have as much cachet. "The Telephone Hour" puzzled audiences because English teens didn't spend their time on the phone gossiping. With Peter Marshall playing Albert and Hermione Baddeley playing his mother, Mae, we soldiered on through the previews. This time Binkie was right: the response was more muted than we had anticipated. When the opening night curtain came down at Her Majesty's Theatre in June 1961, I was, as the Brits say, "gutted." I was sure that my performance as Rosie had let the company down. Like a sullen child, Dolores refused to come out of her dressing room until there was a knock at the door and Binkie came in.

"My dear girl, there is a time for moping and there is a time for getting your arse down to the party in the lobby," he said. "Everybody is waiting to cheer you." I got my "tootie boot" in motion. It's that age-old actor's insecurity. You can be on the receiving end of appreciative applause, and the only person you see at curtain call is the one guy in the front row who looks like he just sucked on a lemon or, worse, is fast asleep. And that anxiety never goes away!

As it turned out, the reviews for *Birdie* were wonderful. Even Bernard Levin, the sourpuss of the *Daily Express*, declared the show to be better than *The Sound of Music* and *The Music Man*. (We loved that last one!)

With his arms full of morning papers, Ed Padula, our New York producer, rode through the streets of London with his head poking out of the car's sunroof, yelling, "I'm king of the world!" What was it that Noel Coward wrote? "Why do the wrong people travel?" John Gielgud was so enamored of *Birdie* that he watched it night after night from the back of the theater. In that gorgeous voice of his, he said, "If they'd asked me, I would have sent this show to the Soviet Union instead of *My Fair Lady*."

During the run of *Birdie*, I got a distressing call from my agent, Dick Seff. Even before I had a chance to do a screen test, the producers of the film version announced that Janet Leigh had been cast as Rosie. I was disappointed; Dolores was pissed off. Gower had declined to direct the movie so George Sidney had stepped in. In Janet Leigh's hands, Rosie would still be Spanish, but her name would be changed to Rosie DeLeon. (Yeah, that one stumped me, too.) And the song "Spanish Rose" would be cut from the film. I had no beef with Janet Leigh; she was a lovely woman. But to add fire to my fury, the producers of the movie asked, "Would it be okay if we sent a crew over to film your matinee performance for reference?" My response? Let me put it this way. Rosie has a number in *Bye Bye Birdie* in which she, furious at Albert, does some damage to a suitcase. It's called "How to Kill a Man." And George Sidney was now the suitcase.

✳

Every Thursday evening, when most of the West End was dark, Binkie would throw a party at his lavish home in Westminster. There the *Birdie* cast would be introduced to some of the brightest talents of England, including Laurence Olivier, Ralph Richardson, Dame Edith Evans, Maggie Smith, and Coral Browne. Their artistry served to raise the bar for us. And yet, these actors were modest about their achievements. Unlike in America, they seemed to embrace their failures as well as their successes. Sure, the English could be snobby, but it didn't penetrate to the theater world. Talent was the great equalizer. There was even an odd affection for losers. Unless they happened to be on a favorite soccer team. On any given night, the pubs were full of rabid fans, uttering the "F-bomb" as though it were punctuation. It even came out of the mouths of the most demure young things. Growing up in a household where profanity was strictly forbidden, I was scandalized.

One evening at Binkie's, the room suddenly quieted down. I turned to see Judy Garland walking in. Like everyone there, I knew her as one of the greatest singers of the century. Just before we'd left for London, she'd had a triumphant return at Carnegie Hall, and the year before that she'd become the toast of London with her concert at the Palladium. She was so vital and charming at Binkie's that I found it difficult to believe this was the same woman who'd filled the tabloids with news of her personal struggles. It seemed as though she'd always been a part of us, even though she was not yet forty. At that moment, I would have given anything to have my brother Hoolie in the room with us. He idolized Judy. A movie and record buff, Hoolie was forever pulling out a copy of Judy's latest record, saying, "Chita, you gotta listen to this!" I was familiar only with *The Wizard of Oz*, but Hoolie's idea of heaven was afternoons at art movie houses playing revivals.

Eventually, our *Bye Bye Birdie* gang retreated to one of Binkie's bedrooms. It wasn't long before Judy joined us. Sitting on the floor, she loved talking about dance, drawing out from us our experiences on Broadway. She recounted how she'd taken Liza, her daughter, to see the show in New York as a fourteenth birthday present.

"And when we came out of the theater," recalled Judy, "Liza turned to me and said, 'Mama, that's what I want to do.' I don't think she had ever really settled on a career in show business. Not until that moment."

All we could do was repay the compliments. We were "gobsmacked" as the English say. There we were in the presence of a legend who was so self-effacing that all she wanted to do was talk about us. When we asked what was next for her, she spoke of a television variety show she was then in the process of negotiating with CBS. A few years later, I'd be honored to be in one of the episodes, singing a duet of "I Believe in You" with her. You can now catch her shows on YouTube. In that same show, you can see me, with my hair piled ridiculously on my head like Marge Simpson, singing and dancing "I Got Plenty O' Nuttin'."

As the party was winding down, Binkie introduced me to a handsome, fashionably dressed young man. "Chita, I'd like you to meet Brian Epstein." Brian had just signed an obscure, scruffy quartet from his hometown in Liverpool. With cunning business sense and great style, he remade them into a mop-topped group in suits and ties: the Beatles. In a few years, they'd be world famous. And in the summer of 1964, Brian asked me to join them in a television special in Blackpool. From there, we flew to London for a "Night of 100 Stars" charity gala before the queen at the Palladium.

✳

To me, Brian and the Beatles epitomized the "Swinging London" that was just emerging. I was never one to embrace the American Beat Generation of Jack Kerouac and Allen Ginsberg. But I had a lot of silly fun with the English Mod scene of miniskirts, the Mersey Sound, Jean Shrimpton, and later, Twiggy. It was right up my Carnaby Street–Westminster alley.

Traveling with the Beatles could be scary. You could get burned from the white heat of their fame. At the time, I had the audacity to think they were not all that great. (As I mentioned, I felt that about Elvis, too.) It wasn't until later that I started to admire their groundbreaking music. In Blackpool, they spent a lot of time trying to crack each other up. John was intense, a bit intimidating; George was shy and quiet; Paul was cute and approachable; and Ringo? Well, Ringo was a frisky puppy. Lovable but not as talented as the rest. At night, Ringo would come to the door of my room in the hotel, looking for company. I sat in the dark, very still, pretending I wasn't at home, until he went running off. There were crowds of women, breathless at the chance to make him feel less lonely.

I saw that frenzy up close at the Blackpool airport as we ran, like a scene out of *Hard Day's Night*, to escape the screaming throngs that had gathered there. I was frightened. I wouldn't have minded if the furor had been for me, but to get trampled for the Beatles? That's like being a casualty in somebody else's war. We managed to board the private jet just as crowds broke through the barricades and ran helter-skelter onto the tarmac. From my window seat, I could see them pouring onto the field like a swarm of bees. The boys were totally nonchalant during this fan frenzy. When the pilot announced that we were in a holding pattern until the police could clear the tarmac, John joked to the pilot, "Can't you just run over 'em?"

I'd never met anyone as subversive as John Lennon before. I never knew quite how to take him. And that came to a head at the "Night of 100 Stars" gala. I performed along with a roster that included Gloria Swanson, Zsa Zsa Gabor, Hailey Mills, Merle Oberon, and Laurence Olivier. The Beatles had been good sports that night, harnessed up and flying around the theater, singing "I'm Flying" from *Peter Pan*. After we each did our bit, we were placed at tables on the stage to watch the rest of the proceedings. I was sitting with the Beatles when gasps came from the audience at a surprise announcement: "Ladies and gentlemen, Judy Garland."

Wearing a red-sequined dress with long sleeves, Judy looked far more frail than she had a couple of years before at Binkie Beaumont's party. Just a month before the gala she had been hospitalized for having "accidentally" cut herself with scissors. Afterwards, she'd been admitted to a nursing home for rest. The Palladium broke out into pandemonium at her appearance. Fans rushed the stage, yelling for her to sing "Over the Rainbow." She tried to quiet them down, saying that she'd only come to show her support and that she wasn't prepared to sing. The crowd just doubled-down. "Sing, Judy, sing!" they screamed.

John then shouted, "Show us your wrists, Judy! Maybe that'll shut them up." I was shocked at his cruelty. I don't think Judy heard. If she did, she ignored it. Because she softly started to sing "Over the Rainbow," and the band picked up on it. The room became so still you could hear a pin drop. The ovation at the end was thunderous. Then, growing even stronger, Judy sang "Swanee." I was mesmerized—and shaken. Not just by her bravery. But also by the energy in the room: the adoration, the ownership ("you're ours!"), and John's cynical outburst. I was disturbed for years by the memory of that night even as my admiration for the Beatles' music grew.

When John was tragically killed by a deranged fan sixteen years later, I realized just how perceptive he'd been on that night in London about the dangers of fame. Both Judy and John had, in their own way, called up the imagined possibilities that lay "beyond the rainbow." And they paid a terrible price for it.

*

Tony and I were serenaded with the classic Italian song, "Volare," seven months into our London run of *West Side Story*. We had just finished a matinee performance when Tony Chardet, our stage manager, brought us down from our dressing rooms and flung open a window at the back of Her Majesty's Theatre. Below, in an alley, three musicians with mandolins and a guitar were belting out Italian songs. That was to get us in the mood for our three-week vacation, which Binkie had suggested we spend in Italy. This included a visit to Corleto Monforte, the ancestral home of the Mordente family.

This visit began a lifelong romance with Italy and especially Positano on the Amalfi Coast, where we stayed at the Miramare, a charming hotel with panoramic views of the Gulf of Salerno and a friendly staff. They fussed a great deal over Lisa, then nearly a year old, and prepared the most delicious meals for us. I was so enchanted by the place and the hotel that I returned again and again with friends and family. Italians! They can talk about food for hours on end, arguing about which region has the best tomatoes, the best garlic, the best olive oil. Even though we gorged on the delicious cuisine, I never seemed to gain weight. That's because the path from the hotel to the Tyrrhenian Sea below was made up of a 352-step stairway, which seemed to get longer and steeper as the years went by. We took turns pointing out the scenery just so we could stop and rest.

The highlight of that first trip was our stay in Rome, which included a pilgrimage to the Vatican's Sistine Chapel and St. Peter's. I'm now not one to wear my Catholicism on my sleeve. But through Katherine, my mother, and Grandma Sallie, it had always been of profound importance to me. When I was growing up we attended Mass as a family every Sunday. I was carried away by the rituals: the Latin, the smell of the incense, the gleaming chalices, and the ornate vestments. It was the best theater in town. Throughout my youth, I was drawn to collecting religious articles. Once I moved to New York, my friend Buzz Miller, a dazzling Jack Cole dancer, joked that he felt like he had to cross himself whenever he entered my apartment. Even now, a medal blessed by Mother Teresa still has pride of place in my house.

So you can imagine how I felt when Tony and I, with Lisa in my arms, entered St. Peter's Basilica along with throngs of worshipers and tourists. Surrounded by its monumental splendor, I wished Mother was with me at that moment, just as I wished that Hoolie had been with me when I met Judy Garland. We had managed to sit in pews close to the aisle down which Pope John XXIII would make his way. I was glad that I'd have the privilege of seeing this Pope in person, rather than another. He had been born Angelo Roncalli and was known as a humble man who remained unaffected by the adoration—as well as the criticism—that was thrown his way. When he opened the doors of the Church to renewal just about that time, he endured a lot of blowback from conservatives.

As we waited, murmurs suddenly filled the air, quickly surging into delirious shouts of "Viva, il Papa! Viva, il Papa! Viva, il Papa." I looked to see Pope John coming down the wide aisle, just a few feet away, carried above us on an elaborate portable throne. The crowd went wild, holding up rosaries, crucifixes, and other religious objects for him to bless, which he did, arms outstretched, turning his face from side to side. I held Lisa high above my head to gain his blessing as he passed. He smiled gently when he saw her, moving his hands in benediction.

✳

In the succeeding decades, I returned to London to work and to Italy to vacation.

After *West Side Story* and *Bye Bye Birdie*, I appeared in the West End production of *Kiss of the Spider Woman* in 1993, and six years later, in *Chicago* as Roxie Hart, this time with the splendid Valarie Pettiford as Velma. I loved presenting my club act there, too, especially at the Palladium, which was the site of so many legendary artists' engagements—none more so than Judy Garland's comebacks there in 1951 and 1964.

One West End show that I let get away was a revival of *Gypsy*, which was to be directed by Arthur Laurents, who'd written the libretto. I'd known Arthur since the 1950s because he'd also written *West Side Story*, and we'd always wanted to work together again. When he asked me to play Mama Rose, one of the greatest roles in all of musical theater, I was intrigued. My hesitation stemmed from the fact that I always looked to create roles, not re-create them. I was apprehensive about comparisons, and Ethel Merman had put her definitive stamp on Rose. I also thought that I was too young to play her. Ethel had been fifty-three when she took on the role, and I was then not yet forty. Also, Rose was loud, pushy, controlling, and ambitious. Which might be okay for some people but not when there are children to be considered. I turned down the offer. I wasn't sure that Arthur ever forgave me until years later he asked me to be in his play *Venecia*, which was about an old Argentine madam dreaming of going to Venice.

I guess it says something about me that I couldn't bring myself to play an abusive mother, no matter how expertly written. But a blind old whore? Count me in!

10

BAJOUR AND OTHER TRICKS UP MY SLEEVE

Anyanka, the gypsy princess I played in *Bajour*, wasn't really as nasty a piece of work as my song in the show "Mean" suggested. She was actually something of a romantic with rough edges, the kind of role that I then excelled at. Though the musical is considered something of an also-ran in the annals of musical theater history, *Bajour* had a rather healthy run of eight months in 1964. It also received a couple of well-deserved Tony nominations for my friends the actress Nancy Dussault and Peter Gennaro, who choreographed.

The musical is probably unrevivable now—even in a concert version—and that's because of its subject matter, gypsies, a word that has since fallen out of favor. *Bajour* was about those people you see in storefronts in some cities, eager to tell your fortune or give you a tarot card reading. They are representative of the Roma, an ethnic group, generally thought to be nomads, who are organized into clans around the world.

In *Bajour*, Anyanka is the daughter of the Moyva King of Newark, who has attracted the eye of a New York City leader, Cockeye Johnny Dembo, played by Herschel Bernardi. Johnny wants to raise his profile by buying Anyanka as a bride for his son, Steve, but needs nine grand to do so. Anyanka is no shrinking violet. She takes one look at Steve—played by a hot, hunky actor named Gus Trikonis—and says to Daddy, "Not a problem! I'll make the money myself by pulling off a bajour." Or words to that effect. "Bajour" is Romani for "a grand swindle."

Ed Padula, who'd produced *Bye Bye Birdie*, thought of me for Anyanka and I'm glad he did. I had a great time, dressed in hoop earrings, lacy shawls, and spangled skirts designed by Freddy Wittop and flashing them around like a dervish. Peter's dances were terrific, and I loved leading the chorus in his wild numbers. There was one super-talented dancer you couldn't miss. He was adorable, swift, and ambitious. His name was Michael Bennett. One regret I have is that, apart from this show, we never managed to work together.

I quickly became friends with Nancy, who played Emily, an anthropologist digging into the Romani subculture. She often joined me for my research trips to the fortune-telling parlors along Eighth Avenue in Hell's Kitchen. I'm as much a sucker as the next person when it comes to psychics and seers. I had my fill of some of the best in the business while I was living in California. But what I picked up from the women in curtained rooms off Times Square was less about my future and more about how to string a person along so they keep dipping into their purse. Once the show was running, I would often get backstage visits from the royal members of the Romani people, who seemed to get a kick out of the show. They weren't in the least hesitant to make themselves quite at home, or swoon over Gus, like almost every woman and a couple of men. I was among them. I relished my love scenes with the handsome young actor.

At the time of *Bajour*, Tony and I were unhappy in our marriage. After *Bye Bye Birdie* in London, we had started to drift apart. My career was going well and his had hit a wall. That can create tensions in any relationship. The last thing he wanted to be known as was Mr. Chita Rivera, and who could blame him? Any man would balk at that. He had tired of performing and had started assisting choreographers, first Gower Champion and then Michael Kidd. But he was at a career crossroads, yet to find his comfortable niche as a director and producer on the West Coast. On top of which his Italian jealousy was beginning to get on my nerves. I can't say I was entirely blameless. Dolores could be a flirt, though I don't think I ever embarrassed him. I hope not.

Tony and I decided to separate, although we worried, like all parents, how it would impact Lisa, who was still very young. As is usually the case when I'm in a crisis, I sought solace and advice from a Catholic priest, Father Shelley, who became a close friend. The Church is pretty strict about marriage vows, and it troubled me that I was going up against the rules. During our sessions, I would sit there and bawl and Father Shelley would listen patiently and then offer me a box of tissues. I was a woman who believed there was only one man in the world for you. You married and stayed married. Then one day, after a lot of soul-searching, I realized I didn't need the tissues. I can torture myself emotionally, but only to a certain point. Then, clarity kicks in, and I know what I need to do. There's always a loss involved. You can't avoid that. Tony and I have maintained an amicable relationship to this day. He's a good man and my heart always skips a little beat when I see him. If he's with a woman, do I feel a jealous pang? Yeah. And I'm glad I do.

I was never unfaithful to Tony while we were married, but once we were separated, temptation came roaring down the pike with Gus Trikonis. You try standing in front of a gorgeous, bare-chested man, singing love songs night after night onstage and then see whether you can stay within your moral boundaries. He was also an extraordinary dancer, which always gets me going. I knew that sex outside of marriage was a no-no, but to tell you the truth, I wasn't all that bothered, good Catholic girl or no. He was just a nice guy whom I cared about deeply, and I know he cared for me. When the run of *Bajour* ended, he moved out to California to pursue a film and television career and intimated that he wanted me to join him there. Though I missed Gus, I felt more comfortable in theater, and Lisa was a big consideration. The separation from Tony was enough upheaval for her to handle, much less another man in her mother's life. As it turned out, Gus fell in love with Goldie Hawn, then in the popular TV series *Laugh-In*, and married her. All I can say is that she has very good taste in men.

I suppose my affair with Gus was just an expression of the gypsy in my soul. I know that the term "gypsy" is not politically correct, but does that mean the classic song is now out of bounds? The last thing I want to do is disparage any ethnic group, but the word "gypsy" has also long described a member of any Broadway chorus. From my earliest days, I, like so many of my peers, was proud to cop to that description. Even after I emerged from the chorus, I considered myself a gypsy. Actors *are* wanderers, taking jobs where they can get them, going to far-flung places just to have a chance to "dance for you," as the lyrics from a song in *A Chorus Line* go.

In fact, I once received the honorary title of Queen of the Gypsies, years after appearing in *Bajour*. There is a tradition of what was once called the Gypsy Robe, but is now known as the Legacy Robe, so as not to offend. In the course of a Broadway season, the robe, decorated with insignia and mementoes from past shows, is passed on from one chorus member to another on opening night. It's usually the one with the most ensemble credits. Cast, crew, and the production team gather in a circle for the onstage ceremony just before the curtain is raised. The recipient, dressed in the robe, walks counterclockwise three times while the assembled company touches the robe for good luck. Curiously enough, the ritual began in 1950 when a robe from the production of *Gentlemen Prefer Blondes* was given on opening night to a chorus member of *Call Me Madam*, my first show. It was then presented, with a feathered rose from one of Ethel Merman's costumes, to a gypsy in *Guys and Dolls*, my second show.

I find it hard to divorce myself from the word "gypsy" because, in the context of the stage, it means so much more than just a chorus dancer. To be called a gypsy—and I still consider myself one—is to honor the loyalties and bonds of the tribe of people who come together to put on a show. There seems to be no substitute for it, maybe because the word has been steeped for so long in theatrical culture. Or maybe I can't let go of it because I'm just a stubborn old broad who feels bound up in the traditions and colorful history it represents.

I like the idea of a robe decorated with a scrapbook of memories. If I had a metaphorical one for 1964, the year of *Bajour*, it would include a program from the 1964 World's Fair in Flushing Meadows, a tribute to the space age that was then dawning. I played a Lady Astronaut in Michael Kidd's *Wonder World*, which included a couple of flyers with jet packs on their backs whizzing around the vast Amphitheater. My title as Lady Astronaut joined two other titles—Miss Jet Away Drive and Miss Gear of the Year—which I'd earned from performing industrial shows. In this imagined robe for 1964, I would also include a postcard of Michelangelo's *Pietà*, brought over from the Vatican, which became the most popular exhibit by far among the 140 pavilions. It left our *Wonder World* in the dust, and why wouldn't it? But what made Miss Gear of the Year eventually shift into double-clutch action after Gus took off for California was a guy. His name was Tom Richmond and I almost married him.

Nancy Dussault and her husband, Jim Travis, brought us together and sparks flew from the beginning. As soon as I saw his kind, handsome face, I thought to myself, "Chita, the turkey is on the table." Tom was funny, gentle, and "a right, proper gentleman," as the Brits like to say. He had his own firm, and though there was some intersection with the arts, he wasn't really involved in show business. That made it ideal when he had to cope with whatever celebrity I had during our decade-long, off-and-on romance. The thing that kind of epitomizes my time with Tom is a pocket-size ceramic green frog. It came into our lives when we were vacationing together at a spa in St. Thomas, and there in the bathroom was this ugly little thing. We laughed so much over it that Tom filched it when we left. Suddenly, the frog was the Zelig of our love affair, going on dates with us, showing up at galas, hitching a ride in our rental cars, tucked in the pillows of our hotel room. Once, at a White House dinner, I looked down to see that Tom had wedged it into the folds of my napkin.

Why didn't I marry sweet, lovely Tom? My daughter, Lisa, would have blamed it on Sister Mary Chita, the good Catholic girl who was forbidden to marry after her divorce. I might have thought that I was sparing her having to deal with a stepfather, though she liked Tom enormously. Maybe it was my own ambition. I always felt supported by Tom in everything I did, and I never got the impression that he felt eclipsed by me. On the contrary, I think he enjoyed accompanying me to my professional engagements. But, in thinking back about this, I see a picture of my legs moving fast. There was never enough time for us to enjoy each other as a committed couple. I was constantly busy and happy to catch him on the fly. Maybe, in turn, he wasn't.

To this day, I get teary-eyed when I see an old couple holding hands, slowly walking through a park, or sitting on a park bench, so content with each other's company that they've almost become one. I've never known that and more's the pity. But you make sacrifices in your life to realize your dreams, and things fall by the wayside, almost without intention. But, oh, what joy I had with Tony, Gus, and Tom! And that never goes away. The songs in my club act veer, like me, toward fun and action. But in the quiet moments, nothing quite revives the memory of loving and having loved as the Great American Songbook. Sometimes you just have to sit back and be lost in the reverie of the greatest gift under the heavens.

11

A HEART ON MY SHOULDER

Sweet Charity

I n 1967, I sat in the back row of the Palace Theatre and witnessed a performance of sheer musical comedy perfection: Gwen Verdon as Charity Hope Valentine, the hopelessly romantic taxi dancer of the seedy Fan-Dango Ballroom. She had the audience eating out of her hand. It wasn't just the way she could play with a top hat as a dancing partner. Or sneak a cigarette while hiding out in a garment bag in a closet. Or perfectly execute small, precise, and isolated movements followed by broad struts across the stage. It was the whole mesmerizing performance. She was one big brass band in one small, carrot-topped clown. Even Gwen's bumps and grinds had an elegance to them. Like the best dancers, she never pretended to be sexy. She effortlessly exuded it because she was so much in touch with her body and what it could do. Musical theater, more than any other art form, allows for that expression, and Gwen embodied it to the nines.

On top of all of that, Gwen could break your heart. When she sang, as Charity, that barn burner of a song "Where Am I Going?," I sniffled into my handkerchief, glad that I was alone in the last row of the orchestra. Suddenly, I felt someone hovering just behind my seat. I looked up to see Bob Fosse, the show's director and choreographer. "Having a good time?" he whispered, his slight body leaning over the standing-room-only divider.

"Uh-huh," I mustered.

He laughed. "You really do get it. You get what we're trying to do."

As if that could ever be in doubt.

Bobby had invited me to see *Sweet Charity* with an eye to casting me in the title role in the national touring production. I was intrigued at the prospect of working with him for the first time. But who could possibly hope to meet the high bar Gwen set with the role? Since I'd met her in 1954 in *Can-Can*, I watched as her star had ascended higher still in such shows as *Damn Yankees*, *New Girl in Town*, *Redhead*, and now *Sweet Charity*. To me, Gwen had become the quintessence of the Broadway musical comedy star, one who had the kookiness of Harpo Marx and the playful sexuality of Carole Lombard. We both gravitated toward playing loose women with an edge. She had her devil's disciple, Lola, in *Yankees* and the barfly Anna Christie in *New Girl*; I had my hooker, Fifi, in *Seventh Heaven* and thieving Anyanka in *Bajour*. Take it from Dolores: bad girls are just more fun to play.

And nobody loved bad girls in musical theater more than Bob Fosse. He'd choreographed all Gwen's shows mentioned above and also directed *Redhead* and *Charity*. A former hoofer himself, who'd started out as a young teen in strip clubs, he brought to Broadway a daring and hip sophistication, the language of the streets. In *Charity*, you could see it reflected in the hormonal jumpiness of the men out for a good time at the Fan-Dango Ballroom. You could see it in the languid posture of the dance hall hostesses looking for their big spenders. (Believe me, moving languidly can be harder than doing jetés.)

Gwen was the perfect muse and match for Bobby from the moment they started working together in 1955 on *Yankees*. They married in 1960 and together redefined and expanded the boundaries of dance on Broadway, becoming one of the most successful husband-and-wife teams in musical theater history. Yet Gwen considered their professional partnership equal if not superior to their marriage. When Gwen was in *Redhead*, Judy Garland said to her, "You must be so proud of your husband's work."

Puzzled, Gwen answered, "Who?" When it came to perfectionism, they were in the same league. Gwen missed her mother's funeral because she had a matinee. Bobby, a workaholic, choreographed all day and even long into the night. That was partly due to his intense competitive streak; he figured all the other choreographers were sleeping.

As I watched *Sweet Charity*, I started to warm to the idea of taking it on. If Bobby felt that I could do it—and he was no pushover—then maybe I would find a way to build on Gwen's achievement. I couldn't hope to equal her. I knew that. But I eventually found the courage to commit to the tour from Gwen herself; I only had to recall what she'd told me in her dressing room during *Can-Can*: "Chita, be more confident!" It was advice I'd never forgotten, and I learned to apply it to Charity, spinning the character out of my own imagination and life experience.

I keyed into the role from the moment I put on the short black dress with a slit up the side—designed by Irene Sharaff—and had the tattooed heart with the name "Charlie" painted on my shoulder. To belong to such a classic musical was another example of being in the right place at the right time. The partnership included not just Bobby's choreography but also the songs by Cy Coleman and Dorothy Fields. Singing and dancing to that score was like having a really great partner to support and carry you. Among my other partners in the show were Ben Vereen, a smashingly talented performer who'd become a dear friend; and James Luisi, who later became famous for his role in *The Rockford Files*. As Vittorio Vidal in *Charity*, he certainly raised my temperature on "If My Friends Could See Me Now." I also loved singing "Where Am I Going?," which is a three-act play in itself. I later incorporated it into my club act and on recordings.

Charity was a marathon of a role. You had to be at the top of your game acting, singing, and dancing. "Triple threat" was not a term in common usage then as it is today. In the early years of my career, the tradition was that singers sang and dancers danced. But I was lucky to have been trained to be a triple threat as early as *West Side Story*. Jerry Robbins was never going to be satisfied with anything less from his cast, and you can believe that Lenny Bernstein and Steve Sondheim were sticklers for diction and pitch. Every lyric had to be perfectly understood and every note hit cleanly and with power. Jeffrey Huard, my friend and musical director, once told me, "Consonants *think*, Chita, vowels *feel*."

Since the day I had walked into Lenny's studio to learn "A Boy Like That," I had sung "from my gut." That meant not just from the diaphragm but from my entire body so that, as Dorothy Loudon once told me, "Chita, you gotta reach beyond the violins." That meant full power and clarity even while dancing my ass off in a number like "America" or "There's Gotta Be Something Better Than This." If you had the proper training, the body would respond with a muscle memory to get you through the number, no matter how tired you might be. Fatigue was never an option.

I've never thought of myself as a great singer. On one level, I consider my voice to be an "instrument" among the others in the band or orchestra. So I was impressed when a musical director said that I might be selling myself short. Ironically, my humility actually made me a better singer than I thought I was. "That humility derails any fear you might have, Cheet," he said. "It lets you concentrate on the job at hand."

That job was to be in the service of the composers. It was their words and music that gave me a door to the character and whatever emotion I was communicating at any given moment. I thought of lyrics as my best friend, and I worked hard to give them their full due and coloration: the dark, ferocious timbre of Lenny and Steve's songs for *West Side Story*, the light, Technicolor wit of Charles Strouse and Lee Adams in *Bye Bye Birdie*, the exuberance of the songs of Cy Coleman and Dorothy Fields in *Sweet Charity*. Singing from the Great American Songbook connected me to the character and the show. But, through the empathy expressed within them, the songs also connected me to the world. I don't think you really can be a triple threat without an engagement, body and soul, with the rest of humanity.

Bobby always used to say that you sing when words alone cannot contain the emotions and you dance when the feelings burst out into movement. That was Charity, leading her imaginary brass band or bursting with glee and wishing her friends could see her now. When it's all blended together, it can give you goose pimples. Even as I'm telling this, I'm sitting here in my kitchen, listening to music with my ass and hands moving. That's how it works.

Bobby was off in preproduction on the film of *Sweet Charity* when the national tour was getting ready, so Robert Linden and Paul Glover put me in the show. But while we were in Toronto with *Charity*, I got a call from Bobby: "How would you like to play Nickie in the movie?" he said, referring to one of Charity's best friends.

Nickie was the one who was determined not to be the "first little, ol' gray-haired taxi dancer." She dreamed of being a receptionist in "one of those glass skyscrapers with my own typewriter . . . and coffee breaks!" I said "yes" faster than one of those lowlifes in the Fan-Dango could step on Nickie's toes. After a screen test, my happiness at making my film debut as Nickie was bittersweet. I was joining a first-rate team as one of Charity's best friends—Paula Kelly, as Helene, was the other. But Shirley MacLaine taking over Gwen's role for the film sat uneasily with me. I figured I knew how she felt because other actresses, Rita Moreno and Janet Leigh, had played Anita and Rosie in the movie versions of *West Side Story* and *Bye Bye Birdie*. As such, I thought that Helen Gallagher had first dibs on Nickie since she was the one who'd created the character on Broadway. To make matters worse, Helen was touring in *Charity* with me when I got word I had the part. I know that's just the way Hollywood works. But it still sucks.

If there was any resentment on Gwen's part that Bobby didn't fight the producers strongly enough to get her the film role, she sure as hell didn't show it. She went so far as not only to coach Shirley on the role of Charity but also to be on the set providing essential help and advice to Bobby when filming began in 1968. She did this even though their marriage had started to falter through his incessant womanizing. They remained joined at the hip not only through their daughter, Nicole, on whom they both doted, but also because Gwen continued to be Bobby's steady rock. During the making of *Charity*, she perched on a ladder, concentrating on every move within a film shot. Her sharp eye could spot if a finger, a shrug, or a hip thrust was so much as a millimeter off. That meant a reshoot. She and Bobby were so attuned to each other that they could complete each other's sentences.

Bobby: "Gwen, I think that maybe Chita . . ."

Gwen: ". . . should be three steps to the left."

Bobby totally relied on her instincts, and she responded with unfailing loyalty. I found it surprising that she took a back seat and let him take much of the credit. Where had that stoicism come from? I wondered. As a child, Gwen had worn large and clunky corrective boots to correct misshapen legs. She cast those off to become the gold standard of Broadway dance. She'd gone into ballet and worked with Jack Cole on the West Coast before scoring big on Broadway. We had both backed into stardom and were equally ambivalent about it. We still thought of ourselves as chorus dancers who'd managed, through luck, talent, and timing, to become well known. The film studios probably thought of us in that way too and so handed the role of Charity to Shirley. She certainly had the goods. Before becoming a film star, Shirley had been a Broadway chorus dancer, getting her break while understudying Carol Haney in *The Pajama Game*. It helps if a Hollywood producer is in the audience when you go on for one of the featured players. Shirley was terrific in the movie, as was Paula, and we all became great friends. But I couldn't help thinking what it would have been like if Gwen had played the role she had so indelibly created. I'll bet it would have been better.

A lot of pressure was riding on Bobby since *Charity* would be his feature film debut. But he didn't show it, at least not to me. Bobby was the type of director and choreographer who could get a performer to do what he wanted either through coaxing, or less pleasantly, through bullying. When I was filming *Charity*, I experienced the sunnier and smoother side of the man. Later, while working on *Chicago*, my friend Tony Stevens would nickname Bobby the Prince of Darkness.

I got a taste of just how seductive Bobby could be when he was blocking the number "There's Gotta Be Something Better Than This." Charity, Helene, and Nickie, sick of the handsy bums at the Fan-Dango Ballroom, sing and dance about escaping their fate for a more sedate existence. The song sends them soaring across a rooftop. Before we shot the scene, Bobby spoke with us in that soft-shoe voice so persuasively that I think each of us would have leapt off the roof if he'd asked us to. The viewfinder dangled from his neck, covered with the ashes of his cigarette. He still looked like the shy, gawky teenager who'd grown up dancing in burlesque halls and cheap comedy clubs and who'd dreamed of being the next Fred Astaire.

When you were around Bobby, what came through was his deep love of women and their bodies. He was a guy who couldn't live without sex. And didn't—time and time again. His understanding of women, especially their great capacity for love, led him to test the depth of it with each new girlfriend. I think he may have tried to make it with practically every female he cast in a show. He never tried anything with me, and I'm not sure I'm not a little upset by that. Unlike so many of the others, I didn't find him particularly attractive. But Dolores would have enjoyed turning him down!

Maybe it was Bobby's intimate familiarity with every curve, joint, and sinew of the female form that allowed him to show his dancers off to the best advantage. And made us want to do our best. If you loved the way you looked, you wanted to be *that*. If it was complicated, all the better. Dancers like to figure it out. What made Bobby's choreography even more intoxicating is that he cut through the sexual tension with humor—mocking sex made it sexier and funnier. Maybe that was something else he had learned in his youth from the comics in burlesque.

Nickie was a hoot to play. So "New Yawk." So optimistic. So . . . cheap. The only time Bobby met the Dolores in me was when I was given the wig Nickie was supposed to wear in the film. I liked Edith Head's costumes for the film, which were exaggerated to the point of satire. But the wig? I hated it. It had this white streak running right up the middle. I begged for a replacement.

"But Chita, I want Nickie to be cheap," he told me.

"Yeah, but do I have to look it?" I pleaded. "Can't I just *act* cheap?" Bobby remained adamant, and my hair looks part skunk in the film.

Just before the three of us were to shoot the rooftop scene concluding "There's Gotta Be Something Better Than This," Bobby took Paula and me aside.

"Listen, you both have done *Charity* onstage," he said, "but this is a heckuva thing for Shirley to step into. So I want you to do your absolute best on every take because when Shirley nails it, that's the one we're going to go with."

So we all lined up with me in front, Shirley in the middle, and Paula in back, having the longer distance to carry through to the end. (Which is the position I wanted. Dancers love to fly!) We did the number and my position was great, but I had moved too far to the left.

"Great! We'll print that one," said Bobby.

"Dammit!" I said.

Shirley, within earshot, asked, "What's wrong, Chita?"

I told her, and without missing a beat, Shirley asked Bobby if we could do the scene one more time. She did it for my sake, though she made it look as though it was for hers. That's called class. Taking care of your buddies. Knowing what it means to be in a chorus. That was Shirley, too.

12

CALIFORNIA, HERE I COME

When the offer of the film of *Sweet Charity* came through, I decided to move to Los Angeles. The best way to go to the West Coast is working, and once the movie was done, the notion of staying on had multiple appeals. For one, my daughter, Lisa, was coming into her teen years and I thought putting her in a school in Los Angeles would be the best path for her. It also wasn't lost on me that Broadway had changed significantly with the advent of *Hair*, the 1968 tribal-rock musical. I loved the show, and Gerry Ragni and Jim Rado, who created it along with Galt MacDermot, were good friends. (Working on the show behind the scenes was a young Merle Frimark, who would later become my longtime and valued personal publicist.) But its hippie sensibility had thrown Broadway off its stride. I was mostly asked to do tours of shows or regional productions of plays, and I figured Los Angeles could be my base of operations as easily as New York.

I'd been flirting with Hollywood and the film business since the success of *West Side Story* had given me a higher profile. Around the same time that Binkie Beaumont had asked me to re-create Anita in London in 1958, I received a call from Marlon Brando. He'd intrigued me since I'd seen him in a corner of Peter Gennaro's dance studio, playing bongos and flirting with the students. Since then, his star had risen only higher in Hollywood, and now he had the chance to direct his first film, *One-Eyed*

Jacks. It was a western and Marlon, in his seductive manner, tried to interest me in playing a Spanish saloon singer and dancer. I was tempted. But my brother Hoolie advised me that I'd be better off going to London with *West Side Story.* He proved so right. *One-Eyed Jacks* turned out to be an expensive fiasco and was jokingly referred to as "Stanislavsky in the Saddle," referring to Marlon's Actors Studio pedigree.

There were other film offers occasionally but nothing that could wean me away from the musical stage. While I was living in Los Angeles, that included a 1969 world premiere of *1491*, a new Meredith Willson musical that was a prequel to Christopher Columbus's voyage to America. The show had been commissioned by Edwin Lester, the veteran producer of West Coast theater as the head of the Los Angeles Civic Light Opera. I had first met Edwin in 1963 on another project, one of the most enticing in my career. It was *Zenda*, a musical adaptation of the Anthony Hope novel *The Prisoner of Zenda* about the political intrigue within the court of a king. His double becomes part of a ruse to avoid a coup d'état. I was cast as Athena, a royal mistress, who, no fool, discovers the plot and is happy to feast at the table of both the king and his double.

The dual role of the king and the imposter was expressly written for Alfred Drake, the iconic musical actor, and I couldn't wait to meet him on the first day of rehearsal. When I arrived, the director George Schaefer told me that he was in the rehearsal room, but when I looked around all I could see was a short, nebbishy-looking man sitting between two girls. As I approached, Alfred rose and, in an instant, was transformed into the Great Man himself. The sudden volt of personality was a lesson to me of how belief in oneself can suddenly transform timidness into the imposing presence and voice of a king. Unfortunately, despite a spectacular and lavish production with music by the veteran composer Vernon Duke and costumes by Miles White, the show never made its planned transfer to Broadway.

The same fate awaited *1491*, in which I was cast as Beatriz, yet another mistress, this time Jewish *and* Spanish, the paramour of Christopher Columbus. I wasn't crazy about the part nor our composer, Meredith Willson. Maybe I still had a chip on my shoulder about his *Music Man* winning the Tony Award for Best Musical over *West Side Story*. What did appeal to me was that John Cullum, a consummate actor, had been cast as Columbus and Jean Fenn as Queen Isabella. But even they couldn't keep the show afloat. It launched in San Francisco and promptly sank, loaded down with a score that sounded more like "Seventy-Six Trombones" than the Latin beat of sevillanas. I recall that the musical also had a bizarre set design. I can still picture John behind a toy-sized steering wheel for the fabled ship, the *Santa Maria*. It couldn't get Columbus out of the harbor, much less across the ocean. We were laughed right out of California.

I was happier in my television appearances on variety shows, like *The Hollywood Palace*, *The Carol Burnett Show*, and *The Julie Andrews Show*. This was mainly because I got to work with my girlfriends Carol and Julie and also choreographers like Alan Johnson and Jack Cole, among the most exacting artists in the business. I had known Alan as an understudy and then, later, as A-Rab in the original production of *West Side Story*. That was before he became the go-to choreographer for Shirley MacLaine, Peter Allen, and several Mel Brooks movies, including *The Producers*, *Blazing Saddles*, and *Young Frankenstein*. The soft-shoe dance that he created for Frankenstein and his monster to "Puttin' on the Ritz" is a classic. Alan also made it his life's mission making sure that the original Robbins choreography for *West Side Story* was faithfully duplicated, including in my show, *Chita Rivera: The Dancer's Life*. A devotee of Jack Cole, Alan had an off-beat style, constantly surprising in the unexpected ways that he could manipulate rhythm. If a musical phrase had four counts, he would cut it down to two or expand it to six. He put a lie to the long-held bias, among East Coast dancers, that their West Coast counterparts—lulled by sunshine, cars, and swimming pools—were inferior. The rivalry was as intense as it was silly.

Anybody who could keep up with Jack Cole, the quintessential West Coast choreographer, had definitely earned bragging rights. His iconic dances in films, TV, and nightclubs gave him the title of "the Father of Theatrical Jazz Dance." It was well-deserved. I had first worked with him on *Zenda*, and I loved his rigorous, athletic, and voluptuous dances. He knew how to frame a woman, empowered and yet feminine, while the men were all about strength, style, and lots of knee slides. He had choreographed "Put the Blame on Mame" for Rita Hayworth and "Diamonds Are a Girl's Best Friend" for Marilyn Monroe. He did the same for me when he choreographed "Blue" on *The Hollywood Palace* variety show. He also danced with me on that number, and he could be full of surprises. He was such a workaholic that sometimes he'd get mixed up on his dances and forget the steps. That could be hair-raising when he was partnering you. Suddenly he would go flying off into the wings and then come flying back in when he remembered what came next. Now you see him, now you don't. Television, which was live then, always had those sorts of surprising moments that kept you on your toes, both literally and figuratively.

I got a disappointing taste of series television in *The New Dick Van Dyke* show, which was the sequel to Dick's amazingly successful bow on the small screen. I jumped at the chance to be reunited with him. But even though the show was being partly written by Carl Reiner, it had little of the wit and charm of the original series. Richard Dawson and I had been cast as Dick's next-door neighbors, and we weren't a good fit. I found the series too constraining and asked to be released from my contract in order to do something more challenging. What called to me was a costarring role in a Chicago production of Oliver Hailey's *Father's Day*.

A few years earlier, in 1970, I had decided to stretch my acting muscles by adding nonmusical plays to my resume. With what only can be described as chutzpah, I started by playing Billie Dawn in a Philadelphia production of Garson Kanin's *Born Yesterday*, opposite John Randolph. Was I terrified to step into the role of the seemingly clueless bimbo so memorably created by Judy Holliday both on Broadway and on screen? You bet. But to paraphrase Eleanor Roosevelt, you should do something every day that scares you. I took that advice with Billie Dawn, and it didn't break me. There's always been something in me, I can't even describe it, that allows me to get past the fear. Maybe it has something to do with what a friend and costar told me years later. He could do his best work, he said, when he realized that what we did as actors was not "falsely important."

My next venture was even scarier: Serafina in Tennessee Williams's *The Rose Tattoo* in New Orleans. I thought, well, if this doesn't expose me as being a fraud all these years, then what can? The risk was worth it. I couldn't possibly turn down such a layered and rich role. Doing it in a city that was so close to the setting of the play itself and that had also meant so much to the playwright was irresistible. As was the opportunity to star opposite Jim Luisi, who'd been my Vittorio Vidal in *Sweet Charity*. As I've said before, God must be Italian. The people, the food, the music, the culture, and . . . the men!

My role as Louise in *Father's Day* in Chicago presented another sort of challenge. Hailey's tale involved three divorced women getting together to air the grievances and advantages of their marital status. Brenda Vaccaro had created Louise in the short-lived Broadway production—only one official performance—but it had a longer life as a regional theater favorite. Louise, loud and brassy, was a kick to play, but I had trouble with her foul language. At one point, she had the line, "Why not play a little Debussy for my pussy?" and she wasn't talking about her cat, either. I balked whenever I came to it. Then I thought up an acceptable take that didn't compromise the character. I elongated it. "Why not play a little De-bus-say for my puss-ay?" Somehow that made it alright for a

Catholic girl to say. Sometimes you have to bend yourself into a pretzel to make some lines work.

Shortly after returning to California, I got an offer to costar with Hal Linden in a production of *Kiss Me, Kate* at the North Shore Music Theatre in Beverly, Massachusetts. I relished taking on the dual role of Lilli Vanessi/Katharine in the musical about a self-involved company of actors putting on Shakespeare's *The Taming of the Shrew*. It was a nice break from playing mistresses and divorcées to take on a woman who sings "I Hate Men." It fit nicely into my career "playlist" that also included "How to Kill a Man" and "Mean." Dolores relished yet another opportunity to throw shade at the opposite sex.

When Hal took on *Kiss Me, Kate*, he was one of Broadway's brightest stars, and he was just about to become a household name in the hit television series *Barney Miller*. We were civil to each other but not exactly cozy. I suppose this worked for the production since we were playing a couple who were at war in "real life" as well as in the play-within-the-play. The reviews for the show were enthusiastic, some of the best in my career. (That's what playing an unqualified bitch can do for you.) But perhaps they were a little too much in my favor for my costar. I noted that from then on, Hal seemed to exert extra muscle in the scene where Petruchio gives Katharine a spanking.

In late 1974, upon my return from the *Kate* engagement, I was beginning to yearn for the restless passion and energy of New York. I could take vicarious joy in my daughter's love of the barbecues, pool parties, and factory mentality of Hollywood. But, to quote Cole Porter, where was the life that late I led? All this paradise—buzzing around in my 280Z Datsun convertible and living in my pretty, itty-bitty pity palace above Mulholland Drive—was taking its toll.

Then, one day, the phone rang. It was Bob Fosse and Gwen Verdon, throwing me a lifeline.

"Hey, Chita, how would you like to do a show with us?"

You could hear my "Yes!" all the way across the San Fernando Valley.

Then Bobby added a sweetener that would change my life. "The songs are gonna be by John Kander and Fred Ebb." I had worked with John when I did a national tour of the Kander and Ebb show *Zorba*, but I knew Freddy only slightly. I would get to know him much, much better. And Freddy, bless him, would get to know me better than I knew myself.

13

A CRAZY CAROUSEL

Chita Plus Two

G rin and grieve," a lyric from *Zorba*, is a phrase that most captures the man who not only wrote it but lived it: Fred Ebb. To say that he was one of my dearest friends and one of the most influential artists in my life, along with his partner, John Kander, would be an understatement. Without them, my resume would be filled with glaring holes and my shelf would be missing a Tony Award or two. Without Fred, I wouldn't be me. Or rather, the sassy version of me—yes, call her Dolores—who with her boys played in nightclubs and concert halls all over the world. All of this because of a heart attack.

Here's how it happened.

A week into rehearsals for *Chicago* in the late fall of 1974, Gwen Verdon and I were taking a lunch break in one of the rooms of the Variety Arts Studios in midtown Manhattan. The cast had just finished a table read of the musical, and we were exhilarated by Fred and John's witty and sophisticated take on Roxie and Velma, a couple of Jazz Age murderesses, played by Gwen and me. With Bob Fosse at the helm as co-writer, director, and choreographer, the smell of a hit was in the air. Gwen was in one corner, practicing how to crochet for a courthouse scene. I was obsessively practicing the steps Bobby had just taught for "All That Jazz," which opened the show.

Suddenly, Phil Friedman, the stage manager, flung open the door, rushed over to Gwen, and whispered in her ear. She calmly lay down her knitting and walked out of the room. The news that Bobby had been hospitalized for "exhaustion" was followed the next day with a grimmer prognosis. He'd suffered a massive coronary and would undergo open heart surgery. The producers vowed that the show would continue, but it might take months for Bobby to recuperate and for rehearsals to resume.

The company was shocked. That was surprising since everyone knew that Bobby smoked a hundred cigarettes a day, ate poorly, and lived on amphetamines. But when you're involved in a show—especially one as complicated and demanding as *Chicago*—you think that great talent and invulnerability go hand and hand. How had his heart even dared to attack him? we wondered. Yet a shot had just been fired over the bow of the most death-obsessed man I had ever known. Thank God he would survive. But, like the rest of the cast, I was at loose ends.

Rocco Morabito, my irrepressible assistant and hairdresser at the time, had an immediate idea.

"Let's go shopping, Cheet!" And we did. Bloomingdale's. But it was only a temporary solution.

After six years in Los Angeles, I'd sold my house on Mulholland Drive and returned to New York, thrilled to be working on a show with Gwen and Bobby. I didn't know John and Freddy as well as them, though I was certainly aware of their soaring successes with *Cabaret*. It had won Liza Minnelli an Oscar and they had polished her star even brighter with *Liza with a Z* in concert and on television. I got to know John better in 1970 costarring opposite John Raitt in the touring production of *Zorba* as the Leader, a sort of one-woman Greek chorus. I sat next to John on the piano in the orchestra pit as he taught me the score, including "The Bend of the Road" and "Life Is." Fred remained distant by comparison.

When we all met up again for *Chicago*, it was the beginning of a friendship that would fuse us together professionally. The incredible talent of Kander and Ebb would bring some of my greatest successes, including *The Rink*, *Kiss of the Spider Woman*, and *The Visit*. More important, Freddy-and-John would become my dearest friends—family, really. Freddy became a brother, my confidant, my rock. Someone who knew me well and had even more confidence in me than I had in myself.

Given how close we became, I was taken aback by what he told me when we first met. Years before, when I was appearing in *Bye Bye Birdie*, he'd often see me in his neighborhood since at the time he lived across the street from the Martin Beck Theatre where the show was playing. He'd wanted to introduce himself but held back.

"I was too scared to say hello," Fred said. "Your resting face looked mean."

After that, I tried to smile whenever I saw him. Which wasn't hard to do. Fred Ebb was one of the funniest guys I'd ever met. But like most people blessed with wit, his humor hid a dark and depressive side. He was the opposite of John in almost every way. Born in New York City, Freddy was the quintessential New Yorker. John, who was born in Kansas City, Missouri, was quiet where Freddy was noisy, calm where Freddy was frantic, and confident in his talent where Freddy was almost crippled with insecurity. He was like a little boy who thought his candy could be taken from him at any minute. John was trim and athletic, while Freddy was stout. He had once written a funny song about his favorite snack:

> *I believe I might do mayhem*
> *Yes, I might destroy myself*
> *If I ever found her missing*
> *From my grocer's shelf*
> *Sara Lee, Sara Lee*

John on the other hand loved limericks, the dirtier, the better. Here is one of the cleaner ones:

> *A wildly obstreperous youth*
> *Got locked in a telephone booth*
> *When hit by the fever*
> *He screwed the receiver*
> *And knocked up a girl in Duluth*

With Bobby sidelined for a few months, the producers of *Chicago* were intent on keeping the company. Freddy knew I was not one to sit around the house, so he came to me with an idea. A scary one.

"Let's put together a nightclub act for you, Cheet," he said.

"Freddy, I can't be in a show. I don't know who I am."

That might have been something of an overstatement. I had a certain sense of who I was, as anybody else might at age forty-one. But I had spent my entire life up to that point hiding behind, in a sense, the characters I played. What I meant was I didn't know who to be as myself to the public. You are so exposed with an audience just a few feet in front of you. I had done a nightclub show previously in the 1960s, namely at hotel casinos in Las Vegas and San Juan, Puerto Rico. I didn't feel I'd been at my best. My backup of two women, Boni Enten and Jackie Cronin, was great, but we didn't exactly fill the showroom. Then there was the occasional heckler to deal with. Once a guy yelled "Take it off!," and I answered, "I will if you will, Bozo!" I wasn't sure I wanted to return to that experience.

As usual, Freddy was leagues ahead of me in his thinking.

"Don't worry, Cheet," he said. "I'll write the act for you. You'll do some of your songs from the shows you've been in, and John and I will write some special material for you. We'll get Ronny to direct and choreograph the act."

Ronny was Ron Field. By that time, he had worked with Freddy and

John on *Cabaret* and *Zorba*. Like them, he'd won a Tony Award and would go on to win two more for *Applause* with Lauren Bacall. Ron, who'd had the inventive choreographer Jack Cole as a mentor, was as opinionated as Freddy. They'd both been born in New York City and were New Yorkers through and through. Ron was also one of the most persuasive men I'd ever met. I was beginning to be intrigued, but was still scared shitless.

"But where will we put it on?" I asked.

"Oh, that won't be a problem," said Freddy. "Ron knows some people."

A few days later, Ron, John, and Freddy took me to a place on West Seventieth Street, a gay bar called the Grand Finale, run by Harry Endicott. He met us at the door enthusiastically and led us into a room that seemed deceptively small with red and black columns and a stage the size of a postage stamp. It seated 250, including the long bar, which sat opposite the stage. The whole place smelled of stale beer and cigarette smoke. The boys could sense my disappointment. I wasn't exactly thinking the Persian Room at the Plaza or the Café Carlyle, but this dive on the Upper West Side? Also, Harry wanted to know if we could be ready in ten days for an opening right after New Year's Day, 1975. The three of them looked at me, panic-stricken. Without missing a beat, they said, "Yes!"

Freddy reassured me. "It'll be great, Cheet. You're not in LA anymore. You're in 'Fun City.'"

❋

I quickly learned that the fun in "Fun City" was being fueled to a large extent by the gay community. New to the nightclub scene were a bunch of small venues, mostly catering to a gay clientele. The clubs had become known as either launchpads for up-and-coming performers or safe and supportive places for comebacks of sorts. In fact, Bette Midler had broken through to mainstream success on the circuit, and it hadn't been at a bar or nightclub. Bette's star-making venue had been a gay bathhouse, the

Continental on the Upper West Side. Barbara Cook, the splendid actress who'd starred in classics like *The Music Man* and *Candide*, had chosen to return after a long hiatus to a series of sold-out nights at the tiny backroom of a gay bar called Brothers and Sisters. And Peter Allen, an irrepressible Aussie who'd been married to Liza Minnelli had recently made a wonderful New York debut at Reno Sweeney, a Greenwich Village cabaret. A few years later this same cabaret would host Edie Beale, the eccentric cousin of Jackie Kennedy Onassis, who had been made famous by the documentary *Grey Gardens*. From Bette to Barbara to Edie. I felt like I was stepping through a looking glass into a crazy wonderland where every night was a combination of Mardi Gras, New Year's Eve, and Gay Pride Day.

From as early as I can remember, my world had always been enriched by gay men and lesbians, both professionally and personally. There'd always been rumors that Doris Jones and Claire Haywood, her partner at the dance school in DC, were on intimate terms. Louis Johnson, my partner at the school and then later one of my closest friends at the School of American Ballet in New York, was fairly open about his sexuality. He made me laugh when I called him on the phone because he would initially answer in a deep, round baritone, "Hello, Louis Johnson speaking." And then the minute he knew it was me, his voice would climb a couple of octaves. "Hey, girl, how ya doing?" My brother Hoolie, whom I was living with at the time, introduced me to his male partners. I embraced them knowing that they were more than how he described them, though it remained unspoken between us.

To be in the theater in New York was to cultivate an admiration for gays and Jews. It is a cliché but true nonetheless. Without Jews and gays, there would be no theater. And no career for someone who owed her start to Arthur Laurents, Stephen Sondheim, Lenny Bernstein, and, now, Fred, John, and Ron. Not only did the gay guys I danced with in the chorus lend my artistry verve and sensuality, but in those early years I found willing conspirators for my silliness as well. There was Earl Lamartiniere, my Cajun friend, who always told me, "Honey, if you get into a fight, don't forget to bring your skillet." And Buzz Miller, who'd practically genuflected when he came into my apartment because of my religious artifacts, and George Marci, a hot-looking Italian American dancer who later changed the spelling of his last name to the less ethnic "Marcy," as one did in those days.

"Georgy Porgy," as we called him, was among my earliest partners in crime for what in Spanish is called *duende*, which loosely translates as "trickster " or "Puck." I'd met George when I was on the road with *Call Me Madam* and he was touring in *Top Banana* with Phil Silvers. We almost always hit the same towns at the same time or overlapped, and so a friendship was born. Back in New York, he was the understudy for Bernardo in *West Side Story*, and the friendship grew. Crazy as a jaybird, Georgy was always trying to crack me up during performance, usually at the most intense moment. I thought the world of him and so did my family, especially my mother, Katherine.

When I was on tour early in my career, I always marveled at how we kids, male and female, slept in the same bed with each other and nothing untoward ever happened. Years later, when I attributed this to the fact that it was a courtliness on the boys' part that kept them from jumping on the girls, a friend responded, "Cheet, did it ever occur to you that the guys had no interest in the girls because they were *gay*?" If Freddy had heard that exchange, he would have chalked it up to "Miss Dove." That was his nickname for me whenever I made some naïve comment or blushed around some off-color remark.

Freddy had fashioned Liza's style out of the raw material of her born-in-a-trunk background and talents. In the same way, he put together my club persona. The show was a little bit of Chita—and a whole helluva lot of Dolores—in the ten days we had to get it up. With uncanny instincts and a deep immersion into the popular culture of the day, Freddy recognized and liberated facets of my personality that I had never thought to reveal in public. I was much too shy for that. Freddy, however, knew that he could cut through my inhibitions. That had already started with the role of Velma in *Chicago*, a musical that was going to go as far as Bobby could take it in displays of flesh and seduction. Both Bobby and Fred knew that my looks, my Puerto Rican heritage, and the rhythm and sound of my voice enabled me to appear more out there, more abandoned than I really was. Just as I trusted Bobby, I put my total faith in Freddy, John, and Ron. I would be game for anything in this new playground.

"I just don't want to be out there alone," I told Ron. "You've got to give me some boys I can hide behind."

Chita Plus Two really gained traction when the "two" of the title were added: Chris Chadman and Tony Stevens. They were both in the ensemble of *Chicago* and were the perfect choices to frame me. Chris was a superb dancer, good looking and sexy with a French beard, crooked grin, and glint of ambition. Bobby was exactly right when, years earlier, he had cast Chris as Lewis in *Pippin*, the narcissistic brother of the title character; and then again as Fred Casely in *Chicago*, the adulterous salesman who ends up in the morgue, courtesy of Gwen's Roxie.

I immediately hit it off with Tony Stevens, born Anthony Pusateri. From the minute I found out that was his real name, I never called him anything else. I liked to tease him. "Tony Stevens? Who's that? I know a cute guy from Missouri named Anthony Pusateri." We both laughed because this echoed my momentary identity as Chita O'Hara. Blessed with inordinate talent, Tony glided through life not only as a Fosse dancer but also as a Michael Bennett one. His diplomatic skills were such that he could bridge the worlds of two men who were wildly competitive. In fact, Tony had been working with Michael on a musical that would become *A Chorus Line* when Bobby "stole" Tony away with the offer not only to be in *Chicago* but to act as his assistant choreographer on the show. As I mentioned before, Tony nicknamed Fosse the Prince of Darkness (and with good reason); in turn, Bobby called Tony Miss Mary Sunshine, which was also the name of the sob sister columnist in *Chicago*, played by Michael O'Haughey. The nickname fit Tony. He was sunny. Also optimistic and caring. And, like Chris, he had great buns!

Buns were not entirely off topic, not any more than our work on the *West Side Story* medley, Jacques Brel's "Carousel," or "All That Jazz" from *Chicago*. Not with Freddy at the helm, writing the act in the hot-to-trot '70s and in the risqué shadow of our now-delayed musical. He knew the Grand Finale audience. Since the Stonewall Riots, which began in June of 1969 on the day of Judy Garland's funeral in New York, gay men had increasingly expressed liberation through their bodies, buffed or otherwise. That carnal carnival had seeped onto the bustling streets of the city. I was impressed with the fearlessness of my gay friends to let their "freak flag fly," as we said then. They lived their lives as they saw fit.

At the same time, Freddy was quick to recognize me as an empowered woman and Latina making my own independent way through the world. We shared a strong sense of going after what we liked, both professionally and personally. And so Freddy, in one number that proved to be a highlight of the act, decided to celebrate a widespread pleasure—the beauty of the male posterior—in a number called "Buns."

Dolores loved the idea, Chita may have had some reservations, but Miss Dove was nowhere to be found. I'd hoisted my own freak flag.

"Do you really think we can get away with it?" I asked Freddy.

"They'll eat it up!" he replied.

And they did.

✳

January 7, 1975, was a frigid night. But if there'd have been windows at the Grand Finale they'd have been steamed the minute Peter Howard, at the piano, hit the keys. Chris and Tony, in skin-tight white shirts and pants, started singing: *Nothing could be sweetah / than to be with Cheeta-Beeta / in the morning . . .*

I made my entrance in a bright red pantsuit and jacket, and Rocco had done up my hair in a cascade of curls. Beyond the blinding lights, I could make out Bobby and Gwen and the cast of *Chicago* along with other friends at the tiny tables in the packed club, including Ben Bagley, the producer of *Shoestring Revue*. Lined up three deep at the bar opposite the stage were mustachioed young men, dressed in the uniform of the day—tight jeans, T-shirts, and bomber jackets—cradling beer bottles. Was I nervous? Preparations for the night had been so headlong and intense, I didn't have a chance to be nervous. Besides, Ethel Merman's advice would cool anybody down: "Nervous? Hell, no! They're the ones who should be nervous. They paid. They want their money's worth."

New York audiences are far from being pushovers, so I was happy to have a secret weapon: "All That Jazz." I was thrilled that Freddy and John had allowed me to unveil it for the first time that night. Not since Lenny had introduced me to "A Boy Like That" in his music studio nearly two decades before had a song seeped into me in such a way. Nobody could write a vamp like John. But this one leading into "All That Jazz" tasted of delirious anticipation; at the same time it gave me a power that could sustain me for the entire evening. Like "Wilkommen," from *Cabaret*, the "All That Jazz" vamp invited the audience to throw away inhibitions, leave their troubles outside, and climb aboard an E-ticket ride to a world of unadulterated pleasure. Pressed tight against one another as we danced and sang on the tiny stage, Chris, Tony, and I did our best to deliver it that night. Judging from the response that grew wilder as the night went on, we succeeded.

As Freddy had predicted, "Buns" and "Trash," the specialty numbers that he and John had written for the act, were among the highlights of the show.

"I love buns," I told the audience, bluntly. "I just love pretty buns. And Chris has pretty buns. And Tony has very pretty buns!" At that, the boys turned around to show the audience just what I was talking about. Then, as if to put a finer point on it, I said to Chris, "Talk with your buns!" At which point, he squeezed them and squeezed them again until we were off and running on the next number. At yet another point, Fred had written "Trash," a vaudevillian number that zeroed in on one of the prevailing moods of the 1970s—an appreciation for the outré personalities of pop culture. It had been celebrated first by Andy Warhol and then by John Waters, the underground filmmaker of *Pink Flamingos*, which starred Divine. He was the inspiration for Ursula in *The Little Mermaid*. John would later go mainstream with the musical version of *Hairspray*, but at the time he was the reigning bad boy of gay camp. Our version of "Trash" eventually included Zsa Zsa Gabor, Leona "the Queen of Mean" Helmsley, Tammy Faye Bakker, Rob Lowe, and, in all fairness, myself.

"Because I never ever will be accused of being *closet* trash," I told the audience. Risqué, yes. But never vulgar. As in *Zorba*, leave it to Freddy to pull out of the shadow of death—Bobby's near-fatal heart attack—a life-affirming and sensual cabaret act by creating a persona that otherwise might well have lain dormant.

✳

"Congratulations, Chita! And remember: Take No Prisoners!"

The message in that telegram came from Liza Minnelli, who caused quite a buzz at the Grand Finale when she and Jack Haley, her husband at the time, came to see the act. In the mid-seventies, she was at her peak, one of the most exciting and popular entertainers of the day. With typical generosity, she then declared that she wanted to present the act in Los Angeles. The boys and I were thrilled. With Liza's backing—she is Hollywood royalty after all—we knew we were in for a great adventure.

That turned out to be an understatement. The venue was, like the Grand Finale, the back room of a gay discotheque, Studio One, in West Hollywood. So a few weeks after we closed in New York, a well-heeled audience wended their way past pairs of buff young men dancing to throbbing pop hits in the disco in order to get to the cabaret. The boys no doubt did double takes when they saw among them Fred Astaire, Cyd Charisse, Ginger Rogers, Gene Kelly, Dick Van Dyke, Gregory Peck, Debbie Reynolds, and other Hollywood stars. Tony and Chris loved the fact that being in a gay bar had to be a first for many of them. But not for Debbie!

Coming back to Los Angeles with *Chita Plus Two* had a special resonance for me. I had just spent six years on the West Coast, not always in the most fulfilling projects. As I bided my time for the phone to ring atop Mulholland Drive, there had been a little New York voice inside of me screaming, "Get me outta here!" Now we were bringing a New York energy to the same factory film town that had snubbed me when it came to the movie versions of *West Side Story* and *Bye Bye Birdie*. The ovations that we received from our idols like Fred Astaire, Gene Kelly, and Cyd Charisse were especially sweet. It wasn't lost on anybody in the room that live performance could bind people together in a way that movies never could.

The inaugural engagements at the Grand Finale and Studio One were the beginning of a career development that would lead to immensely fulfilling experiences all around the globe and up to and including today. What started then was all thanks to the ingenuity of Ron, John, and Freddy and carried on through a succession of directors and beautiful male dancers who flanked me in the act. At times I felt like Roxie in *Chicago*: "Think big, Roxie, get a whole bunch of boys!"

Chita Plus Two became *Chita Plus Three*, and on occasion the act became *Chita Plus Six* and more. Tony and Chris were succeeded by nearly a dozen men who came in and out of the act over the years according to their schedules and mine. Whenever we auditioned for someone to come into the act, I could tell whether they could kick the butt out of a dance just by how they entered the room, walked across it, and threw their bag in the corner. Were they connected to the room, to the people in it? Confident but not cocky? Did they have intensity as well as sensitivity? Did I intimidate them like I had once scared Freddy? If I sensed that, I said, "You're looking at me like I shit ice cream. Well, I don't!" Then with a wink, I added, "But I do drink dragon juice. And you better, too. Cuz I will drain you dry."

Most of all, I looked for whether they could play well with others because they were going to become family in every sense of the word. I found those qualities in Brad Bradley, Lloyd Culbreath, Leland Schwantes, Michael Serrecchia, Wayne Cilento, Alex Sanchez, Raymond del Barrio, Richard Amaro, Robert Montano, and Richard Montoya, among so many others.

As you can tell from the last names, I was partial to Latino and Mediterranean types. Gay, straight, or bisexual, they had power and masculinity in their moves. The similarity of their names became something of a joke when it came to introducing them to the audience. Keeping Amaro straight from Serrecchia, Montano, Montoya, Cilento, or Del Barrio was a tongue-twisting feat in itself. Especially when the boys loved to follow that frisky spirit of *duende* I referred to earlier. To fool with my head, they also made a point of changing places to throw me off. So I usually ended the litany with "Amaro, Montano, Montoya, and . . . I'm Lola Montez!"

Over the years we have crossed continents together, from San Juan to San Francisco, Tokyo to Toronto, London to Las Vegas. We've logged hundreds of thousands of miles on land and sea, bringing the sass and sophistication Freddy devised so many years ago. There are moments, of course, when you find yourself in a motel in Dayton, Ohio, watching the traffic lights outside your window turning from red to yellow to green.

And speaking of green, opening for the likes of Shecky Greene and Engelbert Humperdinck in Las Vegas was lucrative, despite the occasional overserved loudmouth and mobster. One such Mafioso once approached my brother Armando, who, growing disenchanted with his life as a photographer, had just become my manager. It was a baptism by fire because the wise guy told him that if he were to get a certain kickback, he could arrange for me to become a headliner and earn much more money. When Mando told me about it, Dolores answered, breathing dragon flames and speaking, for once, in the third person. "Please tell him that Chita Rivera never pays anybody to entertain for them!" He got the message, and we didn't end up in cement shoes, thank God.

As glamorous and/or prestigious as some of our venues might have been, I treasured discovering the United States in the more eccentric places. I loved calling up Michael Serrecchia and asking, "Do you feel like returning to Swingos Hotel to see Betty?" Swingos, a popular rock and pop hangout in Cleveland, had red-flocked wallpaper, gilt furniture, and gum-smacking waitresses, like Betty, who became an old friend. After shows, we'd go out on the town to local restaurants or bars to wind down. There were nights at gay bars with go-go boys on chairs, trailing dollar bills in their G-strings. And on one Christmas Eve, there we were in Boston at midnight Mass at the Cathedral of the Holy Cross, singing hymns and carols with the congregation as snow gently fell outside.

As the 1970s drew to a close, what we didn't realize is that we were dancing on the lip of a volcano. How could we? We thought the party would never end. But it did, and in its place, came something sad and beautiful just like, as Zorba would say, life.

✳

Looking back on those January nights in 1975 when the club act was born at the Grand Finale, I only now realize just how lucky the timing of the first engagements was, coming as they did just before the start of *Chicago* rehearsals. Freddy had written the act with generous dollops of Chita-as-Velma. She could just as easily have sung "Trash" as I had. Backed by Tony Stevens and Chris Chadman, Velma lived not only in the songs I borrowed for the act from *Chicago*—"All that Jazz" and "My Own Best Friend"—but also in the looseness Freddy had liberated within me. In one of those little miracles of show business, fate and Freddy had conspired to give me a preview of the world of *Chicago* through the club act. It was the best preparation I could've had for the most difficult challenge in my career.

14

A WALK ON THE WILD SIDE

Chicago

At the beginning of almost every performance of *Chicago*, when the stage manager called "Places, please," I took my position in an elevator in the basement below the playing area. It would whisk me, standing in a large cylindrical drum, up to center stage to begin the show. Before that, however, I paced the floor, giving myself a pep talk.

Invariably, the stagehands asked, "Who you gonna be tonight, Chita?"

Of course, my first obligation was to be Velma Kelly, the merry murderess of Cook County jail. But Bob Fosse, our director and choreographer, along with the show's brilliant set designer, Tony Walton, had come up with a spectacular entrance for me. I entered alone onto the stage against a vaudevillian backdrop of dazzling neon. I felt the need to summon up in my imagination a glamorous star in order to carry it off.

"What do you think, boys?" I replied. "Sophia Loren?"

We played the mind game to include Katharine Hepburn, Elizabeth Taylor, Marlene Dietrich, and a host of others. You may laugh but, as Velma, it was up to me to seduce the audience into the world of the musical. Once the elevator reached stage level, the sliding doors of the drum opened to reveal me in a shaft of light, with my back to the audience and a finger cocked in the air. With my hips pulsating to John Kander's intoxicating vamp for my vamp, I oh-so-slowly turned around and waited for a second. Then I sashayed down to the very front of the stage. I looked at the audience with "murder" in my eyes, as Bobby dictated, and invited them to ride with me into a vaudeville of decadence. *Come on, babe, why don't we paint the town* . . .

Looking back, I don't suppose I really needed Sophia Loren or Elizabeth Taylor or their kind as a crutch. I had Freddy and John's dazzling songs, Bobby's erotic choreography, and the armor of Pat Zipprodt's flesh-revealing costume. I also had the confidence of someone who knew what was to come from an impressive cast: Gwen Verdon as Roxie Hart, my partner in crime; Jerry Orbach, as slick lawyer Billy Flynn; Barney Martin, as Roxie's beleaguered husband, Amos; and Mary McCarty as the matron, Mama Morton, "the countess of the clink." To top it off, there was an ensemble of dancers who were the best in the world. They had reached a pinnacle in their careers. Bob Fosse had picked them.

When you're in the process of creating a musical, you never know that you're going to be ahead of the times. That was true of *West Side Story* and it was again the case with *Chicago*. I wasn't thinking of the Watergate scandal or any contemporary headlines reflected in a show that cynically asks, "Whatever happened to fair dealing and pure ethics?" I wasn't that smart. I was focused on Velma and her part in this glittering tale of cuteness and corruption. With all that on my head, how could I or any of us conceive that, after a modestly successful run for *Chicago* in 1975, a revival would become a record-breaking international phenomenon decades later in 1996?

In the latter part of 1974 and into the next year, as we rehearsed in New York and headed off to Philadelphia for the out-of-town tryout, we were just trying to razzle-dazzle audiences with a kind of satirical fun and fury they'd never seen before. I realize now that the making of *Chicago* was what you might call "a perfect storm" of talent, and it was led by a man, Bob Fosse, whom I've always thought of as a flash of lightning in a dark sky.

The journey from first rehearsal to opening night had its share of buffeting winds—you know, "the fits and fights and egos" that affect every creative endeavor. At the time, all we could do was put our heads down, forge ahead, and hope to come out in one piece on the other side. But we did better than that. We came out changed, improved, stronger for the experience. It was as though I had predicted this very thing when, as Velma, I had sung, "In fifty years or so, it's gonna change, y'know. But oh, it's heaven nowadays!"

Chicago was heaven. Hell, too, at times. But, whoa! What a trip!

✳

A musical version of *Chicago* had been on Gwen's mind since the 1950s when she saw *Roxie Hart*, the 1942 film with Ginger Rogers. She liked the idea of adapting it even more after she read the 1926 play *Chicago* by Maurine Dallas Watkin. It had been a hit. The public fell for a pair of devilishly clever young women, Roxie Hart and Velma Kelly, who had parlayed their celebrity as murderers into successful vaudeville careers. When Gwen told Bobby about it, he came quickly on board and they were finally able to secure the rights in the early seventies. For Gwen, it meant a return to Broadway after an absence of nearly a decade. For me, it would mean working again with Bobby since I'd toured in the national company of *Sweet Charity* and danced on a rooftop in his movie version. He'd changed a lot in that time. You start out just wanting to be a hoofer like Fred Astaire and then become an international success. How do you cope with that? His answer came in *Chicago*: "Glamor kills."

✳

If Nickie in *Sweet Charity* was cheap, Velma took cheapness to a whole new level. And I loved her for it. I always thought that I could have made

Pedro Julio del Rivero, my handsome father, forever in my heart.

My beloved mother, Katherine Anderson del Rivero.

My strict SAB dance teacher, Anatole Oboukhoff,
who once threw me under the piano.

As sassy Rita Romano, I'm flanked by
Sammy "Mr. Wonderful" Davis Jr. and Hal Loman.

The original company of *West Side Story*, 1957.
At the piano, Stephen Sondheim, 27, and Lenny Bernstein, an "elder" at 39.

Jerry "Big Daddy" Robbins coaching and coaxing
Larry Kert, Carol Lawrence, and me.

Putting on a happy face was easy with
Dick Van Dyke as my costar in *Bye Bye Birdie*.

You recognize these guys: Paul, George, John, and Ringo,
on July 19, 1964, at the TV program *Blackpool Night Out*.

Poetry in motion, "two moving as one,"
with my beloved Gwen Verdon in *Chicago*.

John Kander, Liza Minnelli, Fred Ebb, and me, prepping for *The Rink*.

Strolling London's Hyde Park with Tony Mordente and our baby, Lisa, while we were both appearing at Her Majesty's Theatre in *West Side Story*.

Joining me in front of a memorial tree for our mother, Katherine del Rivero, is her family who adored her: *(left to right)* Julio, Carmen, Lola, and Armando.

A gathering of the del Rivero and Habib families. Uncle Luciano and Aunt Rita, with whom I lived in the Bronx, sit next to me.

A Catholic girl surrounded by prayerful friends: Father William Shelley, to my right, and behind me is Monsignor Robert Saccoman. To my left, a cleric friend they brought along.

Kissing the ring of Sammy Davis Jr.,
who was my "Mr. Wonderful."

I'm flanked by my costars, the angelic
Brent Carver and handsome Anthony Crivello,
after the opening of *Kiss of the Spider Woman* in Toronto.

Aurora and her rowdy boys in *Kiss of the Spider Woman*: *(left to right)* Robert Montano, John Norman Thomas, Gary Schwartz, and Raymond Rodriguez.

Aurora in her plumage in *Kiss of the Spider Woman* with her boys *(left to right)*: Raymond Rodriguez, Robert Montano, Dan O'Grady, and Keith McDaniel.

After a performance of *Kiss of the Spider Woman* greeting Doris Jones, my first dance teacher and "second mother."

At the opening night party for *Kiss* in Washington, DC, I was thrilled to be reunited with Doris Jones and Louis Johnson, my first dance partner.

I met my close friend Bea "Beady" Arthur on Ben Bagley's *Shoestring Revue* in 1955. I considered her a comic genius.

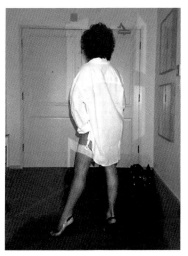

I don't always dress like
this except when
greeting an old flame!

Receiving a Kennedy Center
Honor was the thrill of a lifetime.
Also heart-stopping was when I
temporarily lost one of those earrings
worth the price of a luxury car.

At the Kennedy Center Honors celebration with the men who
"made" me: John Kander, Terrence McNally, and Fred Ebb.

A family reunion on the opening night
of *Chita Rivera: The Dancer's Life*
with Tony Mordente and our daughter, Lisa.

My once-and-always beautiful boyfriend, Tom Richmond.

Dick Van Dyke and I giggle like schoolkids as we rehearse for his guest-starring appearance in *Chita Rivera: The Dancer's Life*.

President Barack Obama and I shared a laugh about his two left feet when he presented me with the Presidential Medal of Freedom in 2009.

Antonio Banderas in *Nine*: "Eat your heart out!"

After losing out four times, I finally won a Tony in 1984 for *The Rink*.
When my name was announced, my mother's spirit came rippling through me.

Grazie Daniele, my dear friend and choreographer, on a break from rehearsing
The Visit in Williamstown, Massachusetts, in the summer of 2014.

Roger Rees, my beloved Anton, always paid a visit to my dressing room just before we went on in *The Visit*.

At a gala benefit for Lenox Hill Hospital with Jerry Robbins and Lisa, I was happy for the opportunity to express my undying gratitude to the staff following my auto accident.

Viva il Papa! I was overwhelmed with joy greeting Pope Francis at the Vatican, decades after my first papal visit with the Blessed Pope John XXIII.

Me and "my greatest production," my daughter, Lisa Mordente.

a good criminal defense lawyer. (I'm addicted to watching crime shows on TV.) Velma in *Chicago* was just the type of person I would have wanted to have as a client. People often asked me if I ever wanted to play Roxie, her rival in the Cook County jail. The short answer is "no." Roxie's cute and conniving, and though I got the chance to play her a couple of times, she will always belong to Gwen. Velma is my kind of girl because she's a fighter, feral and tough. She's not afraid to go as low as she needs to in order to get as high as she wants. The more desperate she became, the more fun it was to play her.

When I first read the script, I thought, "There but for the grace of God go I." I could have been a Velma. You might be scratching your head on that one. How could I relate to a woman who shoots her husband and her sister in a double homicide when she finds them in bed together? It was easy. For Dolores, even easier. I know that I've simply been dealt a better hand of cards to play than the Velmas of the world. Besides, I bought in to her alibi: "They had it coming!" Audiences, for the most part, managed to see that, too, not just for Velma but for all the "chickies in the pen," as Mama Morton put it. At one performance, when Roxie shot her harassing boyfriend, one woman in the audience shouted out, "Shoot him again!" And this was before the Me Too movement.

I liked Velma because she was a straight shooter, so to speak, blunt and practical. To give you a flavor, one of my favorite scenes in the musical is when the female inmates are playing a game of cards. One by one, they cheat. June sneaks a card from under her chair. Liz pulls one out from her wig. Annie has one hidden in her cleavage. All this time, Velma is smoking a cigarette. Finally she exhales a puff and deftly extracts the card that's been in her mouth all along.

Velma's such a wonderful con that when she and matron Mama Morton sing, *Whatever happened to fine morals / and good values / and fine breeding?* you're in on the joke. She's a killer bemoaning the sad state of affairs. Velma leaped off the page and into my imagination almost immediately. I could *see* her doing what she was being asked to do. To me, that's always a very good sign.

On the first days of a rehearsal for a new Broadway musical, all companies are brimming with hope and nervous energy. The ones for *Chicago*, in the autumn of 1974, felt different. There was the excitement of a potential hit in the making, and there was loads of laughter as we read through the script written by Freddy. He gave it warmth and wit; Bobby gave it satire and cynicism. John and Freddy's songs were a Broadway pastiche within a 1920s vaudeville frame. They were hilarious and presentational, such as when an unseen emcee announces the song "My Own Best Friend": "And now Miss Roxie Hart and Miss Velma Kelly sing a song of unrelenting determination and unmitigated ego." Bobby was asking the audience to be complicit in blindly loving the famous, even if they were two cold-blooded murderers. "Would the public buy it?" was a question that was forever hovering over the show.

"A Valentine to show business, etched in acid," is how a writer described *Chicago* later. Throughout the development, there was a tension between the push and pull of these two perspectives. The optimism of Freddy clashed with the pessimism of Bobby, who carried within him a sense of dread. He was mercurial. Happy one day, miserable the next, even though *Chicago* was coming in the wake of a series of triumphs and critical, if not commercial, successes.

Though it got good reviews, the film of *Sweet Charity* was a flop. That didn't make Bobby any more unhappy than if it had been a success. He was a brilliant and complicated artist, and for me to try to figure him out would be a fool's errand. However, I don't think it's too much of an exaggeration to say that he was always a bit more comfortable with failure than with success. Three years after making his film debut with *Charity*, he won an Oscar for directing *Cabaret*, a Tony Award for *Pippin*, and an Emmy for *Liza with a Z*. You'd think winning the triple crown would have driven anybody into leaps of ecstasy. Not Bobby. He checked into Payne Whitney Psychiatric Clinic to cope with all his good news.

"The one thing that Bobby can hold on to is sorrow," said Gwen.

Chicago was obviously a valentine to the woman who'd put up with Bobby for most of their adult lives. At age fifty, Gwen was looking at the show as a passion project for one more hurrah on Broadway. For Bobby, it was a mea culpa for his infidelities. Their twelve-year marriage had ended three years before, and Gwen let on to me that he had since taken up with Ann Reinking, a tall, young dancer whom he'd met on the set of *Pippin*. Annie was talented and had expert technique, but she lacked softness. Nor could she ever fill the niche Gwen occupied in Bobby's life as muse, wife, and mother of Nicole. They never divorced, and she remained the wife, the keeper of the flame, and his closest confidant. I never saw an ounce of resentment in Gwen, on the set of either *Charity* or *Chicago*. That's just how she operated in the world. To Gwen, what mattered was the project at hand. That never changed. During *Chicago*, Bobby may have played around with the dancers in the chorus, but that never stopped him from believing, with good reason, that the sexiest dancer on that stage was his wife.

The professional reunion of Bobby and Gwen, on top of his recent accolades, added to the expectations for *Chicago*. You could see them weighing heavily on him when he walked into the Broadway Arts for that first week of rehearsals. He didn't look well. A steady diet of amphetamines, junk food, sleepless nights, countless cigarettes, and the never-ending quest for perfection can do that to a guy. I've worked with many directors who were less self-destructive than Bobby but no less obsessive. In my entire career, I have yet to collaborate with a director and/or choreographer who was completely satisfied. As the saying goes, "Shows are never finished. They just open."

✳

Once Bobby recuperated from his heart attack, we went to work. It took me a while to get used to his style, which was much more contained and intense than it had been in *Charity*. It didn't help that Bobby wasn't one to give a lot. Forever dressed in black—one day he showed up in blue and I excused myself to get my sunglasses—he was available but not very demonstrative. I love to fly across the stage, so at first I found his choreography for *Chicago* strange, restrictive, and difficult to learn. Tremendous focus and constant repetition were needed to get it right. And it helped to watch the other dancers. At times, rehearsals looked like a hall of mirrors. I was looking at myself while watching them, and they were watching me looking at them while watching themselves. When Bobby saw what we were doing, a rare smile would pass his lips. That is, if there wasn't a cigarette in his mouth. Even after his brush with death, he couldn't bring himself to stop smoking. Out of concern, friends were forever slapping cigarettes out of his lips. I once had the temerity to tell him, "I'll walk off the stage if you don't put that out."

One afternoon, Bobby was choreographing "I Can't Do It Alone." It's the number in the show when Velma, "in an act of desperation," tries to persuade Roxie to take her on as a vaudeville partner once they're sprung from jail. Bobby had me dancing on a chair for what seemed an eternity. The movements were small and subtle.

"Make it less, Chita, less," he kept repeating. At one point, I wondered whether I was moving at all.

Finally, on a break and in an act of desperation myself, I leaned on Tony Stevens, who was now acting as Bobby's assistant choreographer. "Tony, could you please ask Bobby to get me off this damn chair?"

It worked. I was liberated from the chair and wound up eventually using the whole stage, doing flying splits, grand jetés, and even a cartwheel in the number. No disrespect to the chair by the way. I never lost sight that the chair came first; the chair was the star. I said to my understudy, "Be good to that chair, honey, or it will kick you in the ass!"

In the process of working on this and other numbers with Bobby, I realized something that he rarely, if ever, gets credit for. When people think of Fosse choreography, they think of what he himself described as his signature, "the amoeba": the finger-snapping struts, rolling shoulders, sideway shuffles, and gloved jazz hands. But working with me, Bobby used every move, choreographed to the tips of my fingers, to inform and define who Velma was. Building the character was his goal. If I wanted to express desperation, I did it through my body. I learned to enjoy "pulling it back." It was completely different from what my mind and body had thought dance was.

During another session on "I Can't Do It Alone," Bobby pointed to a spotlight on the floor that looked to be a football field away. "Chita, can you jump to there from where you're standing?"

I thought to myself, "Damn, that's far!" When the music started up, I did my best and missed.

"Bobby, I am so sorry. Let me try it again," I said.

He laughed. "Chita, do you see that spotlight just a few feet away? I meant *that* one! Don't kill yourself."

If we all worked hard to please Bobby, it was because we realized that he was working hard for us. Besides, dancers are eager to please, no matter what is asked of them. No matter the pain.

✳

Bobby's brush with death had thrown him into a deep depression that couldn't help but affect *Chicago*. Behind the razzle-dazzle, Bobby was determined to leach out any hint of sentiment. Though the music was ripe and rowdy, the show itself became chillier, meaner, and darker. Bobby had always been a man obsessed with his mortality. Now while we were learning his choreography, he was locked in his own dance of death. He would later explore it in his semiautobiographical film *All That Jazz*, a man writing his own epitaph. The ones who had to deal most with Bobby's mercurial mood swings were the producers, who knew to give him lots of room; Gwen, who must've been used to them by now; and Freddy, who, as the co-writer and lyricist, most often felt the lash.

The company was most protective of Gwen although she could pretty well take care of herself. The dynamic between her and Bobby was fascinating to observe. At times, it could be supportive; at others, contentious and argumentative. Bobby was eager to score a hit with *Chicago* and it wasn't lost on him that four of his six Tony Awards had come in shows starring Gwen. Like any dancer, she could no longer do what she had done in the decades past. But she more than made up for it with a bravura technique and innate comic timing, like in the number "Funny Honey." In the torch song, Roxie laments the stupidity of her cuckolded husband, Amos. In staging it one afternoon, Bobby thought it was a good idea for Gwen to be sitting atop a piano, getting progressively drunker and drunker, legs splayed. I watched it with John and Freddy with increasing alarm. I turned to them and said, "Whoa! What's that all about?" Was he sabotaging her? or did Bobby do that just to get a reaction? He was known for that.

Tony once told me that Bobby and he were watching two women from the cast of *Pippin* arguing outside the theater. It was getting very heated. Tony said, "I'm going to break it up before they come to blows." Bobby held him back. "Don't! I want to see what will happen."

That was exactly the opposite of how I feel in such a situation. I would have wanted to nip it in the bud before it got ugly. Later, when we were doing press for *Chicago*, I got the impression that people wanted Gwen and me to start a feud. There was always that coy question, mainly from women, I hate to add: "So how are you and Gwen getting along?"

"Perfectly," was the answer.

Gwen and I relied on each other's support during the rough development period. Since *Damn Yankees*, she'd always had to carry the show as the star and title character: *Redhead, New Girl in Town, Sweet Charity*.

I'd never had to carry that burden and was glad not to do it on this one. I considered my responsibility was to back Gwen. So I didn't hesitate to agree when she decided to demand that "My Own Best Friend" be her solo number. Bobby had planned it to be a duet. When they began to fight about it, I slipped a note to Tony. "Tell Bobby to give her the song," it read. What did I have to lose? Besides, I thought the song should be hers. Nonetheless, it remained a duet.

Just as Mickey Calin had been Jerry Robbins's whipping boy, so Freddy was the one who took the brunt of Bobby's outbursts and paranoia. It pained me to witness some of Bobby's cruel barbs toward Freddy. Working with John and Freddy on *Chita Plus Two* had drawn me very close to them. Now, after *Chicago* rehearsals, we'd go out for drinks and recapitulate the latest tensions. At one point, Bobby had chewed Freddy out for not having delivered a scene that he had never asked for in the first place. Freddy started to protest and Bobby just kept escalating the rhetoric. Finally, John said he had to physically remove Freddy from the dressing room or the two might have come to blows. They'd learned from Liza Minnelli to walk away when things were in danger of getting out of hand. Liza had told them that during the filming of *Cabaret*, she would put off Bobby if she sensed he wanted to have it out with her about something.

"No, Bobby, we'll talk in the morning," she would tell him. "If we talk now, I'll get upset, and the next day, you'll apologize and send me flowers." Liza preferred doing away with that step altogether.

"Why does Bobby always pick on you?" I asked Freddy. "Doesn't he know how vulnerable you are?"

"Bobby picks on me, Cheet, because I *am* vulnerable," he answered. "And vulnerable people drive him crazy."

Meanwhile, Bobby was driving the company crazy, not to mention the producers. Some of the choreography was so languid, like a slow-motion ballet in water. Tony chalked it up to his depression. "These are the dances of a very depressed man," he said. Freddy and John were forever pleading with Tony to ask Bobby to make it faster. They hadn't written the songs to be played at such a slooooooow pace. There was an upside to it, however. At Bobby's urging, I did learn to take my time while onstage. Like most great directors, he was not afraid of silence, confident that the stage presence of the actor or dancer could fill the void. Let the audience come to you, was his mantra. Don't even try to meet them halfway. Of course, he was right. One of the great contradictions of Bobby was that he had so much contempt for a business he was so good at.

The development of *Chicago* got even more difficult once we embarked to Philadelphia for the tryout. It's a long-standing tradition of shows to go out of town rather than open cold in New York, which would have been its own form of open-heart surgery. There were so many kinks in the show to work out that it was better to do it far away from the prying eyes of the theater buffs who never wasted a chance to take a potshot. (It's even worse now with the internet. More like a colonoscopy.) One of the major kinks in the show was, quite simply, that it was too kinky. Bobby loved to simulate sex onstage. That made sense when he did it in *Pippin*. But for some reason, he thought to embroider Roxie's courtroom scene, featuring the song "Razzle Dazzle" and a brilliant turn by Jerry Orbach as Roxie's slick lawyer, with writhing bodies and orgasmic moans. It distracted from the moral of the show: inviting the audience to own up to being blinded by the flimflam of show business.

Watching a rehearsal from the back of the Forrest Theatre, I was shocked and so were John and Freddy. We couldn't see what seminaked bodies in flagrante delicto had to do with the scene. Freddy and John took it upon themselves to try to convince Bobby to cut the embellishments. For their pains, they were subjected to a nasty tirade from him. They came back fuming. I heard John tell Freddy: "Let's go back to New York tonight. No show is worth dying for." At that moment, the three of us made a pact: "If one of us goes, we all go."

I suppose we meant it at the time. In the process of getting any

Broadway show on its feet, the pressures are so intense and the emotions are so raw that these kind of vows are not uncommon. Instead, we soldiered on in Philly, rehearsing and putting in changes during the day and performing for audiences at night. And, oh, were there ever changes! An entire role—an agent played by David Rounds—was cut. Songs were replaced and new scenes were written. The show was getting even meaner. It was supposed to be cynical, but now Bobby was wringing out the joy as well. The relationship between him and Gwen frayed so much that after one tense disagreement, she said, "They can pack his heart in sawdust for all I care." The three weeks we spent out of town seemed like three years. Poor Tony Stevens was tasked with giving us notes. It got to the point where he was hesitant to give them out at the hotel after a performance. One night I opened the door and standing there was a wrinkled old man. Tony had drawn black circles under his eyes and lines across his face.

"Just. One. More. Note," he said.

Our nerves were shot, our bones ached from dancing on a raked stage, we were bleary-eyed from no sleep and forgetful from having to memorize so many changes. Thank God for one saving grace: the reduced rate for booze at the Variety Club at the Bellevue-Stratford Hotel. That was our refuge. It was also where John and Freddy came up with a smashing song for the finale of *Chicago*. It gave us the ammo to fight another day.

Bobby and Freddy had always struggled with how to end *Chicago*. After Roxie is acquitted in her trial and Velma in hers (offstage), they put together a vaudeville act to take advantage of their notoriety. When Velma suggests the merger, Roxie has a ready answer: "You're forgetting one thing. We hate each other." Velma replies, "Yeah, but there's only one business where that doesn't matter." True. Like I said, Bobby was so good at something he had so much contempt for.

In Philly, the finale had Gwen honking on a sax and me banging on drums as part of a song medley of "Loopin' de Loop" and "It." (If a girl doesn't have "it," she can fuggedaboutit.) Drawing attention to the show's cynical theme, a guy in the audience then jumps up and attacks us as two no-talent murdering "floozies" with a cheesy act. "Why should we cheer for the likes of youse?" It was a sour end to a sour show and nobody was satisfied, particularly Gwen, who wanted Roxie to triumph in the end.

John and Freddy offered to write a new song but Bobby was obsessed with trying to get it right. Finally, in desperation, the producers persuaded him to give in and they approached John and Freddy to ask if they wouldn't mind writing something a bit more sophisticated. They went off and within an hour had composed a new song, "Nowadays." They wrote it so fast that they didn't deliver it until the next day so nobody would think they hadn't worked hard enough on it.

"Nowadays" was a miracle of a song. Its bright optimism reinvigorated the entire show. "You can like the life you're living, you can live the life you like . . ."

The sheer brilliance of John Kander and Fred Ebb. Velma and Roxie figured out that if you don't take responsibility for your actions, then how can you be blamed? The absurdity of it all! Somebody up there may love us, but that Somebody up there is also laughing at us. We're just a bunch of flawed, crazy people trying to make our way out of unforced errors as best we can.

Gwen and I had a ball dancing to "Nowadays," along with "Hot Honey Rag." In our sequined white minishorts, top hats, and canes, lit to reflect every color of the rainbow, we were the personification of the Jazz Age. Bobby had the audacity to present us as "poetry in motion, two moving as one." Each of our movements was perfectly matched to the microsecond. We went all-out on "Hot Honey Rag," as the emcee announced: "Okay, let's pick up the pace, let's shake the blues away, let's make the party longer, the skirts shorter and shorter, let's make the music hotter. Let's all go to town in a fast car and keep it hot!"

And we did, changing into fringed skirts that whipped around in time to the music. I was proud to be next to Gwen. The proximity made me feel taller, bigger, and more accomplished than I had ever felt before in my life. It was, simply, exhilarating. We apparently conveyed that to the audiences as well because they began to like the show.

✳

When *Chicago* opened at the 46th Street Theatre on June 3, 1975, the reviews were divided; some critics were uneasy with just how cynical the show was in presenting two cheerful killers. Parallels to Watergate, the pinnacle of high-level government crime then fresh in the public's imagination, were brought up.

Chicago also had the misfortune of hitting Broadway within months of *A Chorus Line*. That show had been breathing down our backs the entire time, ever since word had gotten out that Michael Bennett was developing a musical about chorus dancers. The buzz around it had just served to make Bobby even more anxious since he was competitive by nature and especially competitive with Michael. He was then part of a group, including Tommy Tune, who were establishing themselves as the Young Turks of Broadway. I'd known Michael for years since he was just starting out as a dancer in *Bajour*, all of twenty-one years old, adorable, sexy, and ambitious. Now, he had developed and directed *A Chorus Line*, first at the Public Theatre and then to its triumphant opening on Broadway.

Tony Stevens had been working with Michael on *A Chorus Line* when Bobby had mischievously stolen him away to work on *Chicago*. So during the show's development, he was forever asking Tony, "Is this better than *A Chorus Line*?" And Tony's answer always came back, "Apples and oranges, Bobby." Tony was right. *A Chorus Line*, with its tear-jerking stories of the dancer's life, was as sentimental as we were cynical, as earth-bound as we were fantastical. It wasn't surprising when they were wholly embraced, and we, in turn, were admired, but with reservations. *Chicago* ran for 936 performances; *A Chorus Line* became, at least for a while, the longest-running show in Broadway history until it was surpassed by *Cats*. It finished a glorious run by clocking 6,137 performances. But Bobby, bless him, had the last laugh.

In 1996, Ann Reinking and Walter Bobbie revived *Chicago* for the City Center Encores! series with "choreography in the style of Bob Fosse." Raves for the show poured in, most of them noting that our celebrity-drenched culture, with the 1995 O. J. Simpson trial (and the subsequent reality shows about the Kardashians), had finally caught up with the musical. Transferring to Broadway, the revival is still running, twenty-seven years later, with more than ten thousand performances.

I have to admit that I wasn't too crazy about the revival when it first opened. When I was asked about it, I always politely said, "It's not the block I lived on." I didn't want to be insulting. Dolores would have said something stronger: What is it the French say? "Sacrebleu!" I just didn't think that it came anywhere close to the radiance of the original version. I have to admit that some wonderful stuff was still intact—the songs and Bobby and Freddy's script. But it was as if they'd forgotten the nail polish, eyelashes, and lipstick by eliminating the contributions of Tony Walton and Patricia Zipprodt. The fabulousness was gone.

From time to time, I was asked to join this version of the show, but I always refused. It didn't seem like a right move. That is, until 1999 when I was approached to do it in London, as Roxie this time. I thought, "Okay. It's London, a fresh start." I had a grand time playing opposite Valarie Pettiford, a firecracker of a talent as Velma, and relished once again being enveloped by John and Freddy's music. (They can never get enough credit for that score!) Playing Roxie again in Las Vegas, I grew to respect the adaptation. What had been sacrificed to keep costs down has been compensated with longer runs, giving more people the chance to see *Chicago*.

Bobby never lived to see the revival. He was only sixty when he collapsed on a sidewalk in Washington, DC, in September 1987 on the opening night of a *Sweet Charity* revival. Gwen was with him at the time and held him in her arms until the ambulance arrived. She was no doubt filled with hope (the middle name of the iconic character she'd created twenty years before) that he might yet survive again.

In the years since *Chicago* had opened, Bobby had won a Tony for *Dancin'*, a compilation of his iconic work, and yet another one for his last show, *Big Deal*. The musical was a change of pace for him. It was, in his words, "about fumblers trying to do something bigger than they were capable of doing and never giving up, that desire to keep trying all the time." That was Bobby. He was forever trying to get it *right* and rarely got the credit he deserved for that. That must've been soul-crushing to someone so sensitive. Bobby always seemed to be dancing in the dark; it was gratifying that his personal song ended on such a bright, sweet, and uncynical note.

At his memorial service, the playwright Steve Tesich described what it was like to call Bobby a friend: "It's like you invite someone to move into your tiny apartment with you. But instead of it becoming cramped and crowded, the space expands and you discover rooms you never knew you had."

That is what Bobby did for me. I discovered rooms within myself, as a dancer and a person, that I never knew I had, and I'm forever grateful to him.

✳

One day, my assistant Rosie got a call from Gwen.

"Hi, does Chita still like giraffes?"

I've never liked giraffes. Monkeys maybe and frogs, but not giraffes.

Nonetheless, a stuffed giraffe arrived at my house, and whenever I look at it, I think of Gwen. Maybe it's the giraffe's long legs that remind me of her.

Gwen, who died in 2000, thirteen years after Bobby, is frequently on my mind. How could she not be? I speak about her lovingly in my nightclub act and I paid homage to her in my autobiographical Broadway show *Chita Rivera: The Dancer's Life*. Graciela Daniele, who directed and choreographed it and who was featured as Hunyak in the original *Chicago*, created a moving tribute to Gwen within the musical.

As the vamp for "Nowadays" began, I said to the audience, "Whenever I hear that, there's only one person I see in front of me, standing in her own special light. No one can replace our costars. Who could?" Then a spotlight materialized next to me and I re-created our dance together, imitating at times that endearing vocal quaver she had. When I came to the lyric "but nothing stays," I turned and bowed to the light as if to say how much I treasured those moments with her.

Years later, I got another chance to acknowledge my debt to Gwen with an inside joke. It had to do with the film of *Chicago* and a call from Rob Marshall, its director. I got to know Rob when he was a chorus dancer on skates in *The Rink*, and during the intervening decades, his career had taken off, first as a choreographer—he made his stunning debut choreographing *Kiss of the Spider Woman*—and then as a director as well. He joined with Sam Mendes for the astonishing 1994 revival of *Cabaret*.

Rob's call to me came when he was casting the movie of *Chicago*, which would be his debut as a filmmaker.

"Chita, are you okay if I cast Catherine Zeta-Jones as Velma?" he said.

I was floored that he had the thoughtfulness to even ask. But that's Rob. He has such loyalty and such respect for the original creative process.

"She's the perfect choice," I answered. "She's so gorgeous I could slap her. And if you don't cast her, Rob, I'll slap you!"

I was touched that Rob also invited me to make a cameo appearance in the film as one of the inmates, although I think I looked like Cher in drag. On the day of the shoot, he gave me a tour of the Cook County jail set and we visited Velma's cell. (Like giddy kids, we even stole a memento from it.) When the moment came to film the scene in which I, looking like a weathered jailbird, gave a husky welcome to Roxie, I turned to Rob with an idea.

"I'm gonna roll one stocking up and roll one stocking down. That's for Gwen. What do you think?" He loved the idea.

I was thrilled for Rob when *Chicago* won the Best Picture Oscar along with one for Catherine Zeta-Jones. (Dolores asks: "What's up with all these actresses winning Oscars for playing roles *I* created?") I told the press at the time, "Tell Ms. Zeta-Jones she can keep the Oscar. I'll keep John's vamp!"

After Gwen died, I was asked to speak at her memorial. It's a daunting assignment at any time, but for Gwen? How do you capture all the special beauty, talent, and joy she brought into our lives? I did my best and ended it with a story Graciela told me about a dream she'd had the previous night.

"In the dream, I saw Gwen dancing with Bobby. But her feet weren't touching the floor. And I said to her, 'How do you do that? Dance without touching the ground?' And she looked at me and smiled and said, 'I always dance like this when I'm happy.'"

Nothing stays—except in the heart.

And that's
Good, isn't it?
Grand, isn't it?
Great, isn't it?
Swell, isn't it?
Fun, isn't it?
But nothing stays
In fifty years or so
It's gonna change, you know
But, oh, it's heaven
Nowadays

15

THE YEARS OF MAGICAL THINKING

I've had an affection for all of my shows, including the flops. I never even considered them as such at the time. Closing notices always came as something of a surprise to me. "Huh? Really?" I have such tunnel vision developing a role that I scarcely bother to handicap a show's chances. On top of that, I never read reviews or Dolores just might invest in a dozen voodoo dolls.

An indication that things were not going all that well was *Bring Back Birdie*, which lasted the shortest—four performances—of all my shows. It ushered in the 1980s, a decade of painfully earned wisdom. Ronald Reagan was president, there was a recession, and Broadway was going through a rough patch, with only half of its thirty-nine theaters occupied. The British invasion and their mega-musicals was just about to begin when *Cats* opened in 1981 in London's West End before transferring to Broadway. Its motto, "Cats, Now and Forever," was considered either a threat or a prediction.

Into this world came *Bring Back Birdie*, written by Michael Stewart, Charles Strouse, and Lee Adams, a sequel to our hit *Bye Bye Birdie*. Set twenty years later, the plot involved Albert and Rose, now with kids of their own, in a scheme to find Birdie, who has disappeared, so that he can appear on a Grammy Awards show. Loyal to the creative team, I was the only one of the original cast to return. Donald O'Connor took on the role of Albert originally created by Dick Van Dyke, and Maria Karnilova was Albert's mother, Mae. Maurice Hines was cast in a new role, Mtobe, an unscrupulous detective who gets mixed up in the foolishness. In a bid for lightning to strike twice, the producers got for the show the Martin Beck Theatre, where *Bye Bye* had played.

Some shows are star-kissed and others are snake-bitten. Once rehearsals started, it soon became clear that the question prompted by the title *Bring Back Birdie* was, uh, "Why bother?" The show was a mess but not for lack of trying, and by some top-notch professionals at that. Donald O'Connor, an MGM musical legend, was a pleasure to work with, but like the rest of the cast, he was at sea. It wasn't his fault. The whole concept was misconceived. Our set designer, the very talented David Mitchell, came up with a wall of video monitors on which would be projected the props. I knew I was in trouble when I was singing about wifely duties, "I Like What I Do," and clothes were projected onto the oven and a turkey was projected onto the washing machine. At one point, I was even chased off the stage by a television. (Don't ask!)

By that time, Dolores was reigning supreme. Friends can remember me coming from rehearsals into Ted Hook's Backstage, a favorite hangout conveniently located next door to the Martin Beck, with steam coming out of my ears. My sister Lola was also the manager there. Over drinks, I sent up an SOS. "They've forgotten their craft, they've forgotten personal feeling, they've forgotten story," I said to anyone who'd listen. "They're so wrapped up in concept that they've forgotten there are real live people onstage."

I finally put my foot down when I was asked to come out onstage in a halter top during a Western saloon scene. (Albert and Rose discovered Birdie in Arizona.) Even worse, at one performance, the top came loose and I grabbed it before there was a major wardrobe malfunction. Lucky for me, I had a friend who generously came to the rescue. The fashion designer Halston remade most of Rose's wardrobe. If a dress can help you get a

Tony nomination, then chalk that up to the red, off-the-shoulder costume Halston devised for my number "Well, I'm Not!" In it, an infuriated Rose declares her independence from Albert, who has strayed with a blond chippie set up by, who else?—his mother, Mae. Choreographed by Joe Layton, the clever number was a showstopper, aided by my partner, Frank DeSal, and the prop of a push broom.

Out of the debacle of *Bring Back Birdie* came a longtime friendship with Maurice Hines, a maestro of tap; stunning Halston designs, some of which proved an inspiration for Marion Elrod, my excellent assistant and seamstress; and meeting Frank DeSal, who became one of my act's backup dancers. Frank and I were able to create at least a little momentary magic before *Bring Back Birdie* went bye-bye.

✳

In the 1983 musical *Merlin*, as a character called the Evil Queen, I sang a song titled "I Can Make It Happen." What I could make happen in the show included turning a black panther into a beautiful girl; transforming a wizard into stone; and summoning through my powers a twenty-foot robot with flashing eyes, wielding a sword. For someone who longed to know the secrets behind magic tricks, the chance to play the role was irresistible.

What I could *not* make happen, as Chita, was working out the convoluted plot. It centered around the Evil Queen's Machiavellian scheme to put her idiot son, Prince Fergus, on the throne, thereby thwarting Merlin's plans to pass the royal title to his protégé, the young Arthur of legend. When I signed on, I knew that all the roles, and the plot for that matter, would be secondary to the reason why everybody was coming to see *Merlin*: to watch Doug Henning, my costar, do some spectacular magic tricks. Scratch that. Not magic tricks, *illusions*.

Doug, an amiable Canadian, then one of the world's greatest

illusionists, made it his mission to elevate magicians in the public's imagination. He'd realized that goal through his TV appearances and having spent several years on Broadway in the 1970s in the smash hit *The Magic Show*, with music by Stephen Schwartz. The show had been nominated for a number of Tonys, including one for Doug. That was something of a magic trick in itself since we were soon to learn that Doug, for all his incredible talent, could not sing, dance, or act. His stage presence was, shall we say, a disappearing act.

Doug's college buddy, Ivan Reitman, had produced *The Magic Show* and wanted to build on the success with *Merlin*. He recruited Elmer Bernstein and Don Black to compose the songs, TV writers Richard Levinson and William Link to write the book, and Theoni Aldredge to design the costumes. That ain't chopped liver. Theoni's sumptuous creations for "EQ," which is how I quickly became known backstage, included six-foot red-and-copper lamé wings. They seemed to operate on their own but were manipulated by little people hidden beneath my costume.

I had also been attracted to the project when I learned that the musical was to be directed by the prestigious British director Frank Dunlop and choreographed by my friend Chris Chadman. When Frank was replaced, Reitman took over his position. A few weeks into rehearsals, what I wished the Evil Queen had the power to do was make him disappear as director. He got to know Dolores a lot better than Chita.

Ivan Reitman was gifted, no question. He would later direct the smash hit films *Meatballs*, *Stripes*, and *Ghostbusters*. But when it came to theater, he was lost. As many film directors who have tried their hand on Broadway have discovered, expertise in one medium does not necessarily translate to another. Nonetheless, *Merlin* had plenty of compensations, not the least of which was a dedicated company of actors, including the distinguished Edmund Lyndeck, as a wizard; Rebecca Wright, a beautiful ballet dancer, as Merlin's unicorn; Michelle Nicastro, as the lovely temptress fashioned by EQ out of a black panther; Christian Slater, then thirteen, as the young Merlin; and, best of all, Nathan Lane as my clueless son, Prince Fergus.

Nathan, making his musical theater debut at age twenty-eight, was yet to establish himself as one of Broadway's comic greats. But he already had the stirring presence to steal every scene and to keep us laughing offstage. I bettered him in that department only once when, at a matinee performance, I made a grand gesture that yanked off my crown and wig so I was left with only a very unroyal stocking cap on my head. I mustered as much dignity as I could for my exit into the wings and then we both burst into giggles.

Nathan couldn't help making fun of the fact that my character never had a real name. "You know, Chita," he said. "On your driver's license, all it would say would be 'Queen, Evil.'" He also couldn't stop marveling at how I managed to turn a four-hundred-pound, eight-foot black panther into Michelle Nicastro before you could say "Abracadabra." Since we were asked to sign a nondisclosure clause forbidding us to describe how the acts were done, all I can say was that it involved distracting the panther. Nathan once asked the animal's handler what would happen if, on a two-show day, the leopard got bored with horse meat and instead had a hankering for the taste of "ingenue." The handler simply responded, "Huh, I never thought of that."

I had my own close encounter with the panther who literally lulled me into complacency because he was such a hypnotic beauty. The more I sang to him, the more I began to believe that he loved me as he tracked my movements and appeared to be listening to me intently. At one point, I got too close to the cage. He took a swipe at me, and I had one fingernail less afterwards. The trainer said, "He wants to make love to you."

I learned my lesson, or thought I did, so I was a bit more wary when we went to a studio to film a commercial for *Merlin*. The trainer had a large basket of meat to distract the panther. But the animal ignored it in favor of watching every movement of my glittery red-and-gold cape. I went over to say, "Nice, kitty," and its growl sent me running. The trainer grabbed me and said, "Stand stock-still. Don't move. He wants to taste you." I had again let my guard down, which is not a good thing to do around wild animals—and some people. Beauty can lull you into a dangerous trust.

We began preview performances of *Merlin* on December 10, 1982, and finally opened on Broadway on February 13, 1983, one of the longest periods of previews in history until *Spider-Man: Turn Off the Dark*. It takes a while to get special effects working well, but the critics had no mercy for the delayed opening and were unkind. Still, we were able to fill seats in the Mark Hellinger Theatre for the next six months. As it turned out, I was grateful to be in a part that was largely a caricature rather than a real character. If need be, I could be EQ on automatic pilot. That was how I had to be midway through the run when tragedy struck. *Merlin* became an unexpected refuge from a personal grief that soon turned into a more universal song of sorrow.

✳

Ironically, the last part of 1983 became a year of "magical thinking" for me. That is how the writer Joan Didion describes imagining that you can influence the outcome of an event over which you have no control. Such as when somebody you dearly love dies and you try to think of everything you can do to somehow prevent that devastating loss. That's how I felt when my brother Armando and my assistant, Marion, woke me on Saturday, July 23, to tell me that my mother, Katherine, had passed earlier that morning.

It was impossible for me to believe that Katherine del Rivero was no longer a part of this world because she'd always been so fully a part of it. I couldn't possibly imagine that she would never again be on the other end of the phone, laughing easily and giving me words of advice, and sometimes criticism. She would not be there to rejoice with me in my career triumphs or commiserate when my heart was broken.

Even when we were not together, my mother was never far away from the center of my being. The "hows" and "whys" that followed in the wake of her passing seemed almost pointless. Katherine had died as she had lived. Selflessly. She never told us that she had a heart condition because she didn't want to worry her family. She had always been fiercely independent, asking for very little and giving so very much.

My friends, who always called her "mother," were saddened to hear of her passing. She, in turn, called everybody "Sugar" in that honeyed voice of hers. Even as I write this, I can picture her presiding over the dinner table at our home on Flagler Place and bringing that same unpretentious elegance to even the most glamorous events. When we got together with friends and family at restaurants like Bob Nahas's Curtain Up or Ted Hook's Backstage, she would sit mid-table, a generous audience for our silly shenanigans, blushing at our risqué jokes.

I believe that mothers give birth to us twice: when they give us the gift of life, and again when they die. I awoke on that fateful day knowing that something inescapable had changed within me. It was a universal but unfamiliar and shifting landscape. Despite the shocking news, I decided to do the matinee of *Merlin* that Saturday. I don't think I would have done it if the play had required an emotional investment on my part. EQ was a role I could do while my mind was elsewhere, as it most certainly was at that time. But I knew with startling clarity, this is what Mother would have wanted me to do. She knew it would be a sanctuary as I began to process the enormity of what had just happened.

✳

Around this time the air all around us was humid with grief. What had started out as a "gay cancer" in 1981 had gained alarming traction by the time mother died. Our sadness at her passing was of a piece with the seemingly endless songs of sorrow now afflicting so many of our friends and colleagues. The earthquake that was the HIV/AIDS epidemic was a long, slow, and torturous one that shook the world beneath our feet. Everybody in theater and dance was profoundly affected by the losses that were unimaginable and far too many. My refrigerator door became covered with photos and prayers for those who were suffering and those who had died. It took a very, very long time before I could bring myself to pull those mementoes down. Life suddenly became incredulous conversations about friends who were facing a terrifying illness at the youthful peak of their powers. These were followed by visits to hospital rooms, the quiet filled with the beeps of heart-monitoring machines and the wheeze of oxygen tanks.

Over the years spanning my career, I had witnessed behavior in the theater both selfless and selfish, ego-less and ego-driven, brittle and bitchy, and kind and supportive. But I'd never seen the theater community rally with such sacrifice and compassion as it did to meet the challenges of the AIDS era. Broadway Cares/Equity Fights AIDS, led by the tireless Tom Viola, was an organization we could pour our energies into as performers. The response to the epidemic was driven in part by anger at the government for its slow response and in part by the hope that a cure would soon be found. In the meantime, there were far too many memorials to attend and condolence notes to write.

✳

The carousel in Central Park is one my favorite places in New York. I used to go there all the time when Lisa was a baby. We'd ride on the horse of her choosing, and as we went round and round, I would look up. There were angels on the ceiling above us, flickering in the colored lights and seem-ingly keeping time to the calliope music. I thought it was so appropriate since Lisa's middle name is Angela. To this day, I still feel as though those angels are surrounding me. Among their numbers are the names of all those who have passed—my mother, Katherine, and my father, Pedro Julio, chief among them. Even now, so many years later, I feel as bound to them as much as I ever did while they were alive. If that is magical thinking, then I find enormous comfort in it.

Entr'acte

Scrambled Eggs with Joe Allen

When *Bring Back Birdie* folded so fast, some people in the theater community thought for sure that a poster of the show would soon end up at the restaurant Joe Allen. On New York's theater row, it is noted for featuring on its walls posters of Broadway flops. I was sure that would never happen with *Bring Back Birdie*, because Joe Allen, the restaurant's owner, and I had great affection for each other. Years earlier, around the time I was in *Chicago*, it had blossomed into a love affair.

I was surprised when Joe showed up at the stage door one night to invite me to supper. I had seen him walking through his restaurant, quiet, almost morose, flashing a sign that seemed to say, "Don't talk to me." I thought that was an odd personality for a restaurant owner, whose stock-in-trade is usually an outgoing, glad-to-meet-you kind of personality. Once we started dating, however, the Joe I got to know was anything but a curmudgeon. He was warm, energetic, and funny; wrote beautiful poetry and letters; and, best of all, had a generosity of spirit.

Born in Queens, Joe sort of wandered through life at first, a teenage father who married and divorced early and then found his calling when he became a bartender at P. J. Clarke's on the East Side of Manhattan. He wasn't particularly interested in theater when he decided to open his restaurant in the district in 1965.

"I came to this neighborhood because it was cheap," he told me. Soon realizing that his business rose and fell in tandem with Broadway, he set out to attract chorus kids with a cheap menu. He also extended credit to them, which most people would have found foolhardy. Yet very few had ever defaulted on a check. In time, headliners and stars joined the post-show revelry at Joe Allen, and the likes of Lauren Bacall, Al Pacino, Elaine Stritch, and Stephen Sondheim became regulars.

Like me, Joe loved dogs, and he was inseparable from Alice, his golden retriever. He would walk through the restaurant with her, New York health codes be damned, and when you saw Alice, you knew Joe was not far behind.

Joe had a treasure trove of show business and New York stories, and I loved listening to them as we sat in his restaurant and I ordered my favorite: the best scrambled eggs in town, prepared by his chef, Henry. He in turn was a great listener—a trait that is so appealing to any woman. I felt very spoiled and well taken care of when I was in Joe's company. We laughed a lot as we surveyed the packed restaurant and swapped tales. He told me that Elaine Stritch, with whom he'd had an affair, had "a money problem." He added that she didn't lack for it, but "she was so cheap that she couldn't part with it." Lauren Bacall, demanding as ever, had made his waiters cry, an unforgivable sin in Joe's book. He loved hiring actors for his staff and took very good care of them, stepping in whenever they needed extra money to survive in the business. One of his most irreverent waiters was Bobby Freedman, a witty Black actor, who seemed to have a ready retort for whatever came at him. He was once serving Sylvia Miles, an actress who was one of New York's most eccentric personalities and who could also be a flirt. When Bobby asked her, "How would you like your coffee?," she responded, "I like my coffee like I like my men." To which Bobby responded, "Sorry, Sylvia, we don't serve gay coffee."

I always felt a little smarter around Joe since he loved and hung out with writers, especially New Yorkers, like Pete Hamill, Ken Auletta, and Jimmy Breslin. With his rough-hewn features and shy manner, Joe would have been right at home in a Damon Runyon short story. Even though his business was a tremendous success, expanding to restaurants in Miami, Los Angeles, Paris, and London, Joe never strayed far from a sense of himself as a smalltime saloon owner. He was the least starstruck person I ever knew. He had little tolerance for anybody with an outsized ego, and that's probably why he put up the posters of flops—to remind people that at any given moment, life could give them a lesson in humility. When he teased me that he was going to put up the poster of *Bring Back Birdie*, I told him that if he did, I'd run off with his chef, Henry. I wouldn't have, of course. Being in love with Joe, even though it was as short as it was intense, was just too much fun.

16

AROUND *THE RINK* WITH
LIZA AND THE BOYS

In the summer of 1984, Liza Minnelli and I were under the camera lights of *Live at Five*, the local New York television program at Rockefeller Center. We were there to promote *The Rink*, the new Broadway musical by John and Freddy that teamed Liza and me as a mother and daughter who were at odds with each other. The show had just opened to a lot of buzz—"Liza and Chita together!"—but less than rave reviews. That meant doing as much press as we could to keep the show running. We were in friendly territory since the host was our buddy Liz Smith, a popular columnist who'd been very supportive of *The Rink*. After some lighthearted banter, Liz, in her good ol' gal way, popped a question:

"Do you ever fight the way you fight onstage? Have you ever had the experience of disagreeing with each other . . . of really being angry?"

"No," I answer softly.

If I was quick off the mark, it was because I knew—and Liz knew—the real answer was much more complicated. The truth? Liza was in trouble, and I was worried that the binges she was going through at the time would seep into, and possibly wreck, the musical. I was doing all I could to keep the show, which meant so much to all of us, from unraveling.

Liza was more direct and honest: "If anything is wrong, if Chita suspects anything is wrong, she'll say, 'This is hot. This feels hot.

Whatever we're having now, feels hot.'" She made a tossing motion and went on with what I had said to her. "There! You want to handle it? I don't. You want to talk about it? Let's deal with it." Then looking at me, she added, "I can't fight with her because she makes me laugh so hard. She never does anything to make me upset."

As Liza said all this on live television, I was wondering just how far she might go. With Liza, you never knew. All through the interview, she had been clutching a small stuffed teddy bear on her lap. Probably a present from a fan who had been waiting as we made our way from the limo and into the television studio. There were so many of them, multitudes of people whose lives she had touched deeply, who were always waiting for a glimpse, to share a word, to snap a photo.

I sat in the studio at *Live at Five*, looking at the puzzle that was my friend and costar: Liza, the extraordinary artist. Liza, the wide-eyed kid always looking for approval. Liza, battling demons that had long been planted within her along with the dazzling talent. She looked so vulnerable that you never wanted to see her hurt again. Men saw the fragility and wanted to marry her; women, the resilience and wanted to be her sister. I saw all of it and wanted to protect her. Dolores? She would have ripped the head off the teddy bear in frustration.

That was the dilemma of *The Rink*. Appropriately, it was the story of a family—the way it's pulled apart through anger, remorse, and confusion and how it comes back together through understanding, love, and forgiveness. What kept the show together is what has always kept families together: the simple faith that "we can get through this." Ours was no different.

✳

"Hey, Cheet, John and I are writing a show for you. We're finally going to win you a Tony Award."

It was Freddy on the other end of the phone. My ears always perked up when "my brother" called. Especially this time. Not at the mention of a Tony. This may seem disingenuous to you, but winning a Tony never really meant that much to me. Wait. Let me qualify that. It didn't mean that much to me *except* when Tony time rolled around. Then all the nominees get infected by the June fever of people saying, "You're gonna win!" or "It's your time!" I usually responded, "It's just an honor to be nominated." Uh-huh. Then Dolores puts on her competitive bitch heels and I think, "I want to win, dammit!" When I got Freddy's call, I had been nominated four times, for *Bye Bye Birdie*, *Chicago*, *Bring Back Birdie*, and *Merlin*. However, Freddy and John gave me the consolation prize of a clever specialty song for my act called "Losing." The audience loved it. I happily fell back on it every time.

When I read Terrence McNally's script for *The Rink*, I wasn't thinking Tony. I was thinking about what a complex and brave piece of work it was. *The Rink* was my introduction to Terrence, the first of what would be three more encounters with his gifted work: *Kiss of the Spider Woman*, *Chita Rivera: The Dancer's Life*, and *The Visit*. I found Terrence, like the title of another one of his plays, to be all about Love! Valor! Compassion! He was yet to receive the well-deserved accolades that would eventually come his way; instead, he'd take some harsh knocks for his courageous plays. I admired his resilience.

Terrence was then in his mid-forties, with his thinning light brown hair, sparkling blue eyes, and goofy smile. He had a wicked sense of humor maybe because, as a born Catholic, he expected life to be what the nuns had taught him: a vale of tears. Our director, A. J. Antoon, had once studied to be a Jesuit priest, so he was also in sync with that philosophy. And our choreographer, Graciela Daniele, who'd been born in Argentina, also knew the catechism of suffering for your sins.

There was a lot of that Catholic penance in Anna Antonelli, my role in *The Rink*. She was the widowed proprietor of a roller rink at a decaying seaside resort who'd had enough of what life had handed down to her: a straying and alcoholic husband, an estranged daughter, and a tough business she had to keep going in a run-down and dangerous neighborhood. As the musical begins, blue skies are opening up for Anna. She has sold the rink to a developer, who plans to level it, leaving her free to go off to Florida with a boyfriend. The bummer to her brighter future comes in the person of her daughter, Angel, who suddenly returns, unmoored and depressed after an absence of seven years. There are lots of fireworks as Angel tries to stop the demolition, opens old wounds, and looks to settle some old scores.

Sound heavy? Not entirely. Not with John and Freddy writing songs like "Colored Lights," "Chief Cook and Bottle Washer," and "The Apple Doesn't Fall." In typical fashion, their songs broke through whatever hurt and recrimination threatened to descend on *The Rink*. I suppose there are a couple of reasons why I have leaned toward dark material during my career. I came of age in *West Side Story*, which has two dead bodies onstage at the end of the first act and another one at the finish. I matured in *Chicago*, which blinded with sequins just how corrupt our society can be. I'm also lucky to be a part of the showbiz family headed by Freddy and John, who never flinched at taking on challenging material. This included the unforgiving world of *Zorba*, the unlikely and courageous prisoners in *Kiss of the Spider Woman*, and the impassioned and flawed heroine of *The Visit*. I go by only one rule when I'm deciding whether to take a role: "Is this a story I'd like to tell?" In the case of *The Rink*, the answer was, "Hell, ya!"

I could identify with Anna Antonelli—her fire, her empowerment, her resolve. I could relate to what it meant to have a failed marriage, despite the best of intentions; to be at odds with a child, who insists she knows better; to struggle to keep your head above water in a business that's flailing; and, as the song in *Charity* goes, just to be "staggering through the thin and thick of it." I also found Anna to be a sister of sorts to a role I had enjoyed playing years earlier, Serafina Delle Rose in Tennessee Williams's *The Rose*

Tattoo. The play is Williams at his most lighthearted. That suited me just fine. No Blanche DuBois or Alexandra Del Lago for me. But an explosive Italian woman who would say a rosary in one moment and look longingly at a hunky truck driver in the next? Sign me up!

As I prepared to play Anna and wondered just who they might cast as my daughter, I got a phone call from Liza.

"Hey, Chita, can we have lunch? I want to ask you something."

Long as I know you're trying.
Long as I know you care.
Long as we pull together we can do anything, anything, anywhere.
I have you.
You have me.
We can make it.
Right to the end of always, down to the finish line.
We can make it fine.

—"WE CAN MAKE IT," FROM *THE RINK*

On an early December afternoon, I made my way through the crowds and holiday booths in the middle of the theater district to get to Charlie's on West Forty-Fifth Street. It was an intimate burger-and-beer joint that had replaced Downey's as a hangout for chorus kids. Craig, the maître d', met me at the door.

"She's already here," he said as he led me to a table at the back that offered a little more privacy. Liza jumped up and hugged me, her sweater mixing with the fragrance of L'Heure Bleue, her favorite perfume. After catching up on the latest gossip, she steered the conversation to *The Rink*.

"Have they cast the part of the daughter yet?" she asked.

"Not as far as I know," I said.

"Now, look, I haven't asked anybody else, but it's your show, so I wanted to ask you first," she said. "What do you think if I played the daughter?"

I was floored. It was a lot to take in at the moment. I could only babble the first answer that came to my mind.

"Stop right there, you can't do this to me," I said. "Don't dangle a little jewel in front of my nose like that. It's not fair. You've got all these other things on your plate, records, concerts. I'll get all excited about the idea, and then it won't happen and I'll get disappointed all over again."

"Well, do you mind if I ask Freddy?" she asked.

"With my blessing," I said.

I knew what Freddy and John's answer would be. They'd be thrilled to have her play Angel. Why wouldn't they? After all, they'd been instrumental in nurturing the vibrant, world-class entertainer she'd become. At age nineteen, she'd starred in their first Broadway musical, *Flora the Red Menace*, and took home a Tony Award for it. Less than a decade later, she became an international star, having won an Oscar as Sally Bowles in Fosse's film version of their *Cabaret*. Shortly after, working again with Bobby, Freddy and John wrote *Liza with a Z*, the concert and TV special. Liza credits Charles Aznavour, the French singer, with having helped her develop her style. But whenever I saw her perform—the wide stance, the jerk of the head, the "cream-of-the-crop-at-the-top-of-the-heap" hand pumping the air—I saw Freddy. In a sense, Liza and I shared the same Big Daddy. We both wouldn't make a move without him.

I had met her in 1969 when she came backstage after seeing *Zorba* in Los Angeles. But we became closer in 1975 when she and her husband, Jack Haley Jr., came to see *Chita Plus Two* at the Grand Finale in New York. That's when she offered to present the act at Studio One in West Hollywood and her fabulous Hollywood friends had turned out in force. Then a couple of months into the run of *Chicago*, Gwen had to leave the show to have polyps on her vocal cords removed. The show was in danger of closing without her, so Liza came to the rescue by stepping in as Roxie Hart for six weeks. Bobby and the producers decided that there'd be no fanfare. No ads proclaiming the casting coup. Every night, there would simply be an announcement by the stage manager over the PA system, "Ladies and gentlemen, the role of Roxie Hart, usually played by Gwen Verdon, will be played by Liza Minnelli." You can imagine the cheers that went up.

When I heard she was going to replace Gwen temporarily, I thought it was a smart move. The box office would get a well-needed boost just at the right time. Liza learned the show in six days, and we made adjustments to give her all the room she needed. She asked Bobby if she could solo on "My Own Best Friend," which had been a duet between me and Gwen. Bobby checked with me and I agreed. I knew she would stop the show with that powerhouse voice of hers, and she did, every night. I enjoyed working with Liza during that time and getting to know her better. Her approach was "take no prisoners," the words of the telegram she had sent me on the opening night of *Chita Plus Two*. *Chicago* had a different vibe when she was in it. There was the nervy anticipation in the audience that comes from seeing a performer at the peak of her powers. Security guards were even stationed in the theater to ensure Liza's safety. At one performance, a maniacal fan tried to rush the stage. I saw him, and before he could hoist himself up to join us, I ran over to the lip of the stage and hissed at him to get his hands off the stage or I'd put my heel through one of them. He slunk off. Score one for Dolores.

Even though Liza was rapturously received, I never thought she outshone me during her short run. She had her strengths. I had mine. She sang more. I danced more. I felt that the pressure was on her to reach the high bar that Gwen had set. And Liza did. When Gwen came back, the show had been energized and audiences were enthusiastic to have her back. We had Liza to thank for it.

The devotion Liza inspired among her following reminded me of the frenzy of her mother's fans. As you may recall, in December 1963, I had appeared on Judy Garland's variety show. I sang a duet with her of "I Believe in You" and later soloed on "I've Got Plenty o' Nuttin'," a kick-ass number choreographed by Jack Cole. Judy had by that time gained a reputation for erratic behavior, but I saw none of it. What I remember most about taping that program at CBS's Television City was the Yellow Brick Road they had painted from her trailer to the studio. It was an honor, and an early Christmas present, to walk that with her.

Now, two decades later, I was costarring with Judy's daughter, Liza, in a new Broadway musical. As we were getting ready for rehearsals of *The Rink* to begin, I didn't doubt that the show's reception would be influenced by her star power. Her casting had turned an intimate musical into an "event." The audience would be coming to see her. I was fine with that. I couldn't match her vocal power, and she couldn't match my dancing. We met on a megawatt energy level. As Liza herself put it, "Chita's a force and I'm a force. It's like two grounding poles and there's this electric current that goes 'Vroom'!" That was what *The Rink* was promising. From the get-go, the pressure was on to deliver that.

What I couldn't have known at the time was the psychological dynamic of being in a musical with Liza about a mother and a daughter. My mother, Katherine, had died just months earlier, while I was in *Merlin*. My emotions were still raw and I felt wounded. But there had not been a lot of unfinished business between us. I had left home very early, and Katherine's role had changed from being the disciplinarian to being supportive and proud of my career. I missed her terribly. But I was glad to have the distraction of being in *The Rink* to fill the void left by her death.

Liza's relationship with her mother had been different. Judy had bestowed on her daughter guts, ambition, and an enormous talent. She was also a cautionary tale of what *not* to do. With Freddy and John's help, Liza had fought like hell to be accepted as a star in her own right and had succeeded. I admired her a lot for that. But stardom for Liza had come at a price. She'd once told me that when she was a little girl, she'd asked Judy, "Mama, what comes after 'Happily ever after'?" The short answer from Judy? "You'll find out."

Liza was finding out. She had since divorced Jack Haley Jr. and was now married, for the third time, to Mark Gero, a handsome Italian American sculptor. Five years into the marriage, she had become fodder for tabloids about her marital and personal problems, some real, some imagined. Maybe the discipline of a Broadway show was just what Liza needed, I thought. As the daughter of a director, Vincente Minnelli, she was used to following dictates. She had proved herself a Fosse dancer, no small task, and was now eager to stretch beyond the glamor and glitter of her concert appearances.

In *The Rink*, Liza spent most of the musical as Angel wearing grubby jeans, with a backpack, and in a hairdo that was a hairstylist's nightmare. As Anna, I had only one costume, smartly designed by Theoni Aldredge, for the entire show. It was a simple lavender shirtwaist dress that had deep box pleats that expanded into a full skirt during the dance numbers. Not showy, not glamorous, just ingenious. It suited Anna perfectly, enhanced by the lighting of Marc B. Weiss. Unlike the other shows of the season, including *La Cage aux Folles* and *Sunday in the Park with George*, there was little in the way of spectacle we could hide behind. Baring our souls in an intimate musical, without a sequin in sight, Liza and I were exposed like never before. We relished the challenge.

*

The rehearsals at 890 Broadway were tough but gratifying. There were lots of changes, with songs cut and new ones added, scenes rewritten. Freddy and John were constants in the room, and I recall Terrence at the back bent over his Smith-Corona, diligently pecking out the new material. The company bonded quickly, since we were all of nine. In addition to

Liza and me, there were Kim Hauser, as little Anna, and six men, playing the "wreckers," a kind of Greek chorus on roller skates. They come into the musical to start dismantling the rink and stick around to play multiple roles as the troubled past of the Antonellis is laid out in flashback. Several of the actors would go on to rise to the top of their profession and became lifelong friends and occasionally collaborators. These included the director Scott Ellis (*The Mystery of Edwin Drood*), the director and choreographer Rob Marshall (*Kiss of the Spider Woman* and *Chicago*, the movie), and Jason Alexander (*Seinfeld*).

As a show develops, there's always a moment when the company collectively reaches a point of consensus. Either you're heading for an iceberg, or something's coming and that something is going to be great. *The Rink* was an entirely original play, not based on a proven movie or book, so we knew we were on the high wire without a net. Yet as we headed toward opening night, *The Rink* grew into a passion project for all of us. It was a first musical for both AJ and Terrence. AJ was best known for directing hard-hitting dramas such as *That Championship Season*. Terrence, then known only as a dramatic writer, would go on to write seven more musicals. Freddy marveled that he had never seen such a happy company. He couldn't wait to go to rehearsals. Years later, reviewing the troubled history of *The Rink*, John cracked, "Which proves that maybe we shouldn't do those ['happy company'] shows."

Even the complexity of some of the material couldn't dampen our spirits. On the contrary, it tended to make us reach for more. At one point, there was a rape scene since the world of the play included the deteriorating neighborhood of the Antonellis' rink. I was anxious about it. The taunting near-rape scene in *West Side Story* had forced me to delve into how women are tragically traumatized all too often. Here I was again. Grazie, who became a friend while we were in *Chicago*, had since won acclaim as a choreographer, including for *The Pirates of Penzance* and *Zorba*. For *The Rink*, she'd come up with a very stylized dance for the dramatic moment of the rape. When the producers saw the scene at a run-through, they complained, "It's too much," and lobbied AJ and Terrence to cut it. Graciela argued to leave it in. They asked for my opinion.

"I trust Grazie's instincts and Terrence's words," I said. "It's difficult, I'll have to brace myself every night for it, but I think it should stay."

After AJ gave notes that night, he addressed the company. "I just want to say that people think of Chita as a dancer and as a singer. I have to say that I think she's proving herself to be, first and foremost, a terrific actress."

"That's very generous of you to say, AJ," I said. "But I just want everybody to know, I'm a dancer and will always be a dancer at heart."

I appreciated AJ's encouragement. We actors can be so vulnerable when we're making creative choices, which means we might be thrown off by any little thing. That's why directors keep the studio doors bolted shut during rehearsals. But the most important thing in the process is to keep the company fused together. Throughout my career, I've made it a point to never let anything separate me from the rest of the cast. I realize the responsibilities that come when your name is above the title. But I wanted to send a signal to the cast of *The Rink* that I was still one of them. I had to support them and, in turn, to be supported by them. The fun was to watch them play their multiple roles.

Scott Ellis, for example, played Lucky, a wrecker, a punk, and, in drag, Sugar. He had quite a good time playing her, flouncing around in a full pink skirt, blouse, pearls, and gloves. At one performance, he flounced a little bit too enthusiastically during one of my numbers. Afterwards Dolores delivered him a note: "Scott, that is the *busiest* skirt on Broadway." Without missing a beat, he retorted, "I learned it all from you, honey!"

During another performance, Rob Marshall, who had been hired as an understudy, was on for the first time and partnering me in one of Grazie's sensational jitterbugs in the show. After completing a series of châiné turns, he slid across the floor as we concluded the number, connecting with me at a point when and where he wasn't supposed to connect. During the applause, I whispered to him, "I think you broke my little finger." Sure enough, I spent the rest of the month with it in a splint. Rob apologized a dozen times, certain that he was going to be fired. He wasn't, of course. He was just too good a dancer and a person. But I've had the pleasure of teasing him ever since.

Previews of *The Rink* played well, but the audience still wanted Liza and me in something other than what they saw as thrift store rejects. She made a call to her pal Halston, and we were soon trooping down to his extravagant studio to be fitted for red sequined gowns for our curtain call. I'd met Halston through Liza after her brief stint in *Chicago*. On a rare occasion, I would meet up with them at some soirée or party, sometimes at Studio 54. I liked Halston a lot. He was kind and generous and always extended invitations to his parties. But I'm not as much of a social butterfly as people think I am. Liza, on the other hand, liked to burn the candle at both ends, and she had the perfect companion for it in Halston. The spangled outfits he made for *The Rink* were fantastic but had little to do with Anna and Angel. It wasn't as if they had decided after the curtain fell to do a double act like Roxie and Velma. But the costume change did the trick. It sent the audience out on a high.

Speaking of high, that was where Liza and I parted ways. I'm no angel. To be in show business is to be around alcohol and an assortment of drugs. It's just part of the territory. I had gotten my first glimpse of the underground scene way back in the fifties. Then there was that time during *Mr. Wonderful* when I came across my friend Jeri between shows at her hotel room with a bunch of jazz musicians sitting around smoking dope. Since then, alcohol has been my choice for relaxation, though I was never a serious drinker. I mean, could you even consider that of someone who would ask for a Tab and a little vodka in a beer glass? Just as I had chosen to smoke more for the color of the cigarette holders than the pleasures of tobacco, esthetics drove my taste in alcohol. As for drugs, I was older when their use became more widespread socially. During the sixties, when everybody was "turning on and dropping out," the mantra was "Never trust anybody over thirty." I was beyond the cut-off date.

My familiarity with harder stuff came only once that I can recall. I was sitting around the room with friends, and they started passing around a drug. I think it was coke or maybe acid. I wasn't sure but at their urging, I thought, "Why the hell not? Just this once." Moments later, I was looking around the room and telling everybody, "I just love you all so much! I really wish I were you!" Everybody laughed. So I repeated it, pointing my finger at each one, "I wish I were you, you, you, you, and you!" (Drugs don't make you any smarter.) The next thing I knew I was in the bathroom with a friend who was holding up my head over the toilet. Not much fun but enlightening enough for me to say, "I won't do *that* again."

I was wary of being too judgmental when Liza's behavior became increasingly difficult to deal with during the run of *The Rink*. What must it be like, I wondered, to have to live up to—as well as escape from—a legend? "Until now, I avoided ever playing a daughter," she once told me, "for fear of what it might bring up." I can't imagine what taking on the role of Angel—who'd been abused by an uncle, betrayed by boyfriends, abandoned by a father—may have conjured up in someone as sensitive as Liza. This at a time when she was also going through disappointments in her personal life.

The trouble started after the opening when the reviews were not what we had hoped for. The critics gave us no extra points for the degree of difficulty in pulling off a dark and original musical. They didn't recognize Liza's daring to play Angel, and she was deeply disappointed. She couldn't seem to break out a new image for herself and now felt stuck in a subordinate role "dressed like a sanitation worker," as one writer put it.

It's tough to be on the receiving end of any criticism and doubly so when you're totally invested in the work, as we all were. Freddy and John felt as though *The Rink* had been everything they'd hoped it could be. When the show didn't get a positive reception, it mattered little to John.

He still loved it. But Freddy had to resist an impulse to turn against it. He felt as though he'd let us down, which simply wasn't true. They'd come through, as usual, with wit and originality. We licked our wounds and took refuge in the work; Liza took refuge in something else.

✳

The first duty of performers is to be fully present when they're onstage. I can't bear it when an actor is off in another world. You can sense it, and the audience can, too. When Liza and I were firing on all cylinders in *The Rink*, it was magic. AJ had done a good job of pairing our sensitivities and strengths. The musical took flight during our duets—"The Apple Doesn't Fall," "Don't Ah Ma Me," and "Wallflower"—and you could sense the audience enjoying every minute of them. We all knew how good it could be, and that made it all the more sad when Liza started phoning it in or wasn't really there. That is, if she made it to the theater at all.

My first impulse when things start to go off the rails is to close the door before things get too hot. "I Don't Want to Know," the Jerry Herman song from *Dear World* that I sang in *Jerry's Girls*, is pretty much one of my theme songs. But I couldn't do that in this case. I saw the insanity, the drama, the craziness, and there was no way to fix it. I had to roll with the punches and do whatever I could to keep the company together and to make sure the audience would never know something was amiss. Liza kept me on my toes. To her credit and mine, I don't think the audience was ever the wiser.

At every performance, after I did my usual preparations in my lavender dressing room, I made a point of going to Liza's, which was painted red. I checked in and could tell what the next couple of hours were going to entail. I kept telling myself that Liza's addiction to prescription drugs and alcohol was a disease, something she herself readily admitted. But you can't very well put that on a card in the lobby of the theater. People had paid top dollar to see us, and it wasn't lost on the company that *The Rink* had opened at a difficult time in the theater. The HIV/AIDS epidemic was starting to gain traction in the community, and we were devastated at the terrible losses. Terrence's boyfriend, the director Bobby Drivas, would be among the first fatalities. The theater became not only a bulwark against the disease but a sanctuary. *La Cage aux Folles* put up a brave front: "The best of times is now." If only we could believe that. In the meantime, it was our obligation to offer at least a bit of escape from the grim headlines.

At one particular matinee of *The Rink*, Liza kept forgetting her lines, and trying to follow her became a game of whack-a-mole. That was when, with some frustration, I confronted her in the way that she later recounted during Liz Smith's interview. I left Dolores back in my dressing room and let Chita handle it. Dolores wouldn't have done any good.

"This feels hot, Liza," I said, referring to the danger she was putting the show in. "Whatever's going on with you feels hot," I said. "Do you want to handle it? Because I don't and I won't."

I couldn't get through to her. Neither could Freddy, who was sympathetic, or John, who was less patient. We felt as helpless as parents with an errant child except this child had her name above the title and the star power to keep the show running. The crisis deepened when Liza started coming to the theater five minutes before a performance or missing them altogether. When Ed Aldridge, our stage manager, made the announcement that Liza would not be performing, the lobby would be crowded with patrons demanding a refund or exchange. On one occasion, Ed came to my dressing room to tell me that there were probably only about four hundred patrons in the Martin Beck, which had more than fourteen hundred seats.

"Do you want to go on, Cheet, or shall we bag it?" he said. I didn't like going on with an understudy, as good as Lenora Nemetz and then Mary Testa were. The show was so finely calibrated between Liza and me that it didn't have the same electric charge without her. I called the company into my dressing room and put the question to them. "There aren't many people out there, but we have a new understudy for Liza, Mary Testa, and she hasn't really had a regular rehearsal," I said. "We could go out there, have a good time, and give her a chance to get her bearings. What would you like to do?"

We went on that night and gave one of the best performances of the entire run of *The Rink*. We were looser and sillier than usual, and the audience of four hundred gave us an ovation that sounded like fourteen hundred.

I can't pretend to tell you that I fully understood what was going on with Liza or what the remedy might have been at the time. She missed the last couple of weeks of her five-month commitment to the show and checked into the Betty Ford Center. I was very proud of her. When the press asked me about it, I simply said, "Thank God! What happened with Liza happens in one way or another to more people than we even know. The most wonderful thing is when they do something about it."

Looking back, I wonder if part of the problem was that Liza had become a star so young. She didn't have a chance to come up through the chorus. That's key for absorbing the discipline and responsibilities of a performer to the creators of a show, to peers, and to the audience. When you are part of an ensemble, you learn to have each other's back. Nothing is more important. It was the courtesy that Shirley MacLaine showed me when we were filming *Sweet Charity*, the respect and professionalism between Gwen and me during the run of *Chicago*, the camaraderie we had at *The Rink*. You never take that for granted. As a member of a company, you're never alone and that can be a tremendous comfort when feelings of loneliness threaten to crush the spirit. Theater can be a gateway drug, too.

✳

June 3, 1984, the Gershwin Theatre, New York.

Freddy and John were true to their promise. I did win a Tony Award for Anna in *The Rink*.

As Robert Preston read the names of the four nominees, my heart was bursting through my chest. But when he announced my name, a calm came over me and I stood ramrod straight. I felt my mother, Katherine, coursing through me—her elegance, her dignity, her beauty. I rose to the podium and joked about having been nominated four times before and losing.

"I'm very happy that I bought the bottom of the dress this year. I've been coming for so many years and losing for so many years, and being quite happy about it, I decided, 'Why buy the bottom of the dress? Nobody sees it.'"

The audience saw the entire dress—black, svelte, and by Halston—and heard me thank those who had brought me to that moment. I saved the last to be a tribute to the woman who most deserved to be acknowledged. The night belonged to Katherine, who had not lived to see *The Rink*. Since I had crashed through the coffee table on Flagler Street in Washington, DC, my mother's love had been my rock, my spiritual guide, the real prize of my life. I felt that this was her last, best gift to me. Holding up the Tony, I said, "Ma, you can relax now."

No sooner had the orchestra played me off the stage when I realized, much to my mortification, that I hadn't thanked Liza, my costar. It threw some cold water on the evening, and I tried to make up for it at several of the following performances of *The Rink*. I usually took the final curtain call at the end of the show, but I gave it to Liza. As the cheers died down, I took Liza's hand and told the audience that when I make a mistake, it's a doozy. And that's what it was, a doozy.

Also nominated for Tony Awards were Liza, Grazie, Freddy and John, and Peter Larkin for his remarkable set. But my win was the sole one so I felt that it honored the efforts of the entire company. *La Cage aux Folles* swept that year. I was pissed, or rather Dolores was, that AJ and Terrence had not even been nominated for their bold work. Beginning in 1993, however, Terrence would have the last laugh. After his nomination and win for *Kiss of the Spider Woman*, he would go on to be nominated another seven times and add three more medallions to his shelf. That's just the way it works. One of the major lessons of Broadway is simple: hang in there.

The only drawback from winning a Tony was that I could no longer sing "Losing" in my nightclub act, which had always been a highlight. At the Tony party afterwards, I told Freddy and John that I'd miss it. Freddy said, "Don't worry, Cheet. I can sing it tonight."

✳

In January 2001, the Drama League honored me at its annual gala. Liza had recently been hospitalized in Florida with a bout of viral encephalitis. It was another malady in a long line of health problems she'd been facing since we were together in *The Rink*. The organizers of the event had informed me that she had sent a telegram which they would read in the course of the festivities. Toward the end of the program, there was a surprise announcement: "Ladies and gentlemen, Miss Liza Minnelli."

In her own quietly heroic way, Liza had flown up to read the telegram in person. Beautifully dressed in a black velvet suit, she made her way across the stage to the microphone to say, "Chita, when I was fifteen, my mother gave me a birthday present: it was you in *Bye Bye Birdie* on Broadway. It was just Mom and me and you on the stage of the Martin Beck. And you changed my life."

As I now recall that thoughtful gift from Liza, the memory of Judy at the London Palladium in the summer of 1964 comes flooding back. How that too was a surprise appearance by her, then frail but indomitable, coming to show support on the "Night of 100 Stars" charity gala.

In *The Rink*, one of my favorite moments was when Scott Holmes, as Dino, my husband, sang a song, "Blue Crystal," to our little daughter, Angel, played by Kim Hauser. It was a fantasy about going to the moon to fetch the gem—a symbol of trust, strength, and compassion—as a gift to her. AJ had positioned Liza to be in the shadows just behind her younger self, watching the scene. A childlike innocence was reflected in both their faces.

In my Tony speech for *The Rink*, I thanked all those "whose faces I'd ever looked into," by which I meant all the artists I've had the privilege of working with. To have looked into the faces of Judy and Liza is to have been blessed twice: Judy with her legendary talent, Liza with her heart as big as the moon.

Entr'acte

Lisa Mordente: The World's Only Living Shark-Jet

For nine months I carried you under my heart
Oh—for nine months, seldom if ever apart
No wonder
I can be annoying, scream and fight,
Sometimes I'm no lady,
Yeah you got that right
So the saying is true
Looka you, looka me.
The apple doesn't fall very far from the tree.

> —"THE APPLE DOESN'T FALL," FROM *THE RINK*,
> BY FRED EBB AND JOHN KANDER

Anyone who has seen my daughter, Lisa Mordente, perform onstage will know that Freddy was onto something when he wrote those lyrics. Even so, I was as nervous as any parent would be on the November night in 1978 when Lisa made her Broadway debut in *Platinum*, which starred Alexis Smith. I didn't need to worry. Ten minutes after she made her entrance as a fabulous rock star dressed in Bob Mackie plumage, I exhaled, thinking to myself, "She owns the stage!" And four years later when she was nominated for a Tony Award for *Marlowe*, a Shakespearean rock musical, her father, Tony, and I were thrilled that Lisa had made good on the promise she'd been showing since she was born. Wait. Make that since she was in the womb.

I was still performing in *West Side Story* six months into my pregnancy. I wouldn't have been surprised if Lisa had danced into the world to "America." Months later, her baby carriage was parked in the wings on any given night when I was performing *West Side* in London. As she grew older, she made herself at home all over a theater, including in the pit with the conductor and musicians, in my dressing room, or backstage with the crew. She never lacked for "honorary" godparents in any of my shows. This included the national tour of *Zorba*, when, at age ten, she joined me onstage as the little girl in the company. When she was sixteen and featured in the ensemble of *Gypsy*, Angela Lansbury took her under her wing, as did Alexis Smith years later. In between, Lisa had a taste of the business on the West Coast, joining Tony, who by then had established himself as a choreographer, director, and producer of television.

Lisa and I never spoke much about her pursuing an acting career. Her love of animals might well have pointed her to a career as a veterinarian. Then one day, after her tour in *Gypsy*, she told me that she had received an offer to appear in the television series *Viva Valdez* as the rambunctious daughter of an East LA family. I was happy for her but sorry that it meant she'd have to leave school. I simply asked, "Would you like to do it?" When she said yes, Tony and I decided she should move in for a time with his brother, Ralph, and his wife, Marian, in Studio City, California. Looking back on that moment, I'm struck by the parallel in our lives. I was the exact same age when I went to my mother, Katherine, and told her that I had the chance to go to New York to study at the School of American Ballet. I also lived with my aunt and uncle but in the Bronx. The universe offers up something, and then it's up to you. You need to recognize it and say "yes"—and your parents have to let you go, as hard as that may be.

At the time, I was in *Chicago* in New York, so I knew I was losing Lisa. I might have felt more abandoned if we had not spent the six previous years living together during my LA period. The chance to spend more time with Lisa in Los Angeles softened the guilt that I think any entertainer has when their work takes them away from their children. That anxiety never goes away. I'm glad that Lisa never identified with what she called "the Carrie Fisher Syndrome," which could result when your mother maintained the aura of "star," as Debbie Reynolds had. That wasn't me. I always left my work behind at the theater or studio and made a point of creating a structured routine for Lisa at home. True to stereotype, the pace in Los Angeles was much more easygoing, with pool parties, barbecues, and long, leisurely Sunday afternoons. Groups of friends and neighbors, Lisa's and mine, kept our house on top of Mulholland Drive buzzing with activity. Freddy Ebb was out there, and we were neighbors with Freddy Curt, who'd been my first dancing partner in *Call Me Madam*. The group kept growing to include choreographers Alan Johnson and Graciela Daniele; Joe Tremaine, the esteemed dance teacher; and the actors Nancy Dussault, Karen Morrow, and Marcia Gregg. Marcia was a wickedly amusing gossip, so of course everybody wanted to sit next to her. Also a part of our clique was Yvonne Othon, who had been in the London cast of *West Side Story* and later in the film. In the 1960s, "Vonny," as we called her, had changed her last name to Wilder. A good choice because, Bronx-born and from Puerto Rican and Cuban ancestry, she was off-the-wall funny. Liza Minnelli also added a lot of sparkle to our group.

Despite the age difference of twelve years, Liza and Lisa had become close ever since meeting in 1969 during the run of *Zorba*. They had a lot in common, the least of which was they were both children of celebrities. Along with Lorna Luft, they hung out together, their restless energy feeding off each other. They listened to records, made up choreography, and watched episodes of *Star Trek*. Liza eventually became Lisa's maid of honor at her marriage to Donnie Kehr, an actor she met while assisting Wayne Cilento on the Broadway musical *The Who's Tommy*. Liza's company was a lifesaver for Lisa. She effectively replaced the high school "besties"—Tracy, Julia, Susan, and Lynn—she had to leave behind when she joined the cast of *Viva Valdez* and later, *Welcome Back, Kotter*.

Lisa eventually rejoined me in New York when she was cast in *Platinum*. She'd just turned twenty. New York was at the time an all-night party, fueled by the city's restless energy and a drug scene centered around clubs like Studio 54. I took part in that energy only occasionally. When you're in a show like *Chicago*, you just want to go home and soak in a tub. A lot of my friends, including Liza and Halston, were burning the midnight oil, often with Lisa in tow. I worried about her coming of age in such an environment. After all, she was half Puerto Rican, half Italian, part Shark, and part Jet. Like her parents, she'd always displayed a fiery and independent streak. The Witch in Stephen Sondheim's show *Into the Woods* expressed the fear of every mother in the song "Stay with Me": . . . *Don't you know what's out there in the world? / Someone has to shield you from the world* . . .

I had learned to do needlepoint while I was in California. I noticed that whenever Lisa went out at night, my stitches became tighter and tighter. So at one point, I decided to write a letter to Liza and Halston asking them to take care of my daughter. If she was going to be out on the town with them, I hoped they'd see to it that she wouldn't get into any sticky situations. They assured me that they would and stayed true to that promise. Lisa, on the other hand, was pissed.

"Mom, you can't make people responsible for me! I'm not a child!" she told me. "If there's an experience I'm supposed to go through and didn't because of that letter, then you messed up!"

When I was in that protective mode, she'd call me "Sister Mary Chita." That was her equivalent of Freddy Ebb's nickname for me, Miss Dove. But when it comes to your children, why not err on the side of caution? Years later, these kinds of scenes between us would not have been out of place in *The Rink*. Here I was playing Anna, mother to rebellious Angel, played by Liza Minnelli, daughter of Judy Garland and a close friend of my own rebellious daughter. I may have drawn on that, but if I did, it was subconsciously. Playing Anna taught me that every mother wants to be perfect and we fall short, no matter how hard we try. As far as children go, the statute of limitations on their resentments has to run out at some point. Until it does, you just have to wait it out.

I realized when Lisa was first laid in my arms as a newborn that she didn't belong to anyone other than herself. But Tony gave her the guts to call people on their bullshit, especially in the business that she had been exposed to since birth. Lisa says I ingrained in her, mostly by example, a feminism to meet the world of men on her own terms. Lisa's favorite of my roles is Rosie in *Bye Bye Birdie*. She likes Rosie's ability to come up with solutions when everybody else is running around like headless chickens. Lisa also loves that Rosie can blow her cool in songs like "How to Kill a Man." Lisa, after all, is the one who coined the phrase "when Mom goes Puerto Rican" about my tirades. She actually likes that version of me more than Sister Mary Chita.

I was never more proud of Lisa than when she decided to play Anita in *West Side Story* at the Burt Reynolds Dinner Theatre in Jupiter, Florida. She'd dated Burt for a while and choreographed *The End*, a black comedy he directed and starred in. When he suggested that she play Anita in a revival, she immediately shot it down. But then he added the sweetener: he would ask Tony to direct and choreograph using the original Jerome Robbins dances. When she told me about Burt's offer, I simply asked, "Do you really want to do it?"

One of the things that Lisa and I like to do is laugh obsessively over TikTok videos of people scaring each other. But there couldn't have been anything more frightening for her than taking on Anita. How remarkable life is! As I sat in my seat at Burt's theater, waiting for the show to begin, I couldn't help thinking that I had carried her in my womb for two trimesters while performing the role I was now about to see her in. I have to admit that it was a little strange—like sitting in a dentist's chair but not having your teeth pulled. But Lisa gave the role her own unique interpretation from the first downbeat to the last. After the performance, all Tony and I could do was beam with pride in her dressing room.

As we embraced, Lisa asked me if I had any notes. "Not one," I said, reminding her that I took notes from her better than she took notes from me. She reminded me that I had once said, while "going Puerto Rican" on her, "You're going to be a wonderful woman if I ever let you live past fifteen!"

Lisa was then twenty-five. I had let her live past fifteen. And I was proved right.

She *had* turned into a wonderful woman.

Entr'acte

Seeing God in the Beat of *Latin Rhythms*

D oesn't she speak with an accent?"

That was the question about me that Meredith Willson, the popular composer of *The Music Man*, asked Edwin Lester, the West Coast producer. They were in the process of casting Willson's new show, *1491*, about Christopher Columbus, and they were considering me for the part of Beatriz, the Spanish mistress of the explorer. I was dumbfounded when my agent, Dick Seff, relayed the conversation to me. It was 1969 and you'd have thought that Willson would have been more savvy. Didn't he realize that just because someone had a Spanish name didn't mean they spoke like someone who'd just fallen off the boat from Veracruz?

As a Latina, I occasionally bumped up against stereotypical notions like those of Willson's, though not as much as Rita Moreno did in Hollywood. The theater, as opposed to the film world, was a bit more relaxed about ethnicities at the time. Besides, I wasn't about to allow myself to be pigeon-holed. I wanted to be considered for a range of roles, and for the most part I succeeded. When I did play Latinas, I was naturally upset when my characters were subjected to racist taunts. In *West Side Story*, as Anita, I cringed at being called a "spic" and "Bernardo's pig" and "garlic mouth" by the Jets. But those exchanges were central to the prejudices that Arthur Laurents's script sought to expose.

In *Bye Bye Birdie*, as Rosie Alvarez, I had to put up with the hostility of Albert's mother, Mae, which she expressed with bigoted slurs. She just didn't think me worthy of her son. I was given the song "Spanish Rose" in order to mock Mae's attitudes of what it meant to be an Alvarez. I didn't like the number. I thought it was stupid and beneath Rosie to sing it. But another part of my brain thought, "Well, it's got to be stupid because it's my response to a very stupid woman." I had found a way to own it. The problem was that, at the time, Latino characters not only were few and far between. They also were being written almost exclusively by non-Latinos. This was across the culture. While writing *West Side Story*, Arthur, Lenny, and Steve had been sensitive to that discrepancy and respected the culture. The creative team of *Bye Bye Birdie* decided to exploit the tension between Mae and Rosie through satire. It was my job to make it clear that I was onto Mae's insults. I decided to fight *fuego* with *fuego*.

In *Chicago*, Velma Kelly was never identified as a Latina once we reached Broadway. But during our out-of-town tryout in Philly, the script called for Roxie to direct a bunch of bigoted slurs toward her. In one scene, she called Velma "a spic" and insisted that all she probably ate were enchiladas and tacos. One of the milder taunts was when Roxie said, "I find people of Spanish origin very jealous, don't you? It must be the hot climate and all those bananas." I can be as jealous as the next person, but I don't think it's because of bananas. And I can be as game as any actor to at least try out what is in the script, which was cowritten by Bobby and Freddy. But Roxie's insults didn't sit well with me. I thought they were unnecessary. There were plenty of other, nonracist ways to heat up the rivalry between Roxie and Velma. I was happy when the references were cut before we got to New York.

It was finally through Aurora in *Kiss of the Spider Woman*, based on the Argentine novel by Manuel Puig, that I was able to relish and celebrate my roots. There was John Kander's Latin-flavored score and Rob Marshall's smoldering dances, particularly in "Gimme Love" and "Where You Are." Since *Kiss* was written by Fred Ebb and Terrence McNally, Latino culture was still being filtered through a non-Latino lens. In fact, with Lin-Manuel Miranda's *In the Heights* and Gloria Estefan's *On Your Feet!* still far in the future, Broadway had almost never had the opportunity to see our people authentically presented in song and dance. Then in 2002, Richard Amaro conceived the idea of *An Evening of Latin Rhythms* as a showcase for Latino talent and as a fund-raiser for Broadway Cares/ Equity Fights AIDS. He asked me to star and host in a series of shows at the B. B. King Blues Club and Grill in Times Square.

Richard, son of a Cuban father and Puerto Rican mother, was born in New York and raised in Miami. He said that the idea had come to him while we were dancing salsa in a club in Dallas. We were on the tail end of the national tour of *Kiss of the Spider Woman* when some of the cast and I decided to go out on the town. We found ourselves in a hot Latin spot and hit the dance floor to the pulsating rhythms of brass and drums. It took me back to my early days at the Palladium, dancing to the music of the two Titos—Puente and Rodriguez.

Richard said, "Cheet, you look like you're having a ball!"

"I am!" I said, sweating up a storm. "When we dance Latin, Richard, we see God!"

Richard was among the many Latin men who'd been part of my club act since its inception. Another one of my boys was Sergio Trujillo, a fantastic dancer who has since gone on to be an amazing choreographer. In 1997, for the show *Chita and All That Jazz*, I asked Sergio to choreograph the number "Ran Kan Kan," which Tito Puente had made famous. I worked really hard on getting the steps down exactly right, rehearsing it again and again at home. When you're dancing salsa, you can expect a lot of eyes on you from purists, looking for any misstep. Another staple of my act has been "La Bamba," a huge hit for Ritchie Valens in the 1950s. I did this number with a maraca in one hand and a banana in the other (maybe Roxie was onto something, after all). We were thrown off at one performance when, before going on, one of the boys had inadvertently eaten the prop.

Latin Rhythms was conceived to show Broadway what Latinos could do, singing and dancing in an authentic way. Richard, as producer and director, with Ariadne Villareal, wanted to re-create those fabled nights at the Palladium. "The real deal," as he put it. To that end, he brought in the one person forever associated with that era, the Grammy-winning Ray Santos, who arranged and conducted the orchestra for the evening. On top of that, he put together an impressive cast, which included several Broadway veterans, such as Raúl Esparza, Daphne Rubin-Vega, Rosie Perez, Andrea Burns, and Natalie Toro. They were joined by a number of the boys from my act, including Richard Montoya, Raymond del Barrio, and Lloyd Culbreath.

We saw God that night—as well as on the additional performances of *Latin Rhythms*. The freedom on the dance floor was exhilarating, 180 degrees away from "Spanish Rose" and Broadway, not a burrito in sight, not a flower in my teeth. Richard and I danced a furious "Ran Kan Kan" and I sang "Our Love Is Here to Stay" to a bolero beat. A high point came when Augie and Margo Rodriguez, the fabled mambo dance duo, took to the floor. I had met them when I first went to the Palladium as a teenager. Now here they were, more than a half-century later, showing us that time had not diminished their energy and commitment.

Mambo, salsa, merengue, cha-cha, samba, conga. We were free to make every non-Latino in the room want to be Latino. After one performance, a reporter asked me whether I had ever desired to "bust out" in any of my Broadway shows to express what I had just been showing on the dance floor. I was kind of thrown by the question. I responded that at times I had been tempted. But in ballet, you are expected to execute what is required of you without deviation. As a musical theater performer, you're obligated to follow the choreographer. I told the reporter that I was lucky to have a nightclub act as a way to bust out.

That is what made presenting the act in Puerto Rico such a pleasure. Performing at the El Caribe Hotel, the Club Tropicoro, and the Centro de Bellas Artes Luis A. Ferré, I felt a special kinship with the audience. How could it be otherwise? "To go Puerto Rican" is not only to be hot-headed, though I surely can be. It also means an abiding love of family, with all our faults, affection for country, with all its faults, and a simple pride, expressed in the flag, *la Bandera de Puerto Rico.*

My brother Hoolie accompanied me and my dancers on those trips and captured on camera the exuberance of our exchanges with the public. They took me to their hearts as we, in turn, took them to ours. The buildings would literally shake with the rush of the energy in the room. I was so moved by the island's people that I ended up buying a condo in the Palmas del Mar complex in Humacao. I spent some of the happiest years of my life there.

I wish I still had that condo. I could float for hours on the affection I encountered when I worked or vacationed on the island. On occasion, I was invited to speak to students at elementary schools in the area and was touched and delighted by the responses of the children. Music seemed to emanate from everywhere—the pastel-colored houses, the restaurants, the clubs, even the schools and ornate churches. The island, like those nights of *Latin Rhythms*, fed the soul, broke loose the spirit, and pulsated with the very rhythm of life.

No wonder it made me who I am.

17

HAVE YOU CRIED YET?

A Jerry Girl Hits a Snag

Well, Chita, you really did a job on yourself," said Dr. John Carmody, when the X-rays came back. "You've suffered compound fractures—a broken tibia and fibula of your left leg. We'll put you in corrective surgery as soon as possible."

A dancer hears the word "break" and the mind goes to the word "finished." But I didn't go there. I couldn't.

"How far can I come back?" I asked, steeling myself for the answer.

"Chita, it's up to you," he said, speaking in that calm, reassuring manner doctors always use.

I looked intently at Dr. Carmody, the orthopedic surgeon at Lenox Hill Hospital. He had a broad, kind face and a walrus mustache that could have been a push broom. I sensed he was telling me the truth. I could hear the voice of Doris Jones, my first dance teacher. "You've got guts, Dolores," she said. "It'll get you through anything."

"Okay, then," I said. "Let's get started."

*

What is it they say about April? That it's the "cruelest month"? That was the case when on April 6, 1986, my 280Z Datsun was broadsided by a taxi as I was making a U-turn on the Upper West Side of Manhattan. It was about midnight when the accident happened. I had volunteered to drop off my boyfriend, Bob Fehribach, and Gail Ricketts, Liza Minnelli's chauffeur, at their apartments. A group of us had just finished a dinner at Curtain Up, the theatrical restaurant owned by my close friend Bob Nahas. We were celebrating the end of another week of performances of *Jerry's Girls*, a Broadway revue of Jerry Herman songs in which I was then appearing with Leslie Uggams and Dorothy Loudon. After dropping Bob and Gail off, I planned to drive to my home, an historic farmhouse in Westchester. I looked forward to a relaxing day off. That was not going to happen.

After hearing the sound of crumpling steel and shattering glass, I remember looking through the broken window at the stricken face of the young Korean-American cab driver who had hit me. Since I was at fault, I felt the need to console him. "I'm so sorry!" I said. "I didn't see you!" In fact, I kept apologizing to everybody. It kept me calm. Gail and Bobby reassured me that they were fine, apart from some minor bruises and cuts. They were more worried about me. I said I was okay, even though my left leg, which had taken most of the impact, was at a weird angle over my right.

A cop peered into the car and said, "Ma'am, stay still until the ambulance gets here. And don't move your leg."

I looked down and saw a bloody, swollen, and discolored limb. Counterintuitively, I moved it. (Nice going, Chita!) Call it a dancer's reflex. I wanted to see how much damage the leg had sustained. It's the fear that every dancer, every physical performer, has from the moment they know their body will be the expression of who they are. Before this, I'd been fairly lucky. A strained muscle here, a torn ligament there. I once suffered a concussion during a dance and figured at least it proved I had a brain. The panther in *Merlin* had nearly torn my nail off. Now I was facing a beast of a different color.

The rest of the night was a blur. Bob Nahas arrived from the restaurant within what seemed like minutes and I wondered how word had gotten out so fast. He told me that Gail had managed to call him and that he then had called my brother Armando. The ambulance arrived soon after, and the cop asked me where I wanted to go.

"To Lenox Hill, to Dr. John Carmody," I said. He had operated on my knee the year before. Bob Fehribach rode with me in the ambulance. I suddenly thought about *Jerry's Girls*. I asked Bob to make sure to call Shirley Herz, the publicist. "Tell her I've had an accident and I won't be able to make Tuesday's performance," I said. Tuesday? How about never?

Another irony of the night came to me later from among the hundreds of telegrams and cards I received from well-wishers. Word got out in the press that one of the passengers in the car had been Gail Ricketts, a chauffeur. A telegram from a wisecracking friend read, "Chita, the next time you're in a car with a chauffeur? Let them do the driving!"

✳

If I needed all the optimism I could muster it was just as well that before the accident I had been performing in the sunniest musical I'd ever been in: *Jerry's Girls*. The show was written by Jerry Herman, the buoyant and boyish composer of such hits as *Mame, Hello, Dolly!*, and *La Cage aux Folles*, and directed by Larry Alford. Choreographing was Wayne Cilento, who'd been one of the boys in my nightclub acts and was now carving out a career as a red-hot choreographer. He'd later strike gold with *Wicked*.

I shared the stage with Leslie Uggams, who'd forged a blazing musical career, winning a Tony Award for her Broadway debut in *Hallelujah, Baby!*, and Dorothy Loudon, who was one of the funniest performers I'd ever worked with. She won acclaim and a Tony Award for her turn as the liquor-swilling meanie Miss Hannigan in *Annie* but had started out in downtown comic revues. Working with Dorothy took me right back to my days in Ben Bagley's *Shoestring Revue*. Like Bea Arthur and Arte Johnson in that show, she couldn't care less whether you liked her or not, found her funny or not. Because of that, she was spontaneous, wicked, and hysterical.

In *Jerry's Girls*, in a solo spot, Dorothy fiddled around at a piano, pretending (or maybe not) to drink from a glass of vodka on the baby grand. She'd placed next to that a goldfish bowl labeled "Kitty." Dorothy then began playing the opening strains of "Hello, Dolly!," Jerry's most popular tune. Within a couple of bars, she looked out at the audience, crinkled her rubber face, and snarled, "I *hate* this song!" The audience roared.

I found the lightness of *Jerry's Girls* to be particularly refreshing after the darkness of *The Rink*. I had only one costume in that show, compared with the dozens of glamorous and beaded Flossie Klotz outfits in our dressing rooms at the St. James Theatre. My favorite, however, was the simple male tux I put on to sing "I Am What I Am," from *La Cage aux Folles*. By that time, the song had become an anthem for the gay community. Since so many of our friends were being afflicted by HIV/AIDS, we found Jerry's songs of indomitability to be even more timely than usual.

The show also had something of a jinx attached to it. Just before we were to open, Dorothy broke her foot after she caught it on part of the set during one of her lightning fast costume changes. That delayed the premiere by a couple of weeks. And now, I had gone and landed in the soup myself.

The producers of *Jerry's Girls* vowed that the show would go on without me. They announced that the seven understudies attached to the show would sub for me. The stage manager was quoted as saying, "The initial reaction was 'Oh, poor Chita!' Then next: 'Okay, we've got a show to put on! Rehearsals [for the new girls] tomorrow.'" The press played up the fact that it took seven women to replace me. I might have allowed myself a self-congratulatory smile at the reports. But I had other things on my mind.

Would I ever dance again?

✳

I took Dr. Carmody at his word. It *was* up to me. After two surgeries, which placed two metal plates and twelve screws in my leg, it was wrapped in a huge cast and I was discharged. I was grateful to the doctors and nurses of Lenox Hill for their extraordinary care. At one point, my depression lifted when a good-looking male nurse, studying my chart, piped up, "You don't look your age." Without missing a beat, I said, "Look again!"

Once home, I was assailed with the doubts that every dancer has when the dreaded subject of life-after-dance arises. I was comforted that I had a couple of nonmusical roles under my belt, including Oliver Hailey's *Father's Day* and Tennessee Williams's *The Rose Tattoo*. I told myself, "Chita, maybe you can be the busiest dramatic actress on Broadway."

But I wasn't ready to "just talk." Not yet. I knew I was in a battle with myself—every time I looked at my exercise bicycle and rowing machine a few feet away from my bed. I never felt like hopping aboard either of them until I reminded myself that five minutes into the exercises I'd be glad I did. Sometimes the pain was so excruciating that I hit the ceiling and started screaming for somebody to peel me off it. Dolores cursed up a blue streak, but my dance training won out. "Just do what you're told to do, Chita!" was the drill.

I don't do misery very well, so I tried to concentrate on placing one foot in front of the other, no matter how long it took. The brigade of angels who always see me through life were soon joined by one more: my physical therapist, Armando Zetina. My recuperation included a daily regimen of exercises plus twice weekly visits to the "muscle therapist" Armando. He was a friendly Latino who liked to joke a lot. I had to discourage that because it hurt when I laughed. "It's a good thing you were in great physical shape when this happened," he said. "This'll go a lot faster because of that."

A month into my sessions, Armando asked, "Have you cried yet?"

I was surprised by the question. Apart from tears of pain when I hit the ceiling, the answer was "no." The next morning, as I hobbled out of the shower with the cast wrapped in plastic, I realized, "Shit, I broke my leg!" And for the first time, I bawled like a baby. It felt really, really good.

Dancers think of their bodies as machines, like a car, if that simile doesn't sound too close to home. So from then on, it was just a question of listening to the progress of the "little people." The healing of my leg felt to me like millions of little people hammering away as the blood vessels rerouted where they were supposed to go. Okay, if this sounds too crazy, you can blame it on Dolores.

Two months after the accident, in June of that year, were the Tony Awards, Broadway's big night. I can't recall how it happened, but I know that I wanted to appear onstage at the ceremony. It's easy to be written off when something like this happens ("Oh, poor Chita!"). I felt the need to show the theater community that I was still alive and kicking—or would be, if the planets aligned and God was good. The year before, at the Tonys, I had been dancing my ass off in a gorgeous red dress, singing "Buenos Aires" from *Evita*. Fate dictated that this year I would be wheeled out on a cart, point to the cast on my left leg, and say, "Well, when you wear a tree on your leg, you might as well show it off!"

My leg was eventually freed from the "tree," thank God. That fall, at the Lenox Hill Hospital annual fund-raiser, I was honored with its first Performer of the Year Award. Larry Kert, Leslie Uggams, and Dorothy Loudon, among others, were on hand to do their special magic. And I received the award from Jerry Robbins, who stood in for all those magnificent teachers responsible for my bouncing back. Of course, the room was full of doctors, including Dr. Carmody, and some of the best-looking guys in New York. They were a cure, all unto themselves. If you're ever in an ambulance and conscious, two words of advice: "Lenox Hill."

Dorothy came onto the stage with a sash that said "Miss Puerto Rico 1949" and proceeded to give me the Miss Congeniality Award, a runner-up no doubt to her sassy self. She also had a Chita Rivera action figure, to which she did things, leaving a crowd, used to stitches, *in* stitches. I would give my eyeteeth to have that doll!

After months of physical therapy, reading books, and doing needlepoint—I got pretty good at it—I received a call from my brother Armando telling me that I had received an offer to star, as La Môme Pistache, in a touring version of *Can-Can*. The plan was to begin by touring throughout Japan and then continue in the States. The musical, directed by Dallett Norris and choreographed by my friend Alan Johnson, was to feature a chorus of the Rockettes, Radio City Music Hall's statuesque beauties. I didn't stop to think that Michael's Kidd choreography, which would be re-created, is some of the toughest in musical theater. I said, "Yes."

It was time.

"You'll be okay," Gary Chryst, the dancer and my good friend said. "But Chita, be prepared. It'll be different."

Gary was right. I felt *different*. For one, the accident had been humbling. I thought it made me a more interesting person, if that makes any sense. For another, I knew there were going to be limitations. A dancer always wants to do 200 percent. Now, I might not be able to do even 100 percent. And, damn, did it ever hurt to do the routines! But when Alan told me that he would adjust the dancing to accommodate the new reality, I told him not to hold back. "I'll give you two splits, Alan. Please, just don't ask for any cartwheels."

Flash forward to the Tony Awards, June 6, 1993. Ben Vereen is at the podium to announce the nominees for Best Performance by a Leading Actress in a Musical. I've been nominated for *Kiss of the Spider Woman*.

As he reads the name of the winner, he says "the award goes ... to the lady whom I love very much and gave me my first telegram when I was sick in the hospital, Chita Rivera!"

In 1992, Ben had been critically injured when he was hit by a car while walking along the side of the Pacific Coast Highway. He recovered after months and months of the same physical therapy I had done years earlier. We embraced and gave each other the knowing look of two dancers who could feel in their bones, "God, how lucky we are to be here, standing on two good legs."

The Tony was a vindication for all the hard work that had gone into *Spider Woman*. So was the Lenox Hill Performer of the Year Award. But I'll tell you what I treasure as the main "award" from that whole adventure: Each year, on January 23, for the past three decades plus, the phone rings and I hear on the other end the sounds of an accordion playing "Happy Birthday." It's my old physical therapist, Armando Zetina, with greetings for another year. He doesn't say much. He just plays on his accordion. When I try to tell him how grateful I am to him and all those who got me through it, he cuts me off. He's too modest to hear my compliments.

So I listen, smile, and say to myself, "Chita, just shut up and dance!"

18

TAKING CHANCES, FACING FEARS

Kiss of the Spider Woman

hen I came to New York to study at the School of American Ballet, I lived in the Bronx on Intervale Avenue with my father's brother, Uncle Luciano, and his wife, Aunt Rita. Luciano was a hardworking man who left home for his job in New Jersey every day. Aunt Rita was a psychic who spoke in tongues. My brothers, Armando and Hoolie, loved to visit her because not only was she a good cook but her paranormal vibes were very entertaining. I was grateful to my aunt and uncle for giving me a home in the city but Aunt Rita scared me when she went into a trance and started babbling. This gave my teenage self the shivers.

I was home one evening and sitting in a rocking chair in the living room after a dinner of arroz con gandules (rice with pigeon peas), pasteles (plantain cakes), and tostones (twice fried plantain slices). Aunt Rita suddenly interrupted the calm and went into a trance. I couldn't make out what she was saying, but Uncle Luciano, who was used to her intense religious experiences, translated.

"She sees someone standing to the right side of your chair," he said.

"Who?" I said, fascinated.

"It's your father, Pedro Julio," he responded. "He's saying something."

"What?" I asked.

"He's saying that he's glad you found us and that you're living here," he answered, tearing up at the appearance of his brother. Then after a pause, he added, "He says that you are too obsessed with death."

It was true. I had been fascinated with the afterlife since, at seven years of age, I came home from school to find my mother, Katherine, and my grandmother, Sallie, weeping. "Your father is gone," my mother said, taking me into her arms. Gone? I thought. How could that be? One moment he was sitting at the dinner table in his white suit and tie, vibrant, laughing, and teasing us. Now he was gone? Where had he gone? It was an unsolvable puzzle. But I couldn't let it go. All I saw at the time were two women crying at the loss, gathering themselves up and determined to move forward as best they could.

The mystery stayed with me, through my teen years with Uncle Luciano and Aunt Rita, through my decades on Broadway, and up to this day. What is death? The Big Sleep, as Raymond Chandler, the crime writer, put it? Shakespeare's "undiscovered country from whose bourn no traveller returns"? Or everlasting life with God and the angels as my Catholic faith promised? If those questions were too much for the greatest philosophers and thinkers, you can imagine how little I could understand about something that had touched me at an early age.

So given my obsession, I was amazed that at a pivotal moment in my life and career, I should be called upon to play Death in the dual personality of a glamorous character: the role of Aurora and the Spider Woman in *Kiss of the Spider Woman*. The irony was that just as Molina tries to elude the seductive enticements of Death in the musical, I almost robbed myself of the role. As often happens in the theater, fate dictated otherwise—even if it took a couple of detours before I landed where I was supposed to be all along.

✳

My first encounter with Aurora and the Spider Woman was hardly life-changing. In June of 1990, Marty Richards, the producer of *Chicago*, and I drove up to the State University of New York at Purchase to support Freddy and John. Their *Kiss of the Spider Woman* was inaugurating the school's New Musicals program. It was geared to help creative teams develop shows free from the pressures of Broadway and the meddling of critics. In theory, the shows, which included *The Secret Garden* and *My Favorite Year*, would creatively evolve during their short runs on the campus.

What Marty and I saw that afternoon was definitely evolving. As usual, Freddy and John had chosen an audacious subject: a musical adaptation of a 1985 Hector Babenco film, starring Raul Julia and William Hurt, which in turn had been based on Manuel Puig's 1976 novel. It is set in the early 1970s in an Argentine prison cell shared by two men who couldn't be more different from each other: Valentin, a fire-breathing Marxist revolutionary, incarcerated for his political activities; and Molina, a flamboyant gay store window dresser being punished for deviant behavior. Much to Valentin's annoyance, Molina is given to flights of fantasy, which he incessantly shares. These involve Aurora, an alluring and beautiful actress of schlocky films whom he worships. The only film of hers that he hates is the one in which she plays a scary incarnation of death known as the Spider Woman.

Freddy had long been fascinated by the story, and he and John had taken it to Hal Prince, who'd directed their *Cabaret*. Hal thought it was such an out-of-the-box suggestion that it just might work. He was taken by the challenge of fusing the harsh political reality with the musical possibilities afforded by Molina's escapist daydreams. They asked Terrence McNally if he would be interested in writing the book. He happened to mention it to his mother, Dorothy, on his regular call to her in Corpus Christi, Texas. "What a terrible idea for a musical," she told him. So, of course, Terrence signed on. Susan Stroman, who was just then coming into her own as a choreographer, completed the team, and off they went to Purchase.

Marty and I were confused by the structure, which told the prison story on one track and the plot of one of Aurora's soapy movies on another. The idea was that the ensemble who played the prisoners would double as the cast of the musical film that danced in Molina's head. The songs were wonderful, as you might expect from Freddy and John. And I'm hooked on soap operas as much as the next person. But the two tracks never meshed. In fact, they warred with each other. I felt, too, that Aurora remained outside the show. She was more of an abstract metaphor than a part of the musical. At dinner after the show, Freddy and John told us that they were aware of the problems and relished the chance to correct them. They almost didn't get the chance.

Despite the fact that the producers asked critics not to review the shows in progress at SUNY, they insisted on coming anyway. They figured that New Musicals was a commercial, ticket-selling enterprise and thus was fair game. The reviews for *Kiss* were negative, including one from the leading critic of the day, Frank Rich of the *New York Times*. He felt that the B-movie subplot overwhelmed the central drama of the prison, which was Valentin's growing alliance with Molina. As I read his review, I was surprised to see that I was mentioned in his analysis of Aurora: "What is needed in this role is not, perhaps, a mysterious reincarnation of Rita Hayworth (which is what Sonia Braga brought to the film) but a dazzling musical-comedy presence of the Chita Rivera sort who has always ignited the flashiest Kander-Ebb songs."

You would have thought this suggestion would have sparked Hal, who had produced *West Side Story* and *Zorba*, both of which I'd been in, to say, "Hey, how about Chita?"

You would have thought Terrence, Freddy, and John also would have chimed in, "Hey, how about Chita?" since they'd expressly written *The Rink* for me.

And, wouldn't Frank Rich's flattering mention have kindled the idea within myself: "Hey, boys, what about me?"

Well, no, as it turned out. I wasn't on anybody's radar, including my own. Maybe it was partly because, after the reviews came out, *Kiss* was left for dead. In the recession of 1990, Broadway was in one of those lulls when half the theaters were dark and investors were in very short supply. Hal had a whopping success with *The Phantom of the Opera*, but just before that, he'd had six consecutive Broadway flops. Freddy and John had been sorely disappointed with the reception for *The Rink*. It took Garth Drabinsky, who was hungry to plant his Canadian flag on Broadway, to pick up the pieces. Garth was a former movie executive and theater owner who saw the potential in *Kiss* at SUNY. He knew Hal because he had produced *Phantom* at one of his theaters in Toronto, which gave him the cash flow to pick up the option on *Kiss*. He insisted on a couple of readings of the musical before a potential premiere of the new version in Toronto in June 1992.

Given a second chance, the creative team put their heads together to come up with a new cast. Who, they wondered, would be the right actress to play Aurora? Who was a triple threat—who could sing, act, and dance? Someone who could add a Latin spice and flash to Aurora? Who had the sensuality to be the seductive siren as the Spider Woman? I spoke up.

"I have just the person for you," I said.

I led them downtown to see a young woman, then making a stir in an Off-Broadway musical, *Song of Singapore*. Donna Murphy, svelte, and imposing, had bowled over the critics as Rose of Rangoon, a low-down torch singer in a seedy bar. I thought she'd be perfect for the role. I didn't know it then, but I was handing to Donna on a silver platter what should have been my role. I thought she would have been perfect, and so did everybody else. But there was an exception. Her dancing was not as strong as her singing and Aurora had to do some strenuous choreography. Thank God for that! When you're destined to play a role, a detail like that can help you out. As the readings approached, the blinders fell off and everybody seemed to slap their heads at once: "Hey, how about Chita?"

Well, what about me? Where was I in my life and career? I was fifty-seven years old and it had been nearly seven years since I had been on Broadway. The previous decade had been a stormy one. *The Rink* had been followed by *Jerry's Girls* and my devastating car accident. I had recovered faster than anybody had expected, presenting my nightclub act in less than a year and then touring in *Can-Can* with the Rockettes. Now I was being offered a role that seemed scarcely to be a role at all. When Terrence gave me the new script, the part of Aurora was identified sketchily, such as "fragment 1" and "fragment 2." What was I to make of all this?

A few years later, people would tell me that my return to Broadway in *Kiss* was one of those classic showbiz stories. I don't know about that. I had been in the business long enough to know that you can do a great show and then be forgotten. That's just the nature of the business. Each time is the first time and it never gets easier. In fact, it gets harder because people expect more. There's a difference between being young and scared to death and being a veteran and dealing with your insecurities. I could be scared in *West Side Story*, but I was young and I knew that if I followed Jerry Robbins's direction, I just might have a career. As you get older, there are so many more things to be afraid of. As any actor will tell you, we're all a bunch of exposed wires out there. The key is to face those fears and then put them aside. Once you've committed, you can't second-guess what you're doing. Or it'll come back and bite you on the ass.

I've always followed my instincts and the trust I place in a creative team. That was true of my decision to take on Aurora. The reviews had been so negative at SUNY that nobody except us had any faith in the future of *Kiss*. By Hal's own admission, it was going to be a rugged road without any guarantee of success. There were pitfalls every step of the way, and we would fall into them. "We're going to be flying blind," Hal told us as we prepared to embark for Toronto after the readings in New York. Good thing there were more than a few miracle workers on board.

✳

She steps to her glass now
All almonds and roses
She's powdered and pampered
The sight of her dark eyes
Igniting the screen
Scorching the screen

—"HER NAME IS AURORA," FROM *KISS OF THE SPIDER WOMAN*

Terrence had revamped the show so that instead of one movie from Aurora's past to parallel what was going on in the prison cell, a series of scenes from various film musicals would be interwoven. This lightened the heaviness of the drama and liberated Freddy and John to write a number of songs, evoking Aurora as a silent film star, a Russian cabaret singer, and a bird of paradise in a gilded cage. Additionally, there was the Spider Woman herself, dressed in black and haunting the stage from a suspended web of wires. It was a groundbreaking set by designer Jerome Sirlin.

On the first day of rehearsal, Hal, his eyeglasses perched on his forehead, explained his concept of integrating the surreal world of Molina's fantasies into the fabric of the play. While the prison cell would remain central, Aurora would emerge through the back of the cell and onto the stage to give flesh to those fantasies. The prison guards and prisoners would transform into an ensemble to support her in the musical numbers, at one point grabbing the bars of the cell to sub as canes in a song and dance.

Although I had known Hal since he'd produced *West Side Story*, this was the first time I was working with him as a director. He had virtually introduced the idea of the "concept" musical with his directorial debut, *Cabaret*, with Freddy and John, and had carried that through in a series of phenomenal successes with Stephen Sondheim on such shows as *Company*, *Sweeney Todd*, and *A Little Night Music*. I'd never been in a concept musical before *Kiss*, so that threw me off at first. I had always relied on the words on the page to help me discover the character. But Aurora and the Spider Woman had virtually no dialogue. They existed only as figments of Molina's imagination. One moment I was a gay fantasia of exalted womanhood, at another, the abstraction of Death.

During the first weeks of rehearsals, I recall being perched on a ladder, which was a stand-in for the web. I watched as Brent Carver, who had been cast as Molina, and Anthony Crivello, as Valentin, played out their scenes. I looked down at the two, wondering what in the hell my relationship to them was, and to the life of the musical. How did I get up here and what was I supposed to be doing?

I didn't feel as though I was bringing anything to the show. I was always on the outside looking in, a disembodied presence except when I took to the stage for my musical numbers. They were entertaining, but what did they have to do with the tale of love, idealism, and sacrifice at the center of *Kiss*? My questions weren't likely to be answered anytime soon. Hal was not really what you'd call an actor's director. He was a smart visionary who could bring all the elements together for the big picture. He could establish a tone that, for example, would allow him to fuse a musical comedy scene in a hospital room with the brutality just outside its walls. But he was leaving it up to me to discover the role for myself. "Take your time, Chita," he said. "You'll find it."

Would I have liked some help from him? You bet. Though I was frightened by the void I had stepped into, I had by then gained the maturity as a performer not to panic. I was calm enough to be totally present in the room, so that I might pick up any clue from what was going on. Little did I know at the time that the answer to my prayers would be Brent, who would do for me what he was doing for Aurora. Give the breath of life.

✳

You've got to learn how not to be
Where you are
The more you face reality, the more you scar
So close your eyes and you'll become a movie star
Why must you stay where you are?

—"WHERE YOU ARE," FROM *KISS OF THE SPIDER WOMAN*

Shortly before rehearsals began, Garth invited me to his office in Toronto to meet my two costars. Anthony Crivello, a handsome Italian American with a forceful personality. He was perfectly cast as the straight and idealistic Valentin, the part created on film by Raul Julia. In the role, Anthony led with his brawn and intellect, in solidarity with his fellow revolutionaries, and showed his sensitive side in scenes with his girlfriend, Marta. Brent Carver, who had been the understudy to Molina at SUNY Purchase, had since been elevated to the role.

Brent was so shy that if he'd been able to fade into the background, he most certainly would have. It's a little difficult to do that if you're five feet, eleven inches in height and have a halo of curly blond hair that makes you seem designed by Botticelli. From the moment I met him, Brent had an ethereal quality, like the Little Prince, only taller and, at age forty, older. He was fair, blue-eyed, and as luminous as a saint. One of the things I noticed most about him were his long and slender fingers. How he ever ended up on the stage of a musical was something of a mystery. One of eight children, he grew up in the small town of Cranbrook, British Columbia. He had distinguished himself for many seasons at the Stratford Shakespeare Festival of Ontario, Canada, a versatile actor with a strong-jawed face, impeccable manners, and baritone voice. During rehearsals, I was mesmerized by his skilled portrayal of Molina.

His innocence reminded me, curiously enough, of Gwen Verdon just as Molina's unbounded passion for his idol, Aurora, reminded me of Freddy, who also had his own idols.

Freddy and John were drawn to writing numbers celebrating diva worship and *Kiss* was no exception. Before we went to Toronto, I was at Freddy's apartment at the Beresford on Central Park West, listening while they played the songs created for *Kiss*. Even the jokey ones made me teary, and they laughed at what a soft touch I was. One night, after I retired to bed, I heard their voices in the work room. I got up, threw on a robe and walked down the hall. I opened the door to find John playing full tilt at the piano and Freddy singing at the top of his lungs. Listening to Freddy belt out "Where You Are" made me realize that he was his own kind of diva and that I was a disciple to his buoyant optimism. That always held up in their work together even though both Freddy and John knew just how shitty life could be, whether in a roller rink or in an Argentine prison.

I, too, have my gay following, but it's been different from that of other musical theater icons. Sure, I've judged Chita Rivera lookalike contests in gay bars and smiled when I've seen a drag queen come down the avenue wearing Anita's purple dress. But I've never been exalted in quite the same manner. I'm more likely to be considered "one of the boys," or a sister, which has suited me just fine.

I must say that the reluctance on my part to claim any sort of diva status interfered with my ability to find Aurora in *Kiss*. I was fearful of the glamor that was called for. I had not yet been swathed in the furs, feathers, and sequins that Flossie Klotz created for Aurora, not to mention the glittering and webbed black body stocking of the Spider Woman. Those costumes would go a long way to help me realize the character, thanks to Flossie's artistry. But it was my close observation of Brent that led to my eureka moment.

One afternoon, during rehearsal, I watched from the ladder as Brent recounted to Anthony's Valentin just who the Aurora of his imagination was. I noticed how he slightly tilted his head, how his long, thin fingers trailed the air, how his eyes closed in remembrance of her elegance and beauty. Most of all, I noticed his emotional nakedness. All of this told me who I had to be for Molina. I knew I could be that by scaling up those small, delicate gestures. Here's the lesson: I might well have missed it altogether had I not been listening and looking intently at Brent during those first weeks. As if to put a finer point on it, we next rehearsed the scene in which Aurora enters the cell, conjured up by Molina. The harsh lights fall away to bathe her in a transfiguring glow. As I came into the cell, I felt Brent's breath on my face and I took it all. From then on, I portrayed Aurora as triumphant and unapologetic. I felt that I could now "ignite and scorch the screen," the way the Molinas of the world liked their divas.

Just after I'd been cast, Hal called me to ask what I thought we should do about choreography for *Kiss*. Susan Stroman had left the project to begin work on *Crazy for You*, which would bring her a well-deserved Tony Award. We needed a replacement.

"Chita, what would you say if we went modern?" he asked. "Take a look at the new Madonna documentary *Truth or Dare* and tell me what you think of this guy, Vincent Paterson."

I went to see the film, about Madonna's 1990 Blond Ambition global tour and was impressed. Vince's dances were inventive and hip and had caused a sensation in pop culture. He had been choreographer not only for Madonna but also for Michael Jackson, Paul McCartney, Björk, Diana Ross, and several other biggies. Maybe Hal was onto something. It would be a gamble, but then *Kiss* was already pushing the boundaries. Vince was based on the West Coast and was young, lean, ambitious, and edgy.

I figured I could always learn something. What I learned was that MTV should be MIA when it comes to Broadway musicals. It was not a good fit.

Midway through the run in Toronto, things came to a head when Vince suggested that I climb onto a table and be the bulls-eye of a dart board. The direction felt totally awkward, without intention or purpose. I knew that it was wrong but I kept counseling myself, "Chita, keep an open mind." Hal was doing such great work in the other rehearsal room, but I felt we were getting nowhere and I didn't enjoy being a target on a dart board. Later during a note session, we were all gathered on the floor and Vince announced to the cast, "This show is not about Chita!" I felt my face turning red. I laughed, but I was insulted. I was the last person to suggest that *Kiss* revolved around me. I kept trying to keep my cool. Then I heard someone saying to me, "This is bullshit!" It was Dolores.

Exit Vince, enter Rob Marshall.

Rob was a divinely inspired piece of advice from my friend Graciela Daniele, who had choreographed *The Rink*. I had sent out an SOS for a new choreographer, first to Jerry Robbins, who wasn't available, and then to Grazie. She had just begun work on *The Goodbye Girl*, but she generously offered to come up to Toronto for a couple of days to help out. "I'm bringing Rob Marshall with me, Chita," she said. "I think you and Hal should seriously consider giving him a shot."

Rob had been one of the "wreckers" in *The Rink*. (Remember?—he broke my little finger dancing a jitterbug with me.) He and his boyfriend, John DeLuca, also an actor and later a producer, were close friends of Freddy and John, so they had often come to see my nightclub act. I loved both of them. Rob was very familiar with my style and knew what to do with me and the ensemble as he overhauled the numbers in *Kiss*.

"Cheet, I think your role as Aurora has been conceived in the wrong way," he said. "They've been thinking of you as Carmen Miranda. That movie poster in the cell of Aurora's *Forbidden Love* is from one of

Ann-Margret's movies. They have you in a bubble bath. It's kitschy and light-hearted. That's just not you. I see you as a Marlene Dietrich. Powerful, passionate, beautiful, and smart."

The light bulb went on. Of course! That was the kind of glamor I had been seeking, but I hadn't been able to put my finger on it. Rob could, and did. From time to time, early in my career, critics had compared me to Dietrich, noting in their reviews my high cheekbones and sultry manner. I thought of the sloe-eyed ambisexuality that she brought to such roles as Amy Jolly in *Morocco*, starring opposite Gary Cooper. You know, the one in which she's singing in a cabaret, dressed in a top hat and tails? At one point, she bends down and kisses a woman on the lips at a front table, and you can see Cooper getting all hot and bothered. And so did everybody else.

"Rob, I'd like to do a number dressed as a man," I said. "I did it for *Jerry's Girls* on 'I Am What I Am' and loved it." He jumped on the idea.

"Perfect! You can be as masculine as you can be feminine, Cheet. They both live in you," he said. "You know that white tux and tails Molina wears for his tango with you at the finale? I see you in that, with a fedora, for the 'Where You Are' number. Then when you're in black and he's in white at the end, it will be a literal manifestation of your relationship."

It was thrilling. "God, Rob, that's so right! It's what Brent and I have been doing throughout the musical. He's playing off me and I'm playing off him. It will fuse us spiritually at the most crucial moment in the musical."

From the beginning, *Kiss* had been one of the most collaborative musicals I'd ever worked on. It was true, what Hal had said at the beginning. We were flying blind. But if you're going to fly blind, it's good to have artists like Rob and Hal, Terrence, Freddy, and John in the cockpit. It was collaboration in the best sense of the word: Generous. Open. Experimental. The combustibility of it all can be, in a word, awesome.

Rob knew in his bones how to give the audience what they wanted. He put this keen insight to good use when, two years later, he joined forces with the director Sam Mendes to create an electrifying revival of *Cabaret* on Broadway. He sharpened those instincts even further directing the films *Nine*, *Into the Woods*, and *Chicago*, which won the Oscar for Best Picture.

In *Kiss*, I had been frustrated with Hal's direction surrounding the number "Gimme Love." In it, Aurora plays this sexy Bird of Paradise, complete with plumage, in a dazzling, all-stops-out number that ends the first act. It concludes with her returning to the cage with the boys grabbing the bars of it and twirling her round and round as the music builds to a huge climax. Hal's cinematic instinct was to bring the lights down on us and immediately go into a somber prison cell scene between Molina and Valentin. But both Rob and I sensed that the audience wanted to break out into applause at the end of "Gimme Love." We wanted them to. We were working our asses off.

There are times to shut up and let the director do his work and there are other times to, well, be a little manipulative. Enter Dolores. Before one preview performance in Toronto, Rob and I gathered the boys around and I told them, "Listen. At the end of this number, I'm going to move into the light and I want you to whip that cage around as fast and fiercely as you can. Don't worry about me. I'll hold on and sing my heart out while you're doing it. Watch. They'll applaud." That night, at the end of "Gimme Love," the boys' sweat was flying as they spun me around and I held on for dear life. Sure enough. The audience broke out into thunderous applause. Hal, bless him, took the cue.

"I think we'll pause after the 'Gimme Love' number," he said during the note session that night. "Give the audience a chance to applaud. Are you okay with that, Chita?" As I said, a great collaboration—taking chances, facing fears.

✳

I enjoyed my scenes as Aurora, especially after Rob put his stamp on them. Playing Death, as the Spider Woman, was another matter. I was a menacing presence to Molina, since it was the only role which Aurora had played that he didn't like. It scared him. Yet I was determined to make the Spider Woman as comforting and alluring as possible. As with all the costumes, Flossie helped me enormously to find both Aurora and the Spider Woman. After putting on the black webbed body stocking and the Louise Brooks bobbed hairdo, I knew it was the Dolores side of me who could guide Molina into the light of redemption, even as he resisted it. I saw the Spider Woman as an ally for both of the men in that cell. It was through the sacrifice of his death that Molina finds purpose in his life, namely, to love another person, which, in the words of *Lés Miserables*, is to "see the face of God."

Since Aurora had once played the Spider Woman in a movie role, I questioned in my mind who I was when I made my appearance as the personification of death. Was I a totally different character as the Spider Woman? Or was I Aurora, re-creating a character from her movie? I decided ultimately that she was clever enough to be both. She is Death, but Death as manifested through Aurora, the pinnacle of the diva glamor that is Molina's lifeblood.

As you may recall, when I was about to make the spectacular entrance devised for Velma in *Chicago*, I felt compelled to conjure up images of glamorous movies stars, like Elizabeth Taylor and Sophia Loren. I didn't need that in *Kiss*, even when I said the lines: "I am beautiful. I am gentle. Kind and warm." I was convinced I had earned the right to say those words. Freddy had always told me, "Chita, you have to learn to act like a star. Then people will treat you like a star. You have to know your own importance." With *Kiss*, I finally arrived at a moment in my life and my career when I could claim that mantle: Chita Rivera, star. Believe me, it has more to do with the power to work with the best in the business than with any of the trappings of success. You can still find me without makeup in a babushka at my home in Westchester sweeping the porch. I was actually doing that one day when a passerby saw me and remarked, "Hey, are you Chita Rivera?" I didn't cop to it. "No, I'm a friend," I said.

I know that stardom is as illusive as Molina's fantasies. It can disappear in an instant. And then you're "Hey, Lady, aren't you whoozis?," as Steve Sondheim wrote. Still, there is enough of the young Chita in me who never felt she could measure up to the regal beauties in the chorus line. So when I did say the line "I am beautiful" to Molina, I had to resist the urge to turn to the audience and say with a wink, "Just kidding!"

✳

When *Kiss* opened in Toronto, the critics were positive. The show had come back from being written off after SUNY. By the time we reached London, the show won the Evening Standard Theatre Award for Best Musical. The Tony Awards in June 1993 were a sweep for us, seven total, including Best Musical. I was proud to pick up my second Tony and was even happier that I was joined by Brent, Anthony, Flossie, Terrence, Freddy, and John. In my acceptance speech, I gave a special shout-out to Garth Drabinsky. I know he's had his trials, literally. But I will always be grateful to him for believing in the show when everybody else had given up on it.

I'm often asked how playing Death changed my view of my mortality. At the time of *Kiss*, I said that I had come to think of the Grim Reaper as someone like the Spider Woman: comforting and merciful. The show had taken the sting out of death in the best way: through a musical. Now, as I face the autumn—well, make that the winter—of my years, I would have to say that it's a Big Question Mark.

Perhaps Death will come in the form of my mother, Katherine, and father, Pedro Julio, and all the lost generations of del Riveros and Andersons. Aunt Rita and Uncle Luciano will be there to say, "I told you so." Boy, will I have a lot of questions for them!

Or maybe Death will come as a welcoming committee of all the friends and colleagues I've lost through the years. We will have so much to talk about.

I can also see Death coming as an angel, with a halo of blond curls, blue eyes, and long slender fingers beckoning me forward. Someone who looks like Brent, who died much too young, at sixty-eight, in 2020. He'll take me in his arms and we'll do a tango. Him in white, and now me in white, too.

Then suddenly, I'll hear over the PA system from another dimension a stage manager saying, "Ladies and gentlemen, half hour."

"Half hour?" I'll extricate myself from the angel's embrace and say, "Sorry but I can't keep the company waiting."

Death will look at me and say with some exasperation, "Actors! Dancers! They always think God will make an exception in their case. It doesn't work that way!"

Then with a wink, he'll say, "Just kidding! Go. You got another show to do."

19

A GORGEOUS BIRD CALLED ANTONIO

The Revival of *Nine*

U p until 2003, I'd been lucky in my career to originate most of my roles, except for the occasional classic like *The Threepenny Opera* or *Born Yesterday*. Being in a revival had never appealed to me. Maybe because I'm not eager to be compared with another actress in the role. Or maybe I felt that I might be too influenced by her performance to find my own footing. Then the director David Leveaux came calling.

I have a weakness for handsome men. Who doesn't? And David is easy on the eyes. On top of which he has a wonderful imagination and sense of humor. He'd taken the trouble to fly out to Los Angeles where I was performing in *The House of Bernarda Alba* as the rigidly controlling matriarch of the title. In the course of a lunch in a fancy restaurant, David explained that he was reviving *Nine*, the 1982 Tony-winning musical for New York's Roundabout Theatre. He wanted me to play Liliane La Fleur, the demanding film producer.

Oh-oh!

Not only was the character named after Liliane Montevecchi, the woman who'd vivaciously originated the role, but she'd won a Tony Award for it. If David was hoping to persuade me to be in a musical revival for the first time, he was on shaky ground. Then he mentioned who was going to play Guido, the womanizing film director in *Nine*. Antonio Banderas.

"This could be good," I suddenly thought.

I'd admired Antonio in several of Pedro Almodóvar's movies, including *Law of Desire* and *Women on the Verge of a Nervous Breakdown*. Unlike a lot of foreign film stars, he'd been able to translate his virile charm to American movies, including in *The Mark of Zorro* and as Tom Hanks's boyfriend in *Philadelphia*. I wasn't aware that Antonio had actually started his career on the stage. He'd acted on the streets of his hometown of Málaga and then at the Spanish National Theatre. Now he'd be making his Broadway debut, acting and singing in a second language. That took *cojones*.

The temptation to be there when Antonio opened in *Nine* was beginning to prove irresistible. Then there were the other perks: the musical itself, based on *8 ½*, the autobiographical Federico Fellini film about the boy within finally becoming a man; Maury Yeston's gorgeous score, with La Fleur's show-stopping "Folies Bergères"; a cast made up entirely of women except for Antonio and one little boy. This was going to be a new one for me. In my club acts and in musicals like *The Rink* and *Kiss of the Spider Woman*, the ensemble had been almost all men. I liked the challenge of sharing the stage with sixteen women and exploring sisterhood for a change. Besides, David had caught me at a vulnerable moment. In *Bernarda Alba*, my costume was a black mourning dress and I wore clunky shoes that made me look like a truck driver. The Chita of my childhood who didn't like "girly things" had long since vanished. *Nine* would be the perfect antidote.

When David asked me whether I was ready to sign on, I replied, "You had me at . . . Antonio."

✳

From the first day of rehearsals, Antonio became part of the company of *Nine*. He entered the room quietly, trying to avoid any attention. The women tried to be professional and adopted a calculated casualness as David introduced him around the room. "Oh, hi!" came the typical response. As we busied ourselves filling out the employment forms, I looked around the room at a cast of women who were so young and pretty that I—no, Dolores—could slap them! These included Mary Stuart Masterson as Luisa, Guido's long-suffering wife; Jane Krakowski as Carla, his seductive mistress; and Laura Benanti as Claudia, his muse. I gravitated toward Laura, who was super talented, funny, and utterly adorable, and Mary Beth Peil, who, as Guido's mother, was as elegant and beautiful as anyone else in the room.

Antonio seemed so unschooled and modest that I felt myself growing nervous for him as we began reading the script and tackling the songs. There he was in this room of seasoned performers, every one of us waiting to hear him sing. When it came to his turn, I held my breath. He began to sing "Guido's Song," a complicated duologue with his neurotic self. As he went on, he grew more assured, making the material his own. He did so without ego, willing to make mistakes. It was a signal to us: "I'm just one of you, trying to do my best." I exhaled. I thought, "Wow, you go right to the middle of it. You don't back off an inch!"

At that moment, I imagined Antonio as a golden bird climbing into the sky with all this power coming from his tail feathers. I saw myself hopping on his back for the ride. Okay. I'm not sure what a psychiatrist would say about that. Probably plenty. I'm not one to analyze myself. All I knew was that my reservations about being in the show disappeared into that sky. I found it a relief not to have to carry a show; David made it clear that we were all principal actors whom he intended to mold into an ensemble based on our individual gifts. His *Nine* was to be warmer and more communal than the original.

Antonio helped to set that tone. As it turned out, Melanie Griffith, his wife, was also making her Broadway debut as Roxie Hart in *Chicago*, which was playing right down the street from us. The better to keep an eye out on him. As Liliane La Fleur, the hard-charging producer, I had no interest in bedding Guido. But I did have one of the sexiest scenes in the show with him. The "Folies Bergères" number had been expanded by our choreographer Jonathan Butterell to include a tango with Antonio. I blindfolded him with a purple scarf and at one point whipped my leg up on his shoulder—and left it there. Then he kissed it. At each performance, I would turn to the audience with a look that said, "Eat your heart out!"

As usually happens, my dressing room soon became a gathering place for the cast. If I wasn't preparing for the show or saying brief prayers, I kept my door open and Antonio was a frequent visitor. He respected and admired musical theater, and as a veteran I was the lucky beneficiary of his attention. In our conversations, the sexually charismatic performer would fall away and in its place would be the questioning boy from Málaga, Spain, who, through a mix of ambition, talent, and luck, had managed to become a movie star. At the time, he had licensed his name to be attached to a series of perfumes that traded on his image. They had names like Queen of Seduction, King of Seduction, Power of Seduction, and Diavolo So Sexy. That made both of us laugh. So *subtle*.

There was something *diavolo* about Antonio, but the fragrances couldn't camouflage the struggles that came along when he became more famous than he'd imagined. He and Melanie had become a Hollywood power couple who were so public, so *Entertainment Tonight*, that it would have thrown anybody off stride. I could see he was satisfied that he had the power to make a revival like this happen. But he also yearned not to lose himself in the hot lights of fame. I wasn't worried because he demonstrated such a commitment to the work. He questioned whether he was doing his best so much that I thought, "Oh, he's definitely got the makings of a theater actor. I hope he sticks with it."

My own challenge in *Nine* was to play a woman who was as French as a baguette topped with foie gras. This Puerto Rican ended up being more Gallic than Liliane Montevecchi. You never heard so many rolled *R*'s in your life. I was also a little more Dolores in this performance than in many of the others. During my "Folies Bergères" solo, I had a lot of fun breaking the fourth wall to talk directly to the audience. This probably would have frightened me except for a couple of things: First, I had the experience of my nightclub performances. (Thank you, Freddy!) Second, the minute I put on Victoria Mortimer's "Swan" dress and stylish heels, I felt I could conquer the world. Still, just as Antonio questioned whether he was doing well enough, so did I. Whenever I stepped to the lip of the stage and looked out, I saw lots of smiling faces. But if I saw somebody who wasn't smiling, I went *there*. "Oh, I'm not enough." You're constantly being judged in the theater and there is no place to hide. Antonio was only voicing what every actor goes through.

Toward the end of my solo, the little boy, who plays Guido at age nine, came from the wings with a gift for me. Our banter charmed the audience, especially when the kid asked me how old I was. I changed the subject! I made the entire cast repeat his name, "Stephen." When I then asked him when the last time was that he heard fourteen beautiful women calling his name, he said, "Yesterday!" (Smart-ass!) Stephen's gift turned out to be a package of "*frrrrrromage*." Cheese. I don't know if that was meant to be an editorial comment on my performance, but I eventually took it to be the gift of *Nine* itself. The show was a singular pleasure in my career, enhanced by the affection the cast members had for each other.

In Spring, Tony nominations were announced for the show and for Antonio. Mary Stuart Masterson, Jane Krakowski, and I were competing in the category Best Performance by a Featured Actress in a Musical. I was only disappointed that Laura Benanti wasn't among us. She not only deserved a nod but a win. *Nine* won the Tony for Best Revival of a Musical and Jane for our category. (Dolores might have had something to say about *that*, but not me.) I was crushed that Antonio lost the Tony to Harvey

Fierstein for *Hairspray*. I love Harvey, but I thought Antonio had the much harder job. He was gracious as usual. "I'm happy for Harvey. But competition in art? I don't believe in it," he told reporters.

I thought, perhaps naïvely, that if Antonio had won the Tony—I mean, it literally had his name on it—he would sign on for another go-around on Broadway. Unfortunately, that hasn't happened—yet. If it does, I hope I'm along for the ride. Once you've climbed onto a magnificent golden bird, you want another chance to soar with him.

Entr'acte

Please Don't Pick Me!
Adventures with *Edwin Drood*

I liked playing Princess Puffer, the madam of an opium den in *The Mystery of Edwin Drood*, a musical set in the London of 1895. She understands and accepts people who enjoy the seedy side of life, and truth to tell, so do I. But the real draw for me to be in the 2012 revival was the creative team, including Scott Ellis, the director, and Rupert Holmes, the writer and composer. They are both very bright guys. They were able to seduce me, without too much resistance, to take on the role. My reservation was how I could ever reach the bar set by the great Cleo Laine, the Brit who'd so memorably created the Princess in the original 1985 production. She could sing the hell out of the score, and Princess Puffer's cockney accent sat much more comfortably in her mouth than it did in mine. I decided not to try to match the matchless Cleo and to rely instead on Scott and Rupert to help me put my own stamp on the devil-may-care dame. Besides, I got to sing "Don't Quit While You're Ahead," which I consider one of my personal theme songs.

One of the perks of growing older is to watch your "kids" evolve into some of the most inventive artists of the day. This was true of Scott, who had been in the ensemble of *The Rink* in 1984. You may recall that, like most of the cast, he played multiple roles, including a construction wrecker and a punk. But he was more of a scene-stealer as Sugar, in pearls, gloves, blouse, and "the busiest skirt on Broadway." He'd since matured into a Tony-nominated stage director as well as holding the position of associate artistic director of the Roundabout Theatre Company, which had done *Nine*. I was in good hands. Rupert, who'd won two Tony Awards for *Drood*, had come out of the pop music world as songwriter and producer for such artists as Barbra Streisand, Judy Collins, and Britney Spears. I liked that he'd initially come from outside musical theater. I think we always need that kind of new blood.

Drood was a rip-roaring musical comedy and I had a ball with the cast that included Stephanie Block, Will Chase, Betsy Wolfe, Gregg Edelman, Andy Karl, and Jessie Mueller. In a minor role was Nicholas Barasch, a very talented and very red-haired fourteen-year-old. I grew fond of him as well as of his family. On certain nights, my old hooker and his young boy were cast as lovers in the show.

This takes some explaining.

The show was based on *The Mystery of Edwin Drood*, the last, unfinished novel of Charles Dickens. In Rupert's adaptation, the solving of Drood's disappearance and murder is left up to the audience. They can choose from a variety of suspects, including John Jasper, Drood's uncle; Rosa, his betrothed; the mysterious twins Helena and Neville Landless; Durdles, the drunken stonemason; or yours truly, Puffer. Once the audience votes on who the murderer is, they are also asked to vote on who should end up as lovers from among the cast.

I always held my breath when the moment came for the voting. I didn't mind being paired as a lover with Nicholas, though it was pretty cheeky of the audience to pick us. It made me look like a cradle robber or worse—which I suppose was the point. The consolation was that we got to sing a reprise of "Perfect Strangers" to each other. The song was gorgeous, though I must say that its romance was lost on our May-to-December pairing. Being chosen as the murderer posed another challenge altogether. Whoever was the unlucky soul then had to sing an involved murderer's confession in a reprise of "A Man Could Go Quite Mad."

My reaction to being chosen? "Shit, shit, shit!"

The problem was that you could forget the lyrics if there'd been a long time, say, two weeks, between being chosen as the murderer. It meant that I had to exit stage left into darkness, where my assistant Rosie held a flashlight on the script to refresh my memory. Then I had to run around the back of the set to enter stage right to sing my confession. I was chosen nearly fifty times during the run of *Drood*. I lost a couple of pounds, almost went mad, and rewarded myself with a vodka and tonic afterwards.

On the first day of rehearsals for the show, Scott brought in a crystal mouse. He explained to the *Drood* cast that this had been my gift to each of the guys on the opening night of *The Rink*. I had forgotten that I'd done that and was touched that he had thought to bring it into the room. It was kind of a lucky omen. That's what I love about the theater. Nothing is lost. It's a living history. There are things that sort of live outside the room itself, spiritual connections that really inform the work.

Sometimes a mouse is more than just a mouse.

Entr'acte

Robert Fehribach: Love and Betrayal

When I first read *The Visit* in 1999, a musical about betrayal, my thoughts went back to a lengthy romantic relationship that I had ended five years before. Even though time had healed the hurt, working on a play like *The Visit* can reawaken emotional residue. I had met Robert Fehribach about the time that *Chicago* was wrapping up its Broadway run, and we hit it off. We had a wonderful chemistry. He was a stagehand, an electrician for producer Cameron Mackintosh's company, masculine, nicely built, and handsome. Bobby resembled the actor William Hurt, with a receding hairline and blue eyes behind wire-rimmed glasses. He had a sweetness and shyness that were irresistible. He was an introvert, so happy for me to be the extrovert in our relationship. Better yet, it was nice to have a man around the house. You know, the kind of guy you could bring home to mother and the kind of guy you could live with—and I did, for seventeen years.

Bobby was a great companion, who easily fit in with both family and friends. Whenever he could get away from the theater, he lit my nightclub act, so he was part of our traveling circus. When we were not working, we relaxed together on vacations in Italy and other places. The bond intensified as we met challenges together. He was in the car when I had my accident; he had been by my side when we buried my mother, Katherine. I cried on his shoulder and he cried on mine.

As the James Taylor song goes, loving Bobby was "as easy as rolling off a log." I appreciated his steady presence and the fact that he was comfortable in his own achievements and never felt eclipsed by mine. I sometimes wondered whether something might be missing, perhaps a little more passion, a little more fire. But then I figured that this Latina burned hot enough for us both and this was how we maintained the delicate balance of our relationship. I thought he would always be around, as reliable as ever—until one day he wasn't. There is nothing like betrayal to make you wonder how you can know somebody for years and never really know them entirely. It's just part of the mysteries we humans uncover about each other, some joyful and some painful.

I have to admit that I was hurt by his infidelity. Who wouldn't be? Did I want to kill him? No. Though Dolores might have had other ideas. What was that song I sang in *Bye Bye Birdie*? "How to Kill a Man"? But Bobby and I had shared too many important moments together, both epic and commonplace, and I didn't want to ever cover those times with a bitter film. Still, I don't do misery very well. So I worked like hell to get the heartbreak behind me as quickly as I could.

Here's a funny detail about our relationship. Before the betrayal, he was always "Bobby" to me. Now, I can't think of him, or even refer to him, by any other name than "Fehribach." I suppose it's because he is now in the rearview mirror. I glance at it every so often and wonder. But not as much as I once thought I would.

20

THE UNKILLABLE CLAIRE ZACHANASSIAN

The Visit

A woman, a butler, two eunuchs, and a coffin enter a bar."

Sounds like a good setup for a joke, doesn't it?

But if instead you said, "A woman, a butler, two eunuchs, and a coffin enter the *stage*," you would have not only one helluvan entrance, but one helluva musical: *The Visit*.

The show was no joke. On the contrary, it was one of the most astonishing events of my life, both on and off the boards. I will carry the memories of it in my heart the way that its lead character, Claire Zachanassian, was said to carry the moon within hers. The description alone of *The Visit* would cause anybody to stop and let it sink in. Claire, a fabulously rich woman, returns to her impoverished hometown of Brachen with an agenda: to persuade its good people to kill Anton Schell, the man who wronged her years before. *A musical?* That would probably be most people's reaction. It wasn't mine.

I knew Freddy and John well enough that I wasn't surprised when they told me that they were working with Terrence on such a chilling piece of theater. As with *Cabaret*, they were back in Europe, this time adapting a drama by the Swiss playwright Friedrich Dürrenmatt. The play had starred Alfred Lunt and Lynn Fontanne on Broadway in 1958 and Anthony Quinn and Ingrid Bergman in the 1964 movie. I wasn't familiar with either of those versions so, late in the year 2000, when Terrence's script arrived, I tore into it with the eagerness of a kid on her birthday. What a delicious and shocking present it turned out to be.

For decades audiences have thought of the story of Claire and Anton as a mythic tale of revenge—the stuff of Medea, Salome, and Pirate Jenny, a role that I once played in a production of *The Threepenny Opera*. Who can blame them? What woman wouldn't have revenge on her mind if, like Claire, she had been seduced, impregnated, and abandoned by an ambitious young man? Who then joined with the townspeople to drive her out in disgrace? To add insult to injury, Anton, to avoid acknowledging that he is the father of her child, convinces a couple of friends to accuse Claire of promiscuity before a corrupt judge. When Claire returns to Brachen, she is ready to settle some scores. Not that she hasn't already. Those eunuchs? They were the guys who lied about her. That butler? The corrupt judge who presided over her hearing. How has she managed to pull all this off? As she sings in the show: *I've got a little secret I'm more than pleased to tell / I married very often and widowed very well.*

Half-Gypsy, half-Jew, born illegitimate. Claire's my kind of woman. Not because she's rich, though it was fun to be swathed in furs and glittering jewels. Nor because she's an avenging fury, though our jailhouse chant in *Chicago*—"He had it coming"—would not have been out of place. No, I like Claire because she wants justice and the truth to be known. And most of all, because she loves Anton, the man who betrayed her. *The Visit* is more than anything a love story. Maybe a little perverse, but a love story nonetheless. Claire doesn't seek Anton's death out of rage. In fact, she never gets angry with him. She's out for bigger game. In the play, she carries one coffin with her. In my imagination, she brings *two*. Her mission is for her and Anton to be bound together in eternal love in Capri on a hill overlooking the Tyrrhenian Sea. And she is unstoppable. Claire has what the eunuchs lack: balls. And that is what attracted me to her and to the musical.

I often got the question from the press how I could play a woman who was essentially a cold-blooded murderer. Easy. I understood her. My personal morality is basic: God sits on one shoulder, my mother, Katherine, on the other. But, as you know by now, I've always been fascinated by people and characters who are on the slippery slope of morality. Give me a good crime show on TV over a musical comedy any day. It's a little bit of "There but for the grace of God go I." But from as early as I can remember, I've loved the complexity of figuring out what makes people go rogue, why people do the things they do. If you look at *The Visit* closely enough, it's really a morality tale driven by Claire. She's waited all her life for this. It's time to hold people accountable. *The world has made me into a whore / And I make the world my brothel now!* That's irresistible.

It's been my luck to collaborate with artists like Freddy, John, and Terrence who've never been afraid to ask the Big Questions: about love, death, betrayal, and what is true and false about us as human beings. *The Visit* asked those questions with a particular panache. As in *The Rink*, the musical was set in a derelict town whose monotone gray is pierced by a luminous Claire. Like the Spider Woman, she's innately theatrical with a flair for the dramatic. In the film, Ingrid Bergman arrived in town with not only a coffin in tow but also a panther. I saw no need for that. I was the panther. Claire stirred the depths of Brachen's despair with a steely command, a raised eyebrow here, a gesture with a cane there.

Oh, right. The cane. There's always a moment in reading a script when the hair on the nape of your neck stands up and you realize, "I know this woman. I can play her." That happened twice as I read through Terrence's script. The first time was shortly after her arrival. Claire and Anton are alone and he moves to embrace her, only to find that her hand is unnaturally firm. It is, in fact, made of ivory. "It comes off," she says, unbothered. "I lost it in a car crash." Moments later, he touches her leg. That, too, comes off. "Wood," she says without a flicker of emotion. "My plane crashed in Tierra del Fuego and I was the only one who climbed out of the wreckage." Then, after a pause, Claire adds, "I'm unkillable." In one adjective, a whole character materialized. What a clue!

Lynn Fontanne was great on Broadway in 1958. But she said there was no way she was going to play Claire with a wooden leg and a ceramic hand. She did not want to limit her movements. At first, I had the same question. I wondered how Claire would be able to move with grace and remain attractive. What would I do with my natural urge to fly?

Then I told myself, "Relax, Chita! If that's the character, so be it. Embrace it." Besides, I knew that Graciela Daniele, my good friend and our choreographer, would manage and even flourish within those limitations. And what a setup for a bunch of cheap jokes.

"Hey Cheet, lend me a hand, will ya?"

"Looks like you got a leg up on the part, huh, Cheet?"

Better yet, I could at my age lift my leg over my head. I just had to unscrew it.

I had another moment of revelation while reading the script. On the night of Claire's arrival, the town throws a banquet in her honor, hoping that she'll come to their financial rescue. She does. Sort of. She rises in all her glory to make a proposition to the people of Brachen: $10 billion to the town and $2 million to each of its inhabitants. The jubilation is cut short, however. She has one condition: that they deliver the body of Anton Schell to her. Not since Salome demanded the head of John the Baptist has there been such a buzzkill. The good people are appropriately outraged by the demand. The mayor, dressed in his robes and medallion of office, gives the answer: "In the name of all citizens of Brachen, I reject your offer. And I reject it in the name of humanity. We shall never accept."

Then with a knowing smile, Claire says the most devastating line in the play: "I can wait."

Like Claire, I too could wait. I had not been the first choice for Claire. Angela Lansbury had been announced for a Broadway-bound production during the 2000–2001 season, and she would have been terrific in the role. But she bowed out to care for Peter Shaw, her ailing husband. I may not have even been the second or third choice as I heard about other names bandied about for Claire. Each time, I thought to myself, "I can wait."

You can't push the envelope when it won't be pushed. Patience can be a fine art when on some intuitive level, you feel destiny is on your side.

Even after I got the role of Claire, there would still be more waiting. I read Terrence's script in the fall of 2000, but we didn't open *The Visit, A New Musical* on Broadway until fifteen years later, on the anniversary of Shakespeare's birthday, April 23. In between, there were other productions of *The Visit*. I starred opposite John McMartin in the world premiere of the musical at the Goodman Theatre in Chicago in 2001, directed by Frank Galati and choreographed by Ann Reinking. Plans to take it to Broadway were interrupted when the tragedy of September 11 made its subject matter too difficult for a traumatized country.

"I can wait."

Another production with the same creative team but with George Hearn as my Anton opened at the Signature Theatre in Arlington, Virginia, in 2008. And once again I waited.

It was worth it. As 2014 dawned, I learned that *The Visit* would once again be resurrected. This time I would be playing Claire in league with a director, John Doyle, and a company of actors who would teach me some of the most blessed lessons of my life and career. Chalk that up to Roger Rees, who was to play my Anton.

This last leg of the twisting journey of *The Visit* started in a summer engagement at the Williamstown Theatre Festival in Massachusetts where I felt as prepared as I would ever be to play Claire. By that time, Chita and Dolores had fused within the role. There I was, pivoting between the most profound romantic yearnings and the haunting mortality of a musical in which a coffin never leaves the stage. As the verdant summer in Williamstown gave way to the chill of winter in New York, the themes of

The Visit seeped into the lives of our happy company in ways we never expected. As art imitated life and vice versa, the events served to bind us. We learned, as Claire herself put it, that "what seemed certain to live, will die."

✳

I had never worked at the Williamstown Theatre Festival before arriving in the summer of 2014 to begin the intensive work on the third version of *The Visit*. The town is the home of Williams College where, in the late 1940s, a young Stephen Sondheim laid down his foundation to become one of the greatest musical theater composers of his generation. I was so psyched to do *The Visit* that I wouldn't have minded creating it in the dank winter of Siberia. But to do it in the full flush of summer, with the scent of jasmine and hyacinth in the air, was a particular pleasure.

The town took on the festive feel of a summer camp around the Adams Memorial Theatre, where we were rehearsing. During breaks, you would see actors come out of the rooms blinking into the sun for a solar recharge. Everywhere attractive young people in tank tops and cutoffs found shade at the picnic tables under the spreading elms. What a recipe for romance. I know I cultivated three of my own that summer. One with our director, John Doyle; another with Roger Rees, my costar; and one with the company of *The Visit*, which included Judy Kuhn, as Anton's miserable wife and my rival; David Garrison, as the mayor of Brachen; and a talented young couple, Michelle Veintimilla and John Bambery, who, as the young Claire and Anton, shadowed Roger and me throughout the musical.

I had not worked with John Doyle before *The Visit*, though I was aware of his reputation. Born in Scotland, he had come out of a small regional theater to introduce the idea of staging musical revivals in which the cast acted and sang and also played instruments. They served as the orchestra. He'd won a Tony Award for directing *Sweeney Todd*, his debut on Broadway. He followed that up with *Company*, with Raul Esparza at the piano. I was assured nobody would be playing an instrument in our version of *The Visit*. I was relieved, though it wouldn't have been the first time. Bob Fosse had momentarily thought it was a good idea for Gwen Verdon to play a sax, and me, a set of drums at the end of *Chicago*.

I liked John. He's a modest and soft-spoken man, slim and nearly bald, with a patient and reassuring manner. His reverence for the theater reminded me of a priest. When I found out he had once toyed with the idea of becoming one, I quickly nicknamed him "Father." That never failed to amuse him. Unlike the previous productions of *The Visit*, John's take was very spare. There was little in the way of scenery. With no place to hide, the cast members had to rely on each other. Scott Pask's design was an open playing area around which lay the ruins of Brachen. It was broken up and framed only by suitcases and the ever-present coffin, which served all sorts of functions: a dining table, a chest, even a car at one point. Scott's design afforded Claire quite an entrance. I came in through the decaying columns, illuminated only by shafts of light provided by the train that had brought me to Brachen. It certainly set the tone for a character whom Anton called "a sorceress."

As a storyteller, John was able to raise the stakes for Claire with clarity and conciseness. The first thing he did was cut *The Visit* down from two acts to one intense act without an intermission. Another of his inspired ideas was the addition of the young Anton and Claire, a pairing that gave the audience a picture of the erotic idyll between them before it all fell apart. It also gave me a vision of my younger self as described by Anton: a wild-haired gypsy running through the woods, "glowing naked, your body glistening from swimming in the stream, your black hair streaming out, slim and supple as a willow. How tender you were . . ."

John, working with Grazie, found the beating heart of the play, and my Claire in this version became more direct, more determined, and more focused on what she had come to Brachen to achieve. What was difficult at first was to nail down, so to speak, my wooden leg. I was called upon to do a lot of standing stock-still and to react to the turmoil that Claire had set in motion. I had to contain all my pent-up energy behind a chilly façade. To ask that of a dancer is a form of purgatory, if not hell. Yet I drew on the lessons I'd learned from Jerry Robbins and Bob Fosse.

"Chita, you can act even with your back to the audience, you don't have to move an inch," Jerry said when we were rehearsing *West Side Story*. "Concentrate. Focus. Bend the audience to your will."

And Bob Fosse taught me about the power of the minimal gesture: "Less, Chita, less."

As imperious as Claire could be, she knew when the joke was on her and went with it. At one point, she sang, *I'm not the woman that I used to be / There's no denying that there's less of me.*

What made more of me was my costar, Roger Rees, one of the great Shakespearean actors and forever Nicholas Nickleby in the 1980 Royal Shakespeare Company adaptation of the Charles Dickens novel. As Anton, he had what most great actors had: the ability to do a lot by doing very little. He, too, had learned restraint from Bob Fosse, who'd directed him in the film *Star 80*. During an interview on the program *Theater Talk*, he told Michael Riedel that during the making of the movie, Bobby would call "action" and then get right up into Roger's face as he said his lines. Out of camera range, Bobby would whisper, "Don't act, Roger, don't act," knowing that he could edit out his interjections later.

On a bright sunny morning when Roger first loped into the rehearsal hall in Williamstown, I could see why Claire would fall passionately in love with his Anton. The striking, slender looks. The gorgeous voice. The full head of salt-and-pepper hair and nearly all-white beard. At first, I was a bit intimidated by his background. He was a classically trained actor, having spent years with the Royal Shakespeare Company. His *Hamlet* for the company had been a triumph, and he'd won a Tony Award in the epic title role of the more-than-eight-hour-long *Nicholas Nickleby*. His experience in musicals was more limited, though he'd received favorable reviews in Terrence's *A Man of No Importance*. Before that he had been fired from the troubled musical version of *The Red Shoes*. It was an indication of Roger's generous spirit that he and his husband, Rick Elice, the writer, were now friends with the director who'd fired him: Stanley Donen.

Like many of the English, Roger had a philosophical approach to success and failure in the business. Even better, he had a self-deprecating and impish sense of humor.

"I'm really a three-foot vaudevillian trapped in a leading man's body," he joked.

Neither of us took ourselves seriously. We had both come up through the ranks and had never forgotten it—me, as a chorus dancer; him, as a spear carrier, third from the left, for his first four years at the RSC. Four years *before* he was given his first speaking part. As I said, patience is an art.

One of the aspects of Claire I sought to avoid was making her too morbid. There was no danger of that because even though the material might have been dark, the atmosphere in the room was light. We worked hard but there were a lot of laughs, too. Maybe it was the summer-camp atmosphere of Williamstown because it wasn't long before we were playing pranks on each other. The prankster-in-chief was David Garrison, who played the mayor of Brachen. He nicknamed me "Sparky" and I called him "E. Bunny." He took me right back to my childhood when my brothers tried to scare the hell out of me. I remember walking into a bathroom stall above which he had rigged a cascade of plastic eggs to fall on top of me. That is, when he hadn't taped the door shut with masking tape. I got back at him by packing a bunch of balloons into the stalls of the boys' bathroom. It got to the point between David and me that I opened the door and found myself staring at an eight-foot-tall inflatable bunny. I sent back a picture of me about to pop it with a hair pin.

Grazie, who was as playful as the rest of us, had a term for our joking around: *duende*. It's a Spanish term, often associated with flamenco, that means "a quality of passion and inspiration." Federico García Lorca, the Spanish poet, further explained that the artistic impulse to create was the result of muses, angels, and the *duende*, which in fairy tales were mischievous sprites like Puck in *A Midsummer Night's Dream*. Lorca said that this mysterious power of *duende* could be present only "when one believes that death is possible." That made a lot of sense as we went about mounting *The Visit*. We forgot that while we were chatting and laughing during breaks, we were often sitting on a coffin.

The Visit was well received by critics and a sellout in Williamstown. It was a nice capper to our summer experience. Broadway, which had been in the show's sights since 1998, finally became a reality sixteen years later when Tom Kirdahy, our producer and Terrence's husband, announced to us that the production would transfer to the intimate Lyceum Theatre. We were to begin rehearsals in February 2015, leading up to an April opening. We left Williamstown for New York, unaware of the curveballs that fate would throw at us.

※

It was winter, snow was falling,
It was winter, you were calling,
And I heard you and I trembled, winter.
And you held me, it was thrilling,
You said always, I was willing,
Then it ended, I remember winter.

—"WINTER," FROM *THE VISIT*

The excitement of regrouping for the first week of rehearsals was dampened when John Doyle, who had been so dynamic at Williamstown, came slowly into the room on two walking sticks. He put us at ease with his usual calm demeanor as he explained that upon his arrival at Kennedy

Airport from London, he had suffered a coronary "event" that put him into the hospital's acute care unit. He related the crisis with such humor and in such a straightforward manner that it took the edge off what might otherwise have upset the company.

There is a resilience to show people that kicks in at moments like these. It's known as "Doctor Show Business." Even if a hurricane of problems threatens to blow your life apart, "places, please" will tell what you have to worry about. Heaven can wait. For instance, in the late summer of 2001, I had experienced another heart-stopping moment when we gathered at the Goodman Theatre in Chicago for the world premiere of *The Visit*. While Terrence sat in the back, pecking away at his typewriter, and John Kander was at the piano, Freddy sat in the front row of the rehearsal room. Oxygen tanks were now his constant companion. It was only then that I realized just how sick he was, and I was shocked and saddened. Freddy always seemed so larger-than-life that I couldn't possibly imagine a world in which he did not exist. There was nothing he couldn't poke fun at, including death.

"Watch out, Cheet," he once told me. "I love you so much that if you get too near my casket, I'll reach up and grab you and take you with me."

I dismissed such talk with a laugh until his death on September 11, 2004, the third anniversary of the event that had prevented *The Visit* continuing to a next step. I remember tearfully going up to the casket and daring Freddy to make good on his promise. I didn't know how I was going to get through losing him. But I did, and it was because of Freddy himself. From the moment we started working together, his love, trust, and confidence had made me stronger than I felt I ever could be. No matter what we were working on, I was moved to validate his faith in me. Freddy's death gave our subsequent work on *The Visit* yet another dimension. We felt that we owed it to his memory to make the show as splendid as he imagined it could be.

As in life, humor and tragedy, vitality and decay lay side by side in *The*

Visit. The story was fairly macabre. We couldn't get away from that, nor did we want to. But a saving grace was always the optimism in the music, striking a balance of moody suspense and bright wit. I mean, you haven't lived until you've danced a tango with a butler and two blind eunuchs who sing of their loyalty to Claire: *We would never leave you, never leave your side, / If we had the balls dear, you would be our bride.*

That was the thing about doing any of Freddy and John's shows. Blind as we might have been about their imperfections, we never lost sight of just how cool and fascinating they were. There'd never been anything quite like *The Visit* on Broadway—and there'd never been anything quite like what it took for the show to reach opening night.

✳

One of the many things I liked about Roger was that he was a Renaissance man when it came to the arts: actor, director, teacher, poet, writer, painter. His husband, Rick, told me that no matter how busy either of them might be on any given day, Roger would insist on a break: "Let's go see something beautiful." They would traipse across the park in whatever weather from their duplex to the Metropolitan Museum of Art. Once there, they would stand in front of a piece of art and let its beauty wash over them. Particular favorites included the long and pale figures of the Spanish artists. Roger had fashioned his "look" in *The Visit* on El Greco's portrait of St. Jerome. He kept a copy of it taped to a shelf in his dressing room next to a quote from *Hamlet*: *How all occasions do inform against me / And spur my dull revenge!* He'd try to stimulate his memory with Shakespeare because he started having trouble remembering his lines.

We soon found out why. Shortly after we began rehearsals, Roger had been diagnosed with a virulent form of brain cancer that in most cases was fatal. Learning of it from Tom Kirdahy, our producer, sent me reeling. *Fatal.* Why did that sound so unreal when it came to Roger? I know this sounds irrational, but if Hamlet, Nicholas Nickleby, and Henry in *The Real Thing* were immortal, how is it that the actor who played them could die? After Tom left my dressing room, I went to see John Doyle. We vowed to do whatever we could to keep Roger in the role he'd indelibly put his stamp on in Williamstown.

"I told him that if he wanted to play the role in a wheelchair, I would stage it in that manner," John said.

We had no idea how the tumor in Roger's brain would progress. The company at large had limited knowledge of his condition. They only knew we were to circle the wagons and protect and support him in whatever way we could. He didn't want us to hover, and we respected his wishes. From the first diagnosis, Roger was a profile in courage. He often came to rehearsals directly from his chemotherapy session, and he gave every ounce of his energy without a hint of self-pity. Now, whenever I hear of actors misbehaving, being late or absent or just walking through a performance, I remember Roger's fierce commitment under the most trying circumstances. He put aside whatever fears he had about "chemo brain" interfering with his artistic process and forged ahead.

A few weeks before the first preview on Broadway, Roger had brain surgery to remove what was then thought of as the last of the tumor. His performance a couple of days after the operation was nothing short of miraculous. We marveled at his ability to hit notes that had eluded him before. At the first preview, Rick said that Roger was the happiest he'd ever been with a performance since his triumph as Hamlet with the Royal Shakespeare Company. Roger had a theory of why he rose to the occasion. With a smile, he shrugged and said, "Maybe because you realize that what you're doing is not falsely important."

The "magical thinking" that all would be well carried him and us through the days, good and bad. If I was the sorceress Claire was reputed to be, I would have done anything to make Roger well. When he arrived at the theater, he would check in with me and again before he left at the end of the evening. He was amused by the two "altars" in my dressing room, a daily and a weekly one. The first was an import from my house that I set up with each new show. It was composed of a statue of the Infant of Prague, holy cards, and pictures of my family and friends. From time to time, I was touched when friends asked if they could contribute something to the altar. I doubt God cares whether a show becomes a hit or a flop. But I do believe in the healing power of prayer to help ailing friends and to encourage me to do my best onstage.

The other "altar" is the one that came into use every Sunday after the matinee performance of *The Visit*. We had Mondays off, so the company would crowd into my dressing room to toast the end of another week. Our communion wine came from my champagne bucket and in the Scotch and other bottles contributed by various cast members. I loved hosting these bacchanals. There were snacks, but what really nourished us was our closeness. One of the great ironies of *The Visit* was that the atmosphere around the show was never negative despite the depressed, greedy villagers, the ever-present coffin, and Claire's homicidal thirst for truth and justice. Our *duende* of frivolity in the presence of death gave us a new kind of clarity. Like Anton, it seemed as though we were "seeing it all for the very first time."

That was true as well of the opening night of *The Visit*, on Shakespeare's birthday. I was overwhelmed and gratified by the reception. The road had been so long and hard for the show that it seemed as though we had climbed Everest itself. *The Visit* now belonged to the world. The ghost of Freddy hung over the performance, as did so many other forces in my life that had brought me to this pinnacle. At the curtain call, as yellow and red roses rained down on us, I looked over to see Roger. His face was radiant with joy and relief. Bathed in the lights, he resembled his St. Jerome. Against all odds, summoning every ounce of energy he could muster, he had reached the finish line. As we bowed to the cheers of the crowd, I thought to myself, "If only they knew . . ."

In the coming weeks, the glioblastoma in Roger's brain increasingly took its toll. He became more forgetful, and his vision started to falter. We put up large signs in bold lettering in the off-stage areas to direct his movements. Rick, devoted as ever, made sure Roger got to the theater. When they arrived, my assistant, Rosie, and Laurie, the stage manager, took over, serving as his dressers and prompting him when necessary. In early May, a couple of weeks after we opened, we had an especially harrowing performance. I was onstage, waiting for him to make an entrance from the wings, and I noticed that he was completely lost. We vamped for time until he could be reoriented, and then we covered up the missteps as best we could. "Live" theater took on a new meaning for all of us, but we were so enmeshed in the world of Brachen that I think I can say without contradiction that the audience never knew anything was wrong. Nor should they have.

The next day, before the matinee, Roger entered my dressing room. I saw his reflection in the mirror and could tell from his expression what he was there to say.

"Cheet, I can't do it anymore," he said, his voice raspy from the exhaustive struggle of the past weeks. "It's not fair. To you. To the company. To the audience. I'm sorry."

Rick knocked at the door and entered. He found us there, weeping in each other's arms.

Tom Nelis took over Roger's role for the rest of the run and did a masterful job. I thought that Roger could now get a well-deserved rest. But that was not to be, at least for a couple of days. Tony season was in full flower, and we had been nominated for five Tony Awards, including Best Musical and one for me, my tenth. At the same time, there are numerous other awards, including the Drama League honors, which involve endless speechifying from the dozens of actors on the dais. Roger and Rick were going to skip it until they were called by the organizers, who told them,

"Chita's going to win the top award for *The Visit*, and we really want Roger to present it to her."

Roger hesitated. "I don't think I can do it," he complained to Rick. "I'll make a fool of myself." Then Rick devised a plan. "Look, all the people on the dais are arranged in alphabetical order," he said. "You and Chita are in the *R*'s and people will be so sick of all the talk that they'll just want to get it over with and go home. So just write something sweet and short." Before they left for the event, Roger grabbed three pieces of paper and scribbled something on each. When it was his turn, he rose to the podium.

He smiled broadly and said, "Chita Rivera." He turned the page. "Chita Rivera." Another page. "Chita Rivera." It brought down the house and became legendary as the best—and shortest—speech in the history of the Drama League.

On July 10, 2015, Roger died. To paraphrase Stephen Spender, he left "the vivid air signed with his honor."

✳

At last! At last!
The old lady pays a visit
But stop and think, just how many lifetimes is it?
Oh, well, who cares?

—"AT LAST," FROM *THE VISIT*

I can't tell you how many times Claire is referred to as "the old lady" in dialogue, lyrics, and even in the translation of Dürrenmatt's German title: "The Visit of the Old Lady." For one of the first times in my career, I was actually playing an old lady. I guess it was God's way of telling me, "Dolores Conchita, you're no longer as young as you think you are."

What is that famous line Bette Davis reportedly had stitched on a pillow? "Old age ain't no place for sissies." You can say that again. I suppose I should be grateful that my life has been full and that my energy level is generally unflagging, even now as I write this. On my fiftieth birthday, while appearing in *Merlin* on Broadway, I adopted the disguise of a little old lady—gray wig, bent frame, and cane—for my arrival at the theater. I figured that I would beat them to the punch.

I needed no such disguise for the last scene of *The Visit*. The body of Anton is about to be delivered in the casket to Claire, the bargain fulfilled. She emerges from the wings having doffed her glamorous appearance in favor of a long black dress and a simple chain. I came in without makeup and my hair, now gray, pulled back in a bun. What a transformation! There were even gasps from the audience. I guess all the glamor that preceded it made the change all the more dramatic.

When I first looked at my reflection in the mirror as the transformed Claire, the years did not pile up as much as they drifted away. There was a hint of my Aunt Lily, my mother's sister, who had lived with us for a while. But what came back in memory at that moment was me as that aspiring ballerina at the School of American Ballet. I couldn't resist doing some ballet steps in my dressing room or striking a couple of Martha Graham poses from *Lamentation*.

This coup de théâtre at the end matched in power a scene that had come earlier during the number "Love and Love Alone," one of the most beautiful songs in the show. John asked Grazie, "Wouldn't it be wonderful if Chita danced with her younger self, Michelle, at the end of the number?" It was an inspired idea. It was a mazurka of sorts, but it was less a choreographed number than a scene without words. I didn't feel hobbled in this number as we swept around the stage in a circular pas de deux. As the music soared, Michelle imitated my gentle moves, a soft challenge dance, involving a shrug of the shoulders, a lift of the leg, a mincing step. These expressions of longing and affection pushed aside, at least for a moment, Claire's crusade for truth and justice. In this joyful cri de coeur Claire seemed to be telling herself that "the old lady" still had the capacity to love. The body might change, but the heart remains constant. For Claire, it was a moment of nostalgia. For me, it was a chance to recall my younger self.

Ask me what I miss of my youth? Dolores would answer without missing a beat: "Everything!" To be honest, I do miss that girl, full of energy, agility, optimism, and hope. Eager to learn, ready for anything that the years, all yet to unfold, might bring her.

Chita would be a little more philosophical. "Gaining maturity and wisdom, such as it is, is a fair trade-off. I'm one lucky girl."

At the end of the number, Michelle and I embraced. As our eyes locked and the music trailed off, two words came to mind from this "old lady" to her "young self":

"Thank you!"

To her and "to all the faces I've ever looked into" what else could there possibly be to say?

> *Suddenly, the chill I knew*
> *Comes the fire of you*
> *You, you, you,*
> *Ask me if dreams come true.*
> *And I answer, you, you, you.*
> *Everywhere you, you, you.*
> *In every dream I dream*
> *There's a specter of you, you, you.*
> *Years have gone by*
> *It is true*
> *Still my heart rushes to*
> *All my memories of you, you, you.*

The End

Afterword

CHITA RIVERA, "LOVE AND LOVE ALONE"

by Patrick Pacheco

I first laid eyes on Chita Rivera on a cold January evening in 1975 at the Grand Finale, a noisy and dingy gay club on West Seventieth. The place was filled to the rafters—a mix of Broadway A-listers at ringside and young men in bomber jackets packed three-deep at the bar. I was just a cub reporter then for *After Dark*, a quasi-gay entertainment magazine. The anticipation was keen for the New York nightclub debut of *Chita Plus Two*, in which the star of the forthcoming musical *Chicago* was joined by Tony Stevens and Chris Chadman on a stage the size of a postage stamp. Chita had just returned to New York from a less-than-happy seven-year hiatus in Los Angeles, and there could've been no better welcome home than the raucous, whistling, stomping ovations that greeted the trio's every bawdy, naughty, hip-swiveling, straight-to-the-heart number.

Chita became mythical to me that night—a singular stardom that glowed even brighter after I saw her in *Chicago*. She remained that way until, years later, as a freelance journalist, I was given occasional assignments to profile her. The first thing Chita did when she met a writer was demystify herself. I was no exception. She was always eager to present herself as anything but a "star"—just one of the chorus kids who happened to have moved into the spotlight. It was an image she cultivated, and it was sincere. But she had a star quality that was undeniable, even to her.

Then in 2004, I received a call from the producer Marty Bell. "We're going to do a show on Chita's life on Broadway," he said, "and Terrence [McNally] doesn't want to do the underlying interviews. So Chita asked us to hire you."

What a gig! I was contracted for three interviews for *Chita Rivera: The Dancer's Life.* What followed were afternoons with Chita, drinking cosmos at the West Bank Café and examining what was then more than four decades of a career and seventy years of a life. She was savvy. She was spirited. She was funny. That throaty laugh! It would start somewhere deep down and slowly rumble up to a high pitch. She laughed loudest at herself. It was the root of her humility and among the many reasons people adored her. "I've never thought of myself as beautiful," she told me once. "My brothers always said I had a face like a chicken butt." What glamorous—and beautiful—star says that about herself?

Chita was also open and honest—up to a point. I got two of the three interviews done when Marty Bell told me I didn't have to do a third one because Terrence thought he had enough. I felt like I had been kicked out of the playground. Worse, I thought I'd only begun to delve into someone who was a deeply private person masked by that cheery bravado.

I got the privilege and honor to delve deeper than I ever imagined when the idea of a book about her life came up many years later. Chita was always reticent to write a memoir. "Who'd care?" she told me. But when the COVID pandemic shut down the lights to which she had always gravitated, her unstoppable energy sought an outlet.

Our first meetings about the memoir were a tango of sorts. What overcame her skepticism was my insistence that she owed it to future generations to share what she'd learned throughout her many years in the theater. She was a stickler that young actors and dancers coming into the business should know their history, the shoulders on which they stood, as she herself had. But open up her private life? Uh, no.

Then I asked her, "After seventy years in the public eye, what is it that people don't know about you?" She replied, "That I'm not nearly as nice as people think I am." I said, "Great! Let's introduce the public to *her*. And let's call her by your first name, Dolores. What your mom called you when you got in trouble. Chita's a nice Catholic girl, but Dolores can cut your *cojones* off!" She loved the idea. We were off and running.

At her home, dressed in black silk pants and blouse with her hair wrapped in a headscarf, she'd make me a grilled cheese sandwich. Between bites of potato chips, we talked in the fading afternoon light (she was never an early riser). Her soft voice painted how she saw her life: a large canvas with spots, blotches, lines of color—like a Jackson Pollock—representing every turn in the road: marriage, motherhood, love affairs, the geniuses she'd worked with, and, especially, the lucky career breaks.

Chita knew she was talented, tenacious, hardworking, and disciplined. But, like every great star, she also knew she was lucky. With equanimity, she talked about how she had not been the first choice, or even the second or third, for roles on which she would place her indelible stamp. She knew she had come up with hundreds of performers who were just as talented, but who had fallen through the cracks. Gratitude poured out of her.

She also wanted me to know in no uncertain terms that the canvas was unfinished. Chita dreaded birthdays. She had so much more to do.

In August 2023, she made her final appearance at the Ice Palace, a gay club on Fire Island. Our lives together had sort of come full circle. She performed that night with Lisa Mordente, her daughter, in an act that sent an audience of all ages and genders into paroxysms of joy and delight. As I watched her, I was reminded of the line from "Sailing to Byzantium" by W. B. Yeats about sages (and artists) being touched by "holy fire." After all these decades, hers burned bright, warm, unquenchable.

During one of our sessions together at her house, I asked her, "Hey, Cheet, which ovation has meant the most to you in your career?"

"What do you mean?"

"You go to the Kennedy Center for the Kennedy Center Honor, and the president, cabinet members, and all these bold-faced names give you a standing ovation. You go to the Tonys, same thing. All the shows, the club acts, the personal appearances. What stands out?"

"I've never given it thought before," she said. "But since you asked, I think it might have been when I came out for the opening night of *The Visit*. The audience just went on and on, and it wouldn't stop. My whole body filled with such love in a way I'd never felt before in my life."

"You wanna know why?" I asked.

She nodded.

"You go to the Kennedy Center, or to the White House, or to wherever you receive all those awards on your mantle, and then you get in the car and go home and wait for the phone to ring." I continued, "On that opening night of *The Visit*, you knew that when that ovation died down, you'd go to work and *earn* that ovation, as you have time and time again for nearly seventy years. You've never lived for the awards or the acclaim. You've lived to give of yourself—body and soul—to whoever came through the doors of the theater, the nightclub, whatever, wherever."

Chita thought for a while, her eyes glistening. "I guess you're right. That's all I've ever wanted to do. I've been so lucky."

AWARDS AND HONORS

Awards for Artistry

1961–2015: Antoinette Perry Award Nominations: *Bye Bye Birdie*, *Chicago*, *Bring Back Birdie*, *Merlin*, *Jerry's Girls*, *Nine*, *Chita Rivera: The Dancer's Life*, and *The Visit*

1984: Antoinette Perry Award for *The Rink*

1993: Antoinette Perry Award for *Kiss of the Spider Woman*

2002: The Kennedy Center Honor, presented by Secretary of State Colin Powell, Washington, DC

2002: The Sarah Siddons Society Award for *The Visit*, Chicago

2006: The San Diego Theatre Critics Circle "Craig Noel" Award for *Chita Rivera: The Dancer's Life*, Old Globe Theatre

2009: Presidential Medal of Freedom, presented by President Barack Obama, The White House

2009: The Helen Hayes Award, Outstanding Lead Actress for *The Visit*, Washington, DC

Lifetime Achievement Awards

2009: The Julie Harris Lifetime Achievement Award

2010: Lifetime Achievement Award from New York Musical Theatre Festival

2013: Elliot Norton Lifetime Achievement Award

2015: The Theatre World's John Willis Award for Lifetime Achievement in the Theater

2016: The Goodspeed Musicals Award for Outstanding Contribution to Musical Theatre

2017: Frank Carrington Award for Excellence in the Arts, Paper Mill Playhouse

2018: The Actors Fund Medal of Honor

2018: Antoinette Perry Award for Lifetime Achievement in the Theatre

2022: Lifetime Achievement Award, the Encompass New Opera Theatre

2022: The Jason Robards Award for Excellence in Theatre, the Roundabout Theatre Company

2023: The Stephen Sondheim Award presented by the Signature Theatre for Important Contributions to the Canon of American Musical Theatre

Awards for Hispanic Representation

1994: Entertainer of the Year Award, The National Hispanic Academy of Media Arts & Sciences (HAMAS)

1994: Honored by The Mayor's Office for Latino Affairs, New York City

2013: Grand Marshal, The Puerto Rican Day Parade, New York City

2015: The Inaugural Latina Legend Award, 100 Hispanic Women, Inc.

2017: The Martina Arroyo Foundation Award

2020: The Raul Julia Heritage Award, The Puerto Rican Family Institute

2022: Lifetime Achievement Award, Hispanic Organization of Latin Actors (HOLA)

Philanthropic and Civic Honors

1995: Mother Hale Award for Caring

2000: The Ellis Island Medal of Honor

2005: The Mayor's Award for Arts & Culture, New York City

2009: The Faces of Inspiration Award from the Robert Bolden School/ P.S. 345, Brooklyn, New York

2012: The Mayor's Spotlight Award, New York City

2013: The 66th John H. Finley Award, presented in recognition of exemplary dedicated service to the City of New York

2018: Chita Rivera: A Living Landmark, awarded by The New York Landmarks Conservancy

2021: Father George Moore Artistic Impact Award from Encore Community Services

Women's Organization Honors

1999: The GEMS Woman of the Year Award, Miami

2003: The Women's Project & Productions Exceptional Achievement Award

2006: "Outstanding Mother" Award, sponsored by The National Mother's Day Committee and *Ladies' Home Journal*

2010: Lifetime Achievement Award from The League of Professional Theatre Women

2017: The Lifetime Spirit Award, LSA Family Health Service/The Spirit of East Harlem

2017: The Woman of Valor Award from the Victory Dance Project

2022: The Eternity Award, Los Angeles Women's Theatre Festival

Awards for Dance

1995: Distinguished Alumni Honoree, the School of American Ballet

2003: The TDF/Astaire Lifetime Achievement Award for *Nine*

2004: The Dance Magazine Award

2006: The Rolex Dance Award

2013: Dizzy Feet Foundation Inspiration Award

2013: Legacy Award, Dancers Over 40

2013: The Jerome Robbins Award

2015: Lifetime Achievement Award, National Museum of Dance, Saratoga Springs, New York

2016: The Legacy Award from the Jones-Haywood Dance School, Washington, DC

2018: Lifetime Achievement in Dance Award from Dancers for Good

Cabaret Awards

2015: Songbook Hall of Fame Honoree, Indianapolis

2019: Broadwayworld.com Cabaret Award, Feinstein's/54 Below

2022: Lifetime Achievement Award, The Manhattan Association of Cabarets (MAC)

Academic Honors

2007: Honorary Doctorate of Fine Arts from Niagara University, Buffalo, New York

2018: Honorary Doctorate of Fine Arts from the University of Florida

2021: Honorary Doctorate of Arts from the Boston Conservatory

ACKNOWLEDGMENTS

Although it is impossible for me to acknowledge everyone who has had a hand in my life and career and, now, in the creation of this memoir, I would like to extend my profound gratitude to:

My wonderful and gifted co-writer, Patrick Pacheco, in whom through our many conversations filled with joy, laughter, tears, and memories, I have found an eternal friend.

To the staff of HarperOne and the family of HarperCollins, who were terrific partners on this project. Thanks are due to Rakesh Satyal, my brilliant editor for his patience and enthusiasm and to his assistant, Ryan Amato; to publisher Judith Curr, associate publisher Laina Adler, senior vice president Lisa Sharkey, as well as to Edward Benitez, my Spanish-language editor, and Aurora Lauzardo, our translator. Kudos to Adrian Morgan and Stephen Brayda, who designed the wonderful cover, production editor Emily Strode, copy editor Jessie Dolch, publicist Paul Olsewski and Aly Mostel, Lucie Culver, and Julia Kent for their marketing skills. David Wienir provided conscientious legal advice throughout the process and thanks as well to lawyers Nan Bases and Eric Zohn. Also deftly guiding this book to publication was Mel Berger, WME's literary agent par excellence and Armando del Rivero, my manager who has my respect and, as my brother, my undying affection.

This book could not have been written without the constant care and solicitude of my personal assistant, Rosie Bentinck, and publicist, Merle Frimark. Their invaluable efforts come in the tradition of the generous support which I have received throughout my life from such helpmates as Rocco Morabito and Marion Rogner Elrod.

Agents and managers are often unsung heroes so I'd like to sing the praises of a group dear to my heart, starting with my first agent Dick Seff, who took a chance on a young actress-dancer. In his stead came my beloved Biff Liff, and dear David Kalodner. Kenny DiCamillo, along with Lee Lessack, expertly handle my cabaret engagements. Aaron Shapiro, "a father figure" in my life, was far beyond just a business manager. He was, along with his wife, Elaine, instrumental in shaping my career with his wise advice. I have since relied on the same smart counsel from Michael Lobel, and Norm Schulman.

Among those who triggered wonderful memories of our cabaret and concert adventures together for this memoir were "my boys": Robert Montano, Leland Schwantes, Richard Montoya, Raymond Del Barrio, Michael Serrechia, Wayne Cilento, Richard Amaro, Frank Mastrocola, Alex Sanchez, Lloyd Culbreath, Bill Burns, Earl Lamartiniere, Spence Henderson, Tim Scott, Frank De Sal, Sebastian LaCause, Sergio Trujillo, and Rob Ashford. A special and honorable mention to my beloved Tony Stevens and Chris Chadman, the original and forever-to-be-remembered "Two" of *Chita Plus Two*. The show always looked gorgeous thanks to my talented lighting designer, Andrew Fritsch.

My beloved friend, the choreographer Peter Gennaro, loved to say, "You get the gig if you can jig." Helping us get to the "jig" were my diligent musical directors, including Michael Croiter, Paul Gemignani, Mark Hummel, Gareth Valentine, Greg Dlugos, Herbie Dell, Gary Adler, David Krane, Carmel Dean, and Louis St. Louis, as well as musicians Jim Donica, David Tancredic, Jason Loffredo, and Alan Herman.

Keeping me agile and on my feet are my doctors, past and present, whose calm and endearing bedside manners also kept me sane. This medical honor roll include John Carmody, Thomas Sculco, Stuart Osher, Barry Kohn, Wilbur Gould, and David Slavit. Complementing their amazing work are my wonderful physical therapists, Armando Zettina and Marika Molnar, and my acupuncturist, Ted Dugas.

While my doctors kept me on earth, my soul was tended to by spiritual advisers with whom I became very close. If I ever get to heaven, it will be due to the guidance of Monsignors Robert Saccoman and Joe Martin and Fathers William Shelley and Doug Haefner. Brother Augustine Towey was always available to offer prayerful guidance to this Roman Catholic sinner.

Throughout my life, I have been honored to help the humanitarian work of such dedicated givers as Tom Viola, who heads Broadway Cares/Equity Fights AIDS. I am in awe of the staff of the Actors Fund Home in Englewood, New Jersey, who provide their residents with tender concern and kindness. The home is administered through the Entertainment Community Fund, headed by Joe Benincasa, which also has established the Friedman Health Center for the Performing Arts in Manhattan. I am continually impressed with the blessed and inestimable work of its medical director, Dr. Jason Kindt and associate medical director, Dr. Louis C Galli.

Any book that covers such a long span of a life and career owes a large debt of gratitude to librarians and archivists. Providing valuable assistance in research were curator Doug Reside, Phillip Karg, Cassie Meyer, Erik Stolarski, photograph librarian Jeremy Megraw, Giovanna Pugliesi (permissions department) and the staff at the Library of Performing Arts, Lincoln Center; Catherine Benson and the staff of the Heermance Public Library, Coxsackie, New York; Michael Robinson and documentarian George Fairfield; as well as Amy Brody of the School of American Ballet and Sandra Fortune-Green of the Jones-Haywood Dance School, Washington, DC. Further assistance came from Mary Chipman, Mireille Miller, and Adam Feldman. Very special thank yous to Paul McKibbins of Kander and Ebb, Inc. and to David "Bone" McKeown, assistant to John Kander.

I would be remiss if I were not to acknowledge and pay tribute to my beloved and extended relatives, the del Rivero and Anderson families, whose beating hearts and souls have made me who I am today.

And, finally, a big and warm embrace to all those many friends, fans, and associates who are unmentioned here. Please know that you remain in my heart with deep gratitude for your love and support throughout my many years.

As my dear and beloved Freddy Ebb wrote, "Ask me if dreams come true / and I answer, 'You, You, You!'"

PERMISSIONS AND CREDITS

We acknowledge the generosity and exceptional efforts regarding permissions for the use of lyrics in the book.

Many thanks to Kevin Thompson of Round Hill Music and Ryan Krasnow of Alfred Music for the lyrics from the John Kander and Fred Ebb songbook.

Thanks to Mitchell S. Bernard, executor of the estate of the late Fred Ebb.

Thanks to Paul McKibbins, music administrator for John Kander and Fred Ebb.

Thanks to Terry Marler for permitting the use of lyrics from the Jerry Herman catalogue.

Thanks to Gerard Alessandrini for the use of the skit "Chita-Rita" from an edition of his show *Forbidden Broadway*.

Page 212: "We Can Make It"
Writers: John Kander & Fred Ebb
Publisher: Kander & Ebb, Inc. (BMI)
©All rights reserved

Page 227: "The Apple Doesn't Fall"
Writers: John Kander & Fred Ebb
Publisher: Kander & Ebb, Inc. (BMI)
©All rights reserved

Page 252: "Her Name Is Aurora" (from *Kiss of the Spider Woman*)
Lyrics by Fred Ebb, Music by John Kander
©1992, 1993 Kander & Ebb, Inc.
All rights by Kander & Ebb, Inc. administered by Warner-Tamerlane
    Publishing, Corp.
This arrangement ©2019 Kander&Ebb, Inc.
All rights reserved.
Used by permission of ALFRED PUBLISHING, LLC

Page 254: "Where You Are"
 Writers John Kander & Fred Ebb
Publisher: Kander & Ebb, Inc. (BMI)
©All rights reserved.

Page 283: "Winter"
Writers: John Kander & Fred Ebb
Publisher: Kander & Ebb, Inc. (BMI)
©All rights reserved

Page 289: "At Last"
Writers: John Kander & Fred Ebb
Publisher: Kander & Ebb, Inc. (BMI)
 ©All rights reserved

Page 291: "You, You, You"
Writers: John Kander & Fred Ebb
Publisher: Kander & Ebb, Inc. (BMI)
©All rights reserved.

Photography Insert

Unless otherwise noted, photographs are part of the author's personal collection.

Pages 2 (*bottom*), 3, 4 (*top*): Friedman-Abeles © New York Public Library for the Performing Arts.

Pages 5, 9, 14 (*top*): Martha Swope © Billy Rose Theatre Division, New York Public Library for the Performing Arts.

Page 13 (*bottom*): Joan Marcus.

Page 16 (*bottom*): Gene Reed.